HUMAN RIGHTS WATCH BOOKS

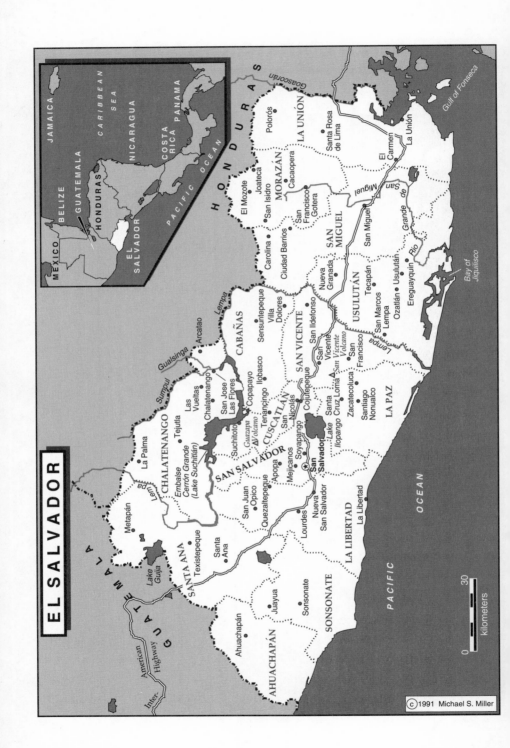

EL SALVADOR

EL SALVADOR'S
DECADE OF TERROR
HUMAN RIGHTS SINCE
THE ASSASSINATION OF
ARCHBISHOP ROMERO

AMERICAS WATCH

HUMAN
RIGHTS
WATCH
BOOKS

Yale University Press   New Haven and London

Americas Watch was established in 1981 to monitor and promote observance
of internationally recognized human rights in Latin America
and the Caribbean. Human Rights Watch also includes Africa Watch,
Asia Watch, Helsinki Watch, Middle East Watch, and the
Fund for Free Expression.

Set in Times Roman type by
The Composing Room of Michigan, Inc.

Printed in the United States of America by
Vail-Ballou Press, Binghamton, New York.

Library of Congress Cataloging-in-Publication Data

El Salvador's decade of terror : human rights since the
assassination of Archbishop Romero / Americas Watch.
    p.   cm. — (Human rights watch books)
Includes bibliographical references and index.
ISBN 0-300-04939-0
1. Human rights—El Salvador—History.   2. Political
persecution—El Salvador—History.   3. Violence—El Salvador.
4. El Salvador—Politics and government—1979–
5. El Salvador—Foreign relations—United States.
6. United States—Foreign relations—El Salvador.
I. Americas Watch Committee (U.S.)   II. Series.
JC599.S2E42   1991
323.4'9'097284—dc20   91-20365 CIP

The paper in this book meets the guidelines for permanence and
durability of the Committee on Production Guidelines for Book
Longevity of the Council on Library Resources.

10   9   8   7   6   5   4   3   2   1

CONTENTS

FOREWORD

To defend human rights is a humanistic, religious, and ethical commitment that each individual and all societies must make. To be indifferent or noncommittal in the face of human rights violations is symptomatic of a very serious lack of values. Ironically, even though the societies of the world have made considerable progress in setting human rights policies, this is still a time of serious violations to personal dignity.

The history of each nation is filled with occasions of shame, humiliation, and pain, as well as moments of pride and glory. The 1980s will remain a shameful and humiliating period in Salvadoran history, in large part because those in power have maintained conditions that violate the political, cultural, and fundamental rights of all Salvadorans. It has been a decade of great pain for the Salvadoran people. We demanded recognition of our inalienable rights, and in response, thousands were tortured, murdered, arbitrarily jailed, or disappeared.

In *El Salvador's Decade of Terror,* Americas Watch, a distinguished nongovernmental human rights organization, documents many malignant abuses against the dignity of the human spirit. The testimony set forth here serves as a public denunciation of those responsible not just for the deeds but also for the context in which they occur. The book methodically describes the legal system that makes these crimes possible, identifies those responsible for the violence, and records its victims: clergy, church workers, political activists, journalists, peasants, union members, health workers, students, teachers, and human rights monitors. It analyzes a government strategy that evolved from massacres conducted by ground forces to indiscriminate killing by aerial attacks to a rule of terror featuring targeted assassinations. Violations committed by the Farabundo Martí National Liberation Front, or FMLN, are also carefully documented.

Americas Watch also contributes a valuable analysis of international law as it applies to domestic armed conflicts. It critiques FMLN procedures for summary executions as rudimentary and inconsistent with the obligations of an insurgent force under international humanitarian law. (Some of the relevant standards embodied in international humanitarian law need to be updated and made more precise and detailed. The international community should also make an effort to ensure wide acceptance and ratification of new instruments by all member states. This would be a first step in making armed conflict less gruesome and inhumane.)

In a thoroughly researched analysis of the interconnected problems of the judiciary, its nonexistent administration of justice, and the impunity enjoyed by the military, Americas Watch accurately concludes: "The impunity of the armed forces and the death squads flows from the weakness and corruption of the judiciary and the overwhelming strength of the military and paramilitary groups." The murder of the archbishop of San Salvador, Msgr. Oscar Arnulfo Romero, best illustrates these weaknesses.

The role of the United States in El Salvador is immense and complicated. Since 1976 three successive U.S. administrations have failed to improve human rights in El Salvador through their foreign policy. Americas Watch addresses this failure with great honesty and seriousness. For Salvadorans, U.S. policy has represented one of the chief obstacles to improving human rights in a conflict that has already taken more than eighty thousand lives. We have had to struggle against our own problems, and in addition, we have had to carry an even greater burden: to fight the policies of the U.S. government toward El Salvador. Now the reader will gain a better understanding of our plight, thanks to the efforts of a U.S.-based organization that has come to our country, shared in our daily effort to end human rights violations, and painstakingly researched and documented the abuses we have suffered. Bearing witness to those crimes is undoubtedly an outstanding contribution to making our world more humane.

El Salvador has been subjected to many horrors for many years. With testimony from Americas Watch and other groups, we can work toward a better society, where human rights will thrive. Before this dream can come true, however, the people of the United States must realize that their own government has yet to sign or ratify most international human rights treaties. Who or what are the obstacles to a U.S. commitment to human rights? It is the task of every U.S. citizen to reflect on, then investigate and ultimately remove, those obstacles, in order to promote human rights not just for all of their fellow citizens but for all people. Without a firm government commitment, the perception will remain that people in the United States believe they are endowed with inalienable rights while others are merely pawns to be manipulated, regardless of the resulting loss of human dignity. Humankind is at tremendous risk unless all nations can agree to apply international human rights standards. I am hopeful that this struggle for universal human rights will continue.

María Julia Hernández
Director
Tutela Legal
San Salvador

PREFACE

A dozen years have passed since the tragedy of political violence in El Salvador grabbed the attention of the United States. The growth of a radical opposition movement led to the uneasy combination of reform and repression that characterized the military government born of the October 1979 coup d'état. The United States decided to enter the fray to avoid "losing" El Salvador to a leftist insurgency, and the huge amounts of military aid sent since then have been the source of endless, though often misguided, debate among U.S. policymakers.

Through the years, three administrations have avoided making El Salvador into "another Vietnam," keeping U.S. casualties low while Salvadorans have fought and died by the tens of thousands. Although opposition in the United States among those informed about U.S. policy toward El Salvador remains high, it does not have the urgency or priority that could jeopardize continuation of the policy.

The debate goes on, however, even if obscured from time to time by developments in Nicaragua or Eastern Europe and more recently by the war in the Middle East. Central to the debate has been the issue of human rights. If at first the Reagan administration tried to make human rights take a back seat to national security concerns, it soon found a way to present its policies as designed to foster respect for the rights of Salvadorans. The long history of abuses described in this book should dispel any notion that U.S. policy has effectively promoted human rights in El Salvador, even if one accepts the premise that doing so has been an objective. The Reagan and Bush administrations have succeeded in ensuring that the conditions imposed by law on foreign military assistance are not taken seriously. Arguing against all evidence, they have claimed that some of the repellent acts did not happen; that if they happened, they were not perpetrated by government forces but rather by some obscure right-wing force; or that government forces may have committed atrocities in the past but, thanks to U.S. influence, are now showing greater respect for human rights.

The murder of Archbishop Romero in 1980 and the massacre of six prominent Jesuit intellectuals, their housekeeper, and her daughter in 1989 bracket a tragic and violent decade in Salvadoran history. The fact that the Jesuit murders were carried out by officers and troops from the elite Atlacatl Battalion, created, trained, and armed by the United States, makes clear that U.S. assistance is not buying human rights protection for the people of El Salvador. In both cases, and in thousands of others in the intervening years, U.S. officials clung to the notion that the military was not responsible. In the Jesuit case, they discounted reports of military involvement for two months, until the weight of the evidence made the army's role impossible to ignore. It is almost certain that the murder of Father Ignacio Ellacuría and the others was engineered at the highest level of the army, and it is absolutely certain that the high command acted repeatedly to cover up its involvement, sometimes with the collusion of U.S. Embassy officials.

Following the Jesuit murders, the U.S. Congress finally reconsidered the enormous amount of military aid funneled to the Salvadoran army and halved the amount requested by the Bush administration. President Bush reinstated the aid within several months, however, thereby diluting the unequivocal message the Congress wanted to send. The administration argued that guerrilla violence against civilians and their receipt of weapons from abroad warranted renewed assistance; it ignored the lack of progress in the Jesuit case, a clear congressional prerequisite for aid to flow. Thus, while professing to want justice for those slayings, the administration has sent contradictory signals. The long-standing pattern is to allow so-called security concerns to override human rights imperatives.

The Salvadoran army knew for almost the entire decade that threats to reduce U.S. aid were hollow gestures. As this book shows, Salvadoran authorities have produced results when faced with serious U.S. demands, only to reverse those gains as soon as the spotlight is off. Behind the U.S. unwillingness to exert greater pressure is the implied threat of catastrophic violence: if the United States pulls out altogether, the armed forces will resort to a full-scale bloodbath of the sort they inflicted on their fellow Salvadorans in the late 1970s and early 1980s, and destroy the country the way the Guatemalan army did in Guatemala when left to its own devices. There is reason to take such a threat seriously. But the argument itself shows that U.S. policy has been helplessly mired in the rationalization of El Salvador's tragedy, unable to resist this most unusual sort of blackmail.

El Salvador's Decade of Terror chronicles the developments in this bloody conflict over many years in which Americas Watch has closely monitored the human rights situation and participated in the debate over El Salvador in the United States. It is written from the vantage point of an organization that has dedicated substantial energy and resources to obtaining accurate and timely evidence about the human rights situation there. Sweeping changes in El Salvador over the decade notwithstanding, human rights violations have continued at unacceptably high rates. Many abuses have occurred in the heat of combat; still others have claimed victims far from the battleground. Hopes that peace initiatives, made as early as 1984, would bring an end to the war, or at least humanize the conduct of the fighting by government and guerrillas, proved illusory for many years. In spite of false starts, both sides to the conflict are currently engaged in serious and intense negotiations, mediated by the United Nations, which hold the promise of preventing the bloodshed of the 1980s from indefinitely staining El Salvador's future.

Building on a trend started with the 1975 Helsinki accords and the 1987 Central American peace plan, the Salvadoran talks have intimately linked the issues of security and human rights. Although the conclusion of the peace negotiations does not appear to be at hand, a detailed and comprehensive accord was reached on human rights in July 1990. The warring parties' compliance with the historic agreement will be verified for the foreseeable future by a U.N. monitoring mission, even without further progress toward ending the war. Another significant interim agreement concerns establishment of a "truth commission" to investigate the most serious abuses of the past. A key issue the parties are committed to address is reform of the armed forces, ending its role in the torture, murder, disappearances, and other abuses that have characterized its behavior. These developments are promising not only for the establishment of respect for human rights in El Salvador but for the precedent they set for keeping human rights at the fore in resolving other civil conflicts.

In spite of the endless tragedy described in the following pages, the Americas Watch experience in El Salvador has been a source of inspiration for Human Rights Watch work around the world. These pages are written in profound admiration for colleagues who promote fundamental freedoms in their own country while running enormous personal risks and for the millions of Salvadoran citizens who, against terrible odds, have not stopped demanding justice. Because of them we feel that there is some hope for the future in El Salvador.

Juan E. Méndez
Executive Director
Americas Watch
Washington, D.C.

ACKNOWLEDGMENTS

Human Rights Watch and Yale University Press express their appreciation to the J. M. Kaplan Fund for making this joint publishing program possible.

This book is the product of many people's efforts and, like anything written by Americas Watch about the country, owes its deepest debt to the countless Salvadorans who have provided information and testimonies over the years. Above all, we are grateful to Salvadoran human rights monitors, whose courage and tenacity we greatly admire.

The report was prepared by a team of authors from Americas Watch: Anne Manuel, associate director, edited and updated chapter 1 from *Report on Human Rights in El Salvador* (1982), wrote chapter 6, and edited the entire manuscript; James A. Goldston, Orville Schell fellow, wrote chapters 2, 5, and 9; Aryeh Neier, executive director of Human Rights Watch, wrote chapters 3, 4, and 7; and Cynthia J. Arnson, associate director, wrote chapter 8 and the portion of chapter 5 covering U.S. aid to El Salvador's police. Jemera Rone, counsel, did research during five years' residence in El Salvador that has formed the basis of our knowledge of the period 1985–90, and she commented on various versions of the manuscript. Martha Farmelo and Karen Plafker provided substantial research assistance, and Polly Bone wrote the bulk of the human rights chronology, which Allyson Collins updated. Patricia Sinay compiled El Salvador: Vital Statistics, and Gloría Martínez provided the full names in Spanish for the List of Acronyms.

VITAL STATISTICS

Official Name: Republic of El Salvador.
Area: 8,260 square miles; shares borders with Guatemala and Honduras.
Population: 5.2 million.
Ethnic Groups: Mestizo, 92 percent; Indian, 6 percent; European origin, 2 percent.
Religious Groups: Roman Catholic, almost 100 percent.
Official Language: Spanish.
Government:
Elected democratic government: Executive branch headed by a president (Alfredo Cristiani).
Unicameral legislative assembly.
Independent, politically appointed judiciary.
Major Political Parties: Nationalist Republican Alliance (ARENA); Christian Democratic Party (PDC); Democratic Convergence (CD), a 1988 alliance of the unarmed parties on the political left, including the National Revolutionary Movement (MNR), the Popular Social Christian Movement (MPSC), and the Social Democratic Party (PSD); the National Conciliation Party (PCN); and the Nationalist Democratic Union (UDN).
The Insurgency: Farabundo Martí National Liberation Front (FMLN), consisting of the Popular Forces of Liberation (FPL), the People's Revolutionary Army (ERP), the Armed Forces of National Resistance (FARN), the Armed Forces of Liberation (FAL), and the Revolutionary Party of Central American Workers (PRTC).
Economy:
Gross National Product (GNP) per Capita: $940 (1989).
Foreign Debt: $2 billion.
Exports: A mixed economy; heavily agricultural—coffee is 65 percent of the total.
El Salvador is a party to the following human rights treaties:
Convention on the Prevention and Punishment of the Crime of Genocide; signed April 27, 1949, ratified September 28, 1950.
Convention on the Political Rights of Women; signed June 24, 1953.
Convention Relating to the Status of Stateless Persons; signed September 28, 1954. With reservations.

International Covenant on Civil and Political Rights; signed September
21, 1967, ratified November 30, 1979.
International Covenant on Economic, Social and Cultural Rights; signed
September 21, 1967, ratified November 30, 1979.
Optional Protocol to the International Covenant on Civil and Political
Rights; signed September 21, 1967.
American Convention on Human Rights; ratified June 23, 1978.
Protocols I and II of the Geneva Convention; ratified November 23, 1978.
International Convention on the Elimination of All Forms of Racial
Discrimination; accession November 30, 1979.
International Convention on the Suppression and Punishment of the Crime
of *Apartheid;* accession November 30, 1979.
Convention on the Elimination of All Forms of Discrimination against
Women; signed November 14, 1980, ratified August 19, 1981.
Reservations: Article 29.
Convention Relating to the Status of Refugees and Protocol Relating to
the Status of Refugees; accession April 28, 1983.
El Salvador is not a party to the Convention against Torture and Other
Cruel, Inhuman or Degrading Treatment or Punishment.

ACRONYMS

ACLU American Civil Liberties Union

AFL-CIO American Federation of Labor and Congress of Industrial Organizations

AGEMHA Association of Treasury Ministry Employees (Asociación General de Empleados del Ministerio de Hacienda)

AID Agency for International Development

AIFLD American Institute for Free Labor Development

ANDES National Association of Salvadoran Educators (Asociación Nacional de Educadores Salvadoreños)

ANEP National Association of Private Enterprise (Asociación Nacional de la Empresa Privada)

ANSESAL Salvadoran National Security Agency (Agencia Nacional de Seguridad Salvadoreña)

ARDE Revolutionary Action for Extermination (Acción Revolucionario de Exterminio)

ARENA Nationalist Republican Alliance (Alianza Republicana Nacionalista)

ASID Salvadoran Association of Democratic Indians (Asociación Salvadoreña de Indígenas Democráticos)

ASTTEL Association of Telecommunications Workers (Asociación Sindical de Trabajadores de Telecomunicaciones)

ATA Anti-Terrorism Assistance

BPR Popular Revolutionary Block (Bloque Popular Revolucionario)

CASU Anticommunist Command for Salvation of the University (Comando Anticomunista por la Salvación de la Universidad)

CD Democratic Convergence (Convergencia Democrática)

CDD Democratic Defense Commands (Comandos de Defensa Democrática)

CDH Human Rights Commission (Comisión de Derechos Humanos)

CDHES-NG Nongovernmental Human Rights Commission of El Salvador (Comisón de Derechos Humanos de El Salvador-No Gubernamental)

CEAT Special Antiterrorist Command (Comando Especial Antiterrorista)

CIA Central Intelligence Agency

CITFA Transmission Instruction Center of the Armed Forces (Centro de Instrucciónes de Transmisíones de la Fuerza Armada)

CNR National Coordinator for Repopulation (Coordinadora Nacional de Repobladores)

COCAFAN Ghost Busters Commando (Comando Caza Fantasmas)

COMADRES Committee of Mothers and Families of the Detained, Disappeared, and Assassinated of El Salvador (Comité de Madres y Familiares de Presos, Desaparecidos y Asesinados Políticos de El Salvador)

CONADES National Commission of Displaced Persons of El Salvador (Comisión Nacional de Desplazados de El Salvador)

COPREFA Press Office of the Armed Forces (Comité de Prensa de la Fuerza Armada)

CORELESAL Revisory Commission on Salvadoran Legislation (Comisión Revisora de la Legislación Salvadoreña)

COSOR Eastern Solidarity Committee (Comité de Solidaridad del Oriente)

CRIPDES Christian Committee for Displaced Persons of El Salvador (Comité Cristiano Pro Desplazados de El Salvador)

CRM Revolutionary Coordinator of the Masses (Coordinadora Revolucionaria de Masas)

DEA Drug Enforcement Agency

DNI National Intelligence Directorate (Directorio Nacional de Inteligencia)

DRU United Revolutionary Directorate (Directorio Unido Revolucionario)

EPS Protective Salvadoran Army (Ejército Protector Salvadoreño)

EPSA Protective Army of Santa Ana (Ejército Protector de Santa Ana)

ERP People's Revolutionary Army (Ejército Revolucionario del Pueblo)

ESA Secret Anticommunist Army (Ejército Secreto Anticomunista)

FAL Armed Forces of Liberation (Fuerzas Armadas de Liberación)

FAPU Front for Unified Popular Action (Frente de Acción Popular Unificada)

FARN Armed Forces of National Resistance (Fuerzas Armadas de la Resistencia Nacional)

FARO Eastern Region Farmers' Front (Frente de Agricultores de la Región Oriental)

FBI Federal Bureau of Investigation

FD Democratic Front (Frente Democrático)

FDR Democratic Revolutionary Front (Frente Democrático Revolucionario)

FEASIES Federation of Independent Associations and Unions of El Salvador (Federación de Asociaciones y Sindicatos Independientes de El Salvador)

FENASTRAS National Federation of Salvadoran Workers (Federación Nacional de Trabajadores Salvadoreñas)

FMLN Farabundo Martí National Liberation Front (Frente Farabundo Martí para la Liberación Nacional)

FPL Popular Forces of Liberation (Fuerzas Populares de Liberación)

FUSS United Federation of Salvadoran Unions (Federación Unitaria Sindical Salvadoreña)

IACHR Inter-American Commission on Human Rights

ICITAP International Criminal Investigative Training Assistance Program

ICJ International Commission of Jurists

ICRC International Committee of the Red Cross

IDHUCA Institute of Human Rights of Central American University (Instituto de Derechos Humanos de la Universidad Centroamericana)

INCAFE National Coffee Institute (Instituto Nacional del Café)

INM International Narcotics Matters

ISTA Salvadoran Institute for Agricultural Transformation (Instituto Salvadoreño de Transformación Agraria)

LP-28 Popular Leagues of February 28 (Ligas Populares 28 de Febrero)

MACA Central American Anticommunist Hand (Mano Anticomunista Centroamericana)

MIPTES Independent Movement of Professionals and Technicians of El Salvador (Movimiento Independiente de Profesionales y Técnicos de El Salvador)

MNR National Revolutionary Movement (Movimiento Nacional Revolucionario)

MPSC Popular Social Christian Movement (Movimiento Popular Social Cristiano)

ORDEN Democratic Nationalist Organization (Organización Democrática Nacionalista)

PCES Salvadoran Communist Party (Partido Comunista de El Salvador)

PCN National Conciliation Party (Partido de Conciliación Nacional)

PDC Christian Democratic Party (Partido Demócrata Cristiano)

PRS Salvadoran Revolutionary Party (Partido Revolucionario Salvadoreño)

PRTC Revolutionary Party of Central American Workers (Partido Revolucionario de Trabajadores Centroamericanos)

PSD Social Democratic Party (Partido Social Demócrata)

SICAFE Coffee Industry Union (Sindicato de la Industria del Café)

SIU Special Investigative Unit (Comisión de Investigación de Hechos Delectivos)

STECEL Lempa River Hydroelectric Commission Workers' Union (Sindicato de Trabajadores de la Comisión Hidroeléctrica del Río Lempa)

STISSS Salvadoran Social Security Institute Workers' Union (Sindicato de Trabajadores del Instituto Salvadoreño de Seguro Social)

UCA Central American University, José Simeón Cañas (Universidad Centroamericana José Simeón Cañas)

UCS Salvadoran Communal Union or Salvadoran Peasant Union (Unión Comunal Salvadoreña)

UDN Nationalist Democratic Union (Unión Democrática Nacionalista)

UNICEF United Nations International Children's Emergency Fund

UNOC National Union of Workers and Peasants (Unión Nacional de Obreros y Campesinos)

UNTS National Unity of Salvadoran Workers (Unidad Nacional de Trabajadores Salvadoreños)

USTR U.S. Trade Representative

EL SALVADOR'S DECADE OF TERROR

I would like to make a special appeal to the men of the army, and specifically to the ranks of the National Guard, the police, and the military. Brothers, you came from our own people. You are killing your own brother peasants when any human order to kill must be subordinate to the law of God, which says, "Thou shalt not kill." No soldier is obliged to obey an order contrary to the law of God. No one has to obey an immoral law. It is high time you recovered your consciences and obeyed your consciences rather than a sinful order. The church, the defender of the rights of God, of the law of God, of human dignity, of the person, cannot remain silent before such an abomination. We want the government to face the fact that reforms are valueless if they are carried out at the cost of so much blood. In the name of God, in the name of this suffering people whose cries rise to heaven more loudly each day, I implore you, I beg you, I order you in the name of God: stop the repression.

—Archbishop Oscar Arnulfo Romero, March 23, 1980

1

A BRIEF HISTORY

For the past decade El Salvador has stubbornly occupied the world stage because of a bitter internal conflict that has claimed the lives of tens of thousands of civilians. Why has Salvadoran society become so polarized? Why, despite pressure from abroad, has it proved impossible to enact reform within a peaceful climate? Why do social tensions that erupted in the past—as long ago as 1932—now rage in a seemingly endless civil conflict? As James LeMoyne, a former *New York Times* correspondent in El Salvador, recently wrote, "El Salvador is at war because it is one of the sickest societies in Latin America. Its archaic social structure remains basically colonial. Despite some efforts at change, a tiny urban elite and dominating caste of army officers essentially rule, but do not effectively govern, an illiterate, disease-ridden and frustrated majority of peasants and urban slum-dwellers. Order is often imposed by violence; there is not now, nor has there ever been, a just legal system. The rebels, in short, have had ample cause to lead a revolution."[1]

El Salvador's social indicators tell part of the tale. It is a very poor country, lacking strategic or mineral resources and attracting little foreign investment. The economy is overwhelmingly agricultural, with more than half the population living off the land, much of which is rugged terrain unsuitable even for subsistence farming.[2] El Salvador has by far the highest population density in Central America: 652 people per square mile versus an average of 136 per square mile in the rest of the isthmus.[3] The average per capita GNP is estimated at nine hundred U.S. dollars, and 20 percent of the people receive 66 percent of the national income. Seventy percent of the rural population lives in absolute poverty, measured as the inability to afford food providing a minimum of nutritional requirements. The level of social amenities remains extraordinarily low, particularly in the countryside, where an average of four people share a room and 85 percent of all houses lack electricity, running water, and proper sanitary facilities. Only 37 percent of Salvadorans have access to medical care; life expectancy is fifty-nine years at birth.[4] Half of all Salvadoran children under five are malnourished, and 15 percent suffer from severe malnutrition;

1

among those Salvadorans displaced from their homes, 75 percent of the children are malnourished.[5]

Like its Central American neighbors, El Salvador experienced a dynamic process of land concentration and eviction from the land over the last century. It began during the coffee boom of the late nineteenth century, when communal lands farmed by indigenous peasants were abolished in favor of private property and reached a second, acute phase during the cotton and sugar booms of the 1950s, 1960s, and 1970s, when the number of landless peasants increased in alarming proportions. In the meantime, the military and paramilitary law-enforcement agencies kept a progressively tighter rein in rural areas in an attempt to stifle social protest at its inception. Nor has the concentration of land in fewer hands been reversed, the enactment of a few social reforms in the 1960s and an agrarian reform in 1980 notwithstanding. The impoverished rural workers have grown ever more militant as their economic plight has continued to deteriorate, while the security forces respond to their challenge with ever-greater brutality.

The legislation that abolished communal patterns of land tenure was enacted in February 1881. The coffee boom was already under way, and previous legislation had specified that at least half of a communal landholding had to be dedicated to commercial crops, a demand that few indigenous peasants could afford to fulfill, given the five years it takes a coffee plant to bear fruit. During the latter part of the nineteenth century, the heyday of laissez-faire liberalism, similar legislation was enacted all over Latin America, but in El Salvador the laws were actually enforced. Given the intensive labor requirements of coffee cultivation, the new magnates needed a regular supply of labor power more than they needed legal title to the land itself. In rural areas, new police forces were established to help officials evict and control the population. When widespread unrest broke out in the major coffee regions toward the turn of the century, a new mounted police force, the precursor of the National Guard, was created, first in the coffee departments of Ahuachapán, Sonsonate, and Santa Ana and then throughout the country.

The system was refined further over the next fifty years. The Agrarian Law passed in 1907 gives some indication of the virtual slavery to which rural workers were reduced. Landless laborers could be arrested for vagrancy and had to carry work books registering their work obligations. Agrarian Law judges, assisted by the army, were appointed in each village to keep lists of all day laborers and arrange for the capture of all those who ran away from the estates. In 1912 the state created the rural National Guard and the *patrullas cantonales,* consisting of army reserve units carrying out regular police patrols.

Popular pressure built up through the 1920s, and when the bottom fell our of the coffee market during the Depression, it finally erupted in the uprising of

1932, which led to the slaughter popularly known as *la matanza* (the massacre). The previous year the oligarchy had been sufficiently disturbed by popular unrest to acquiesce in the election of a reformist liberal named Arturo Araujo, the last civilian to be elected president until 1984. Within months, as demonstrations and strikes escalated markedly, Araujo was obliged to surrender power to a military officer, Gen. Maximiliano Hernández Martínez. General Hernández Martínez swiftly fused together the repressive apparatus, bringing the National Guard, the National Police, and the patrullas cantonales under the direct jurisdiction of the Defense Ministry. After a peasant uprising in the west of the country had been suppressed, he retaliated with a "scorched earth" policy that cost up to thirty thousand lives. This massacre is one of the most important political events in the history of El Salvador. The government held El Salvador's small Communist party to blame for the uprising and arrested and executed its leader, Agustín Farabundo Martí. His name is now internationally known, because of its adoption by the insurrectionary movement, the Farabundo Martí National Liberation Front (FMLN), which has fought in El Salvador throughout the 1980s and into the 1990s.

General Hernández Martínez, who ruled for twelve years, paved the way for the system of government that, except for one brief interlude in 1960–61, survived intact until 1979. Throughout this period, presidents were chosen from among the ranks of the military and invariable appointed civilian cabinet members who represented the interests of the now-entrenched coffee oligarchy.

After the Second World War, the Salvadoran economy underwent significant transformations, which in turn had their effect on both political party structures and the attitudes of the military toward popular pressure groups. Some industrialization took place in the capital city of San Salvador and such regional towns as Santa Ana. The industrial working class was for the first time permitted the freedom to organize trade unions and provided with social welfare benefits and a minimum wage structure. During the Alliance for Progress era of the 1960s, substantial U.S. aid poured into urban industry. Within the framework of the Central American Common Market, El Salvador developed substantial light industries in processed foods, paint, paper products, and the assembly of prefabricated items. Many of its exports went to the neighboring country of Honduras, until this market was cut off by the "soccer war" of 1969.

By 1960 organized labor had gained such influence in urban areas that the military overthrew its own incumbent president and installed a provisional government that included labor representatives. The experiment was short-lived, and another military coup brought Col. Julio Rivera to power in 1961. However, for the urban sector at least, the nature of the government had undoubtedly changed. The Christian Democratic Party (PDC), of which José

Napoleón Duarte was a founding member, was established in the 1960s, and Guillermo Manuel Ungo's social-democratic National Revolutionary Movement (MNR) was founded in 1965. The Christian Democratic Party rapidly gained support, emerging as the dominant opposition party in the March 1964 municipal elections, and it increased its share of the vote through the remainder of the decade.

But rural El Salvador was a very different society. The formation of trade unions remained illegal for agricultural workers, and any attempt at organization was ruthlessly suppressed. The Agrarian Law of 1907, as amended in 1950, stipulated that National Guard members keep order on private estates and that law enforcement officials be appointed by the landowners themselves; it made provisions for the summary eviction of unwanted tenant farmers, for the local mayor and police to destroy the homes of "malefactors," for people out at night to be detained indefinitely by the police on suspicion, and for the national Guard to arrest anywhere, at any time, laborers who failed in their obligations to landowners. It was still a society of virtual serfdom.

The dramatic expansion of commercial agriculture put increased pressure on the land. Until about 1950 commercial farming was restricted to large-scale coffee cultivation in the highlands. But new crops, primarily cotton and sugar, gradually took over the entire Pacific lowlands, forcing squatters and former subsistence farmers into the position of landless laborers. The most significant expansion occurred during the Alliance for Progress when cotton acreage alone went up from 106,000 acres in 1960 to 302,000 acres in 1965. One researcher estimates that landless rural workers rose from 11 percent of the labor force in 1961 to 29 percent in 1971 and 40 percent in 1975.[6]

In other parts of Latin America, the twin poles of the Alliance for Progress were reform (primarily land reform) and counterinsurgency. In El Salvador the privileged classes equated land reform with communism, and the very term brought back memories of 1932. The U.S. government did not press for land reform at that time, but it laid a strong emphasis on suppressing counterinsurgency and upgrading the police forces. There was—perhaps surprisingly—no violent uprising in El Salvador in the 1960s. But the United States feared the acute social tensions could lead to violence, as an internal evaluation of the U.S. Public Safety Program, prepared in 1967, makes clear: "The Public Safety Program in El Salvador is 10 years sold and the advisors have efficiently trained the National Guard and National Police in basic tactics so that authorities have been successful in handling any politically motivated demonstrations in recent years. . . . With the potential danger that exists in a densely populated country where the rich are very rich and the poor extremely poor, El Salvador is fortunate that the Guard and the Police are well trained and disciplined."[7]

During the late 1960s an additional element appeared in the Salvadoran security apparatus in the form of an eighty-thousand-strong paramilitary network, the Democratic Nationalist Organization, known as ORDEN, which penetrated every hamlet in the country and established an elaborate system of internal espionage. ORDEN was organized by Gen. José Alberto ("Chele") Medrano, who had received assistance from U.S. intelligence officers[8] and was assassinated by guerrillas in 1985. The rural vigilante force is widely recognized as one of the precursors of the "death squads" of the late 1970s and 1980s.

As a result of the fraudulent 1967 elections and the labor unrest that occurred in the next two years, tensions were high by the early 1970s. In 1972 the Christian Democrat José Napoleón Duarte who later became president and social democrat Guillermo Ungo (who later became head of the opposition Democratic Revolutionary Front, which was allied with the guerrillas), ran for election together as, respectively, the presidential and vice presidential candidates of an electoral coalition that campaigned on a platform of human rights and social justice and sought to end forty years of military dictatorship through the ballot box. Blatant fraud by the military deprived them of victory in the February 20 election. The elections of March 12 to fill municipal council and the Legislative Assembly seats were also marred by irregularities, and voters nullified a large portion of the ballots in protest. When political violence intensified, rebel military officers led an unsuccessful uprising on March 25. Suppression of the uprising is said to have cost as many as a hundred lives, with another two hundred injured.[9] In the subsequent wave of reprisals Duarte, who had publicly backed the coup attempt, and numerous political and military leaders were detained and tortured.

With the avenues of peaceful change closed off, several armed opposition groups announced their formation. The Popular Forces of Liberation (FPL), born in 1970 from a radical faction of the Salvadoran Communist Party (PCES) in alliance with left-wing university students, appeared first. The People's Revolutionary Army (ERP) sprang up in 1971, and the Armed Forces of National Resistance (FARN) formed from an ERP splinter group in 1975. The groups differed in military and political strategy; ERP, for example, turned to sabotage and individual acts of violence while the others emphasized building popular support. Not until October 1980 would these guerrilla groups join with the Armed Forces of Liberation (FAL) and the Revolutionary Party of Central American Workers (PRTC) into a unified command.

One effect of the renewed land concentration in the 1960s and 1970s was peasant flight to the cities, creating a new class of slum dwellers. They— together with urban workers disillusioned with official unionism, university students and low-paid teachers—enabled mass organizations to arise outside the traditional party structure. First to be formed, in 1974, was the Front for Unified Popular Action (FAPU), composed primarily of urban workers. The following year the Popular Revolutionary Block (BPR) appeared; it was the largest and most radical group, deriving the bulk of its support from the peasantry. Finally, the Popular Leagues of February 28 (LP-28) was set up in 1977 within the student population of San Salvador. Although each organization developed links with the guerrillas, FAPU with FARN, BPR with FPL, and the LP-28 with ERP, they manifested distinct political and social characteristics, and there was often rivalry, particularly with FAPU, which the others accused of having "reformist tendencies." All concurred, however, on the necessity of implementing a wide-ranging program of reforms and bringing down the military regime through mass action. The government of Col. Arturo Armando Molina (r. 1972–77), under pressure from the U.S. Embassy, attempted to counter the growing tensions by enacting a limited agrarian reform supported by a government-favored peasant organization, the Salvadoran Communal Union (UCS), which claimed 100,000 members and received extensive support from the U.S.-based American Institute for Free Labor Development (AIFLD). An agrarian transformation act was passed in 1975, but the reform program never got under way. The first stage was to have been extremely limited, distributing only fifty thousand acres of land to twelve thousand peasant families. To the rural oligarchy the reform was an attack on the concept of private property, the provisions for generous compensation notwithstanding. Powerful landowner associations, such as the Eastern Region Farmers' Front (FARO) and the influential National Association of Private Enterprise (ANEP), launched a publicity campaign against the project. The military itself was divided, and the conservatives prevailed.

Like the balloting held in 1972, the presidential elections held on February 20, 1977, were marked by intimidation, violence, and fraud carried out on a massive scale by the government. Predictably, Gen. Carlos Humberto Romero, the official candidate, was declared the winner.[10] On February 28, police fired on thousands of demonstrators protesting election fraud in downtown San Salvador, leaving nearly one hundred dead.[11] The leftist group LP-28, formed soon thereafter, took its name from this massacre.

Under General Romero all talk of reform was replaced by an escalating campaign of repression and political killing, which was amply documented by such organizations as the Inter-American Commission on Human Rights (IACHR). The victims included people from almost every sector of society, including politicians and priests, but poor peasants and rural workers again bore the brunt of the repression. The victory of the Nicaraguan revolutionaries in July 1979 turned the scales against General Romero. Military officers perceived him to lack the political skill to extract the reforms from the armed forces and oligarchy needed to avoid a repetition of the Nicaraguan experience in El Salvador, so they staged a military coup against the general in October 1979.

The officers were by no means united among themselves. At one end of the spectrum were the younger and more progressive officers, grouped around Col. Adolfo Arnoldo Majano; at the other end were conservatives who nevertheless saw the need for a new public image. This group was led by Cols. José Guillermo García, later named defense minister, and Jaime Abdul Gutiérrez. Initially committed to reforms, the first junta of the new government included five members: Majano and Gutiérrez, representing the military, and Guillermo Ungo, Román Mayorga of the Catholic University, and Mario Andino, representing the private sector.

Unhappily, the initial promise of the junta to prevent the slide into civil war was not realized. Changes in the military were not far-reaching: although reform-minded younger officers were promoted, conservative military leaders mounted a determined effort to preserve the command structure. General Romero and a number of other military figures identified with the extreme right wing, such as Maj. Roberto D'Aubuisson, were displaced, but hard-line officers were placed in top positions, including Colonel García as defense minister, Col. Carlos Eugenio Vides Casanova as director of the National Guard, Col. Carlos Reynaldo López Nuila as director of the National Police, and Col. Nicolás Carranza as vice minister of defense. While the mass organizations viewed the new government with deep skepticism and mounted continuous pressure for speedy reforms, the government itself was deeply divided over the way to handle the popular movement.[12]

The junta stated its intention to restore the rule of law, create a climate of peace, and recognize "the validity of the current [1962] Constitution . . . and all laws . . . that govern the institutional life of the Republic" (Decree 1, Article 4). On October 16, 1979, it declared a general amnesty for all political prisoners and Salvadorans in exile, and in November it dissolved ORDEN, the rural vigilante force, and created a special committee to investigate missing political prisoners, which was granted autonomy and full powers to carry out its task. Composed of the attorney general, a member appointed by the Court of Justice, and "an honorable citizen" appointed by the junta, it was given sixty days to carry out the investigation and submit "a detailed report." On November 23, 1979, the commission recommended prosecuting former officials of the last two regimes, as well as prohibiting jails or other detention facilities in the headquarters of the armed or security forces—which, it said, facilitated illegal detention and the use of torture—and compensating families of political prisoners who had disappeared.

On December 3, 1979, the Ministry of the Presidency announced that the Attorney General's Office had been instructed to investigate and obtain sufficient evidence to begin proceedings against those officials and that compensation would be paid to families of missing persons and to police killed by the guerrillas. These instructions were never carried out, nor were the civilian members of the junta empowered to carry out the special commission's other recommendations. Political detainees remained imprisoned, and ORDEN, though officially proscribed, continued to operate with impunity, in complicity with the security forces.

In the months following the coup there were demonstrations, strikes, and occupations of ministries and embassies, led by popular organizations demanding a halt to the repression. These protests were crushed with a savagery arguably greater than that employed by General Romero. Col. Majano and some officers under him attempted to halt the rising violence with which the security forces acted against the protesters but found they had only limited authority within the regular army and virtually none over the National Guard and the Treasury Police. These security forces were the nerve centers of rightwing terrorism, many of their personnel belonging to the various paramilitary groups of death squads. By the end of 1979 the activities of the death squads had become so extreme, and so clearly identified with the government forces, that the civilian members of the junta made executive control over the armed forces the central issue of their continued participation in the government.

The military took firm hold over the next few months. Early in January 1980 the military rejected civilian attempts to exercise control over the armed forces, thus precipitating the resignation of two of the three civilian junta members— Guillermo Ungo and Román Mayorga—as well as all civilian cabinet members. This exodus is popularly referred to as the fall of the first junta.

On January 22, 1980, to commemorate the forty-eighth anniversary of the rebellion of 1932, the Revolutionary Coordinator of the Masses (CRM), a coalition of mass organizations, orchestrated an enormous demonstration in San Salvador, the largest ever held in the country. Guards and sharpshooters on the rooftops of the National Palace attacked the demonstrators, leaving many civilians dead. As in the case of past massacres, sources disagree about the exact number killed; one says "more than twenty," another "at least 52."[13]

On February 8, 1980, the junta placed itself beyond all legal restraints with the announcement that it would recognize the validity of the Constitution of 1962 only insofar as it was "compatible" with the objectives of the regime and its "line of government" (Decree 144, Article 1). On March 6, 1980, the junta declared a nationwide state of emergency, which was renewed every thirty days, with only one brief interruption in the course of seven years, and which significantly changed the nature and administration of the legal system. During each state of emergency constitutional protections of basic liberties have been suspended; special criminal procedures promulgated by the government have granted jurisdiction over politically motivated crimes to military courts and have bestowed undue powers on police and army personnel with respect to criminal suspects.

Many of the civilians who had not left with the fall of the first junta stayed on just until March 1980, by which time they too resigned and left the country, charging that they had no effective voice with a government that increasingly concentrated control in the hands of the military. "We have not been able to stop the repression," the former junta member Héctor Dada Hirez said upon resigning, "and those committing acts of repression in disrespect of the authority of the junta go unpunished. . . . The chances for producing reforms with the support of the people are receding beyond reach."[14] With the fall of these "first two juntas," the center-left alternative was effectively closed. The military was back in control. At this point the junta recruited Duarte, leaving the Christian Democrats alone in alliance with the armed forces.

In April 1980 many former government officials who had left the first two juntas, Ungo among them, combined with the various civilian political groups, nonaligned trade unions, and professional organizations to form the Democratic Front (FD). This group soon reached agreement with the Revolutionary Coordinator of the Masses on a common program of reforms and action, which led in turn to the establishment of the Democratic Revolutionary Front (FDR). Since that time, the FDR has been the political arm of the revolutionary opposition, incorporating liberal and social-democratic elements, as well as those of the Marxist left.

At the same time, the various guerrilla groups had been moving toward greater unity, setting up a united command structure, known as the United Revolutionary Directorate (DRU). In October 1980 they incorporated the small military forces of the Communist party, establishing the Farabundo Martí National Liberation Front. By mid-1981 the FMLN had five thousand combatants, compared with fifteen thousand in the combined Salvadoran Armed Forces (excluding the security forces). Armed confrontations between the military and the guerrillas intensified.

The move toward open warfare was accelerated by the assassination on March 24, 1980, of Oscar Arnulfo Romero, archbishop of San Salvador, who had championed the cause of the poor and used his influence to promote a political solution to the conflict. In his last homily, Romero had called on the junta's troops to disobey orders to fire on their fellow citizens. With his death El Salvador lost its most revered leader of peaceful resistance to political violence.

For the rest of 1980 the reformist image the Salvadoran government sought to project through the agrarian reform program was repeatedly tarnished by events. Colonel Majano, considered the principal progressive force within the military, was forced out of the junta by the conservative colonels García and

Gutiérrez and sent into exile. In November, six leading members of the Democratic Revolutionary Front including its president, the former agriculture minister Enrique Alvarez Cordoba were kidnapped from a meeting in San Salvador by a large group of heavily armed plainclothesmen. Their mutilated, bullet-ridden bodies were discovered later by the side of a road. In early December, National Guard troops raped and murdered four U.S. churchwomen on an isolated road outside San Salvador. That same month, to bolster the junta's waning image, the Christian Democrat José Napoleón Duarte was elevated to the provisional presidency of what became the fourth transitional government since October 1979.

In January 1981 the FMLN launched an inauspiciously named "final offensive," which failed to spark a general insurrection but prompted a rampage by the military and security forces that took the lives of thousands of suspected civilian guerrilla supporters. Soon after the failed offensive, the guerrillas began to press for a negotiated settlement to the conflict. The effort to promote negotiations received the support of the acting archbishop of San Salvador, Arturo Rivera Damas, who in 1981 began what became nearly a decade of attempts at quiet mediation between the government and the rebels.

Mexico and France also supported negotiations, and in August 1981 they recognized the FD-FMLN as a "representative political force." President Daniel Ortega of Nicaragua proposed at the U.N. General Assembly in 1981 that negotiations be internationally supervised. The United States, however, with a newly inaugurated Republican president, adamantly opposed negotiations. The Reagan administration adhered to a Cold War view of the Salvadoran conflict, seeing in it not an indigenous conflict born of inhuman living conditions and appalling human rights abuses but rather a "textbook case of indirect armed aggression by Communist powers through Cuba," as a State Department white paper put it.

In an effort to "draw the line" against communism, in the words of then Secretary of State Alexander Haig, the Reagan administration deepened its military ties with El Salvador. In 1982 it began training Salvadoran soldiers in the United States, and military aid, which had been extremely limited under the Carter administration, rose from $5.7 million in "nonlethal" military equipment in 1980 to $35.5 million in 1981 and $82.0 million in 1982 (see app. A for a table on U.S. aid to El Salvador).

Duarte's accession to the presidency of the junta had failed to slow the country's political polarization or limit the savagery of the military forces, security forces, and allied death squads. In January 1981 two U.S. labor advisers and the head of the Salvadoran land reform agency were gunned down as they drank coffee in the Sheraton Hotel in San Salvador. Political killings of civilians by government forces and death squads reached an estimated peak of nearly fourteen thousand in 1981, according to the legal aid office of the Archdiocese of San Salvador. In 1982 nearly six thousand civilians were killed.

In March 1982, El Salvador held elections for a constituent assembly, in what one historian has described as "a genuine if far from clean contest between the right . . . and the extreme right."[15] Although Duarte's Christian Democratic party came away with a plurality in the assembly, the right-wing Nationalist Republican Alliance (ARENA) party, in coalition with the traditional military-based National Conciliation Party (PCN), named the extremist Roberto D'Aubuisson president of the lawmaking body. The left did not participate in the election, at least in part out of fear. Many years later, the *Washington Post* reported that the dentist friend D'Aubuisson named as head of security for the assembly, Héctor Antonio Regalado, had allegedly used his position to mount a death squad operation on the second floor of the assembly building.[16]

In April 1982 the assembly, under military suggestion, named a business-man, Alvaro Magaña, the provisional president of the country, and in one of its first acts, it suspended key provisions of one of three components of the agrarian reform program, the so-called Land-to-the-Tiller Plan (Decree 207), which allowed peasants to buy the small plots of land they had been working as tenants. Massive evictions of tenants ensued.[17]

The guerrillas' growing strength was demonstrated by their December 30, 1983, attack on the El Paraíso military base, where they killed at least one hundred soldiers, and the sabotage just two days later of the Cuscatlán bridge. By 1984 the insurgents apparently exercised control over the northern thirds of the departments of Morazán, La Unión, Chalatenango, and Cabañas, as well as along the southeastern coast and around the Guazapa volcano near San Salvador.[18]

In March 1984, El Salvador held a presidential election that seemed to be largely free of fraud, although tainted by allegations that the U.S. Central Intelligence Agency (CIA) heavily financed the campaign of the winner, Duarte, to prevent ARENA's D'Aubuisson from winning.[19] As in the 1982 elections, left-wing parties, concerned about the safety of candidates and supporters, did not participate. Nor did the left participate in legislative and municipal elections held in March 1985, after which Duarte's Christian Democrats won a working majority in the Legislative Assembly. Their fear was well grounded: not only had soldiers murdered the six top leaders of the FDR in November 1980 but several other FDR and allied union activists "disappeared" in October 1982 and Víctor Manuel Quintanilla Ramos, the highest ranking spokesperson for the FDR remaining in El Salvador, was murdered in October 1983.[20] The government made no attempt to guarantee the physical safety of FDR activists should they choose to participate in the elections.

The economic crisis had deepened severely by 1984, with GNP down by nearly a quarter since 1978; the cost of living had more than doubled in the same period. Wages in the urban sector had fallen by over 40 percent in four years. Popular pressure on the government increased as conditions worsened; labor unions engaged in a growing number of strikes as workers grew more disillusioned with and defiant of government policies.[21] The economic misfortunes of the nation intensified when a major earthquake hit San Salvador in October 1986, killing at least one thousand people and leaving thousands more homeless.

In October 1984, President Duarte surprised the Reagan administration, which had made clear its strong opposition to negotiations, by holding an unprecedented meeting with FMLN leaders in the village of La Palma in embattled Chalatenango Department. Although the meeting gave voice to popular demands for peace, the positions of the government and the guerrillas appeared all but irreconcilable. During the meeting President Duarte reportedly proposed that the FMLN lay down its weapons under a guarantee of amnesty and become a political party competing in elections. He also reportedly offered to help resettle former guerrillas who wanted to live outside the country. A month later, in a second round of meetings at Ayagualo, the guerrillas demanded participation in a provisional government that would arrange new elections and reorganize the military.[22] The talks broke down and were not resumed for several years.

Aside from the dramatic gesture of the La Palma and Ayagualo meetings, Duarte's presidency seemed paralyzed from the start. Having campaigned on broad promises of land reform, prosecution of notorious human rights crimes, negotiations with the guerrillas, and an end to corruption, he failed to produce significant movement on any of these fronts. The land reform program remained stalled, reaching only 77,296 peasants by 1987; the U.S. Agency for International Development (AID), which designed the program, had initially planned on 300,000 beneficiaries.[23] Of the five human rights cases that Duarte promised to investigate, only one, the 1981 murder of two U.S. labor advisers and the Salvadoran head of the land reform agency, achieved a measure of justice with the conviction and sentencing of two low-ranking National Guardsmen. The intellectual authors of the crime, well-connected officers and businessmen, were never tried. And reports of widespread corruption in the Christian Democratic administration at a time of severe economic decline may have been the primary reason for the party's resounding defeat by ARENA in the 1989 presidential elections.

Duarte failed to accomplish any of his professed goals both because of his weakness relative to the traditional twin powers of Salvadoran society—the army and the oligarchy—and because of his own progressively rightward drift. Examples of military insubordination to the commander in chief abound, from his inability to fire his own air force commander after the latter's role in the

Iran-*contra* supply line became public,[24] to his inability to have a powerful colonel arrested after witnesses linked him to a multimillion-dollar kidnapping ring.[25] The Iran-contra scandal erupted when the U.S. Justice Department revealed in the fall of 1986 that profits from the secret sale of arms to Iran had been diverted to the Nicaraguan contras. The diversion took place when the Congress had banned military aid to the contra rebels.

Inaction aside, Duarte was always quick to defend the military against accusations of atrocities. When the army massacred then unarmed peasants in San Vicente Department in September 1988, for example, Duarte was quick to suggest that witnesses who blamed the army were not to be believed. "Obviously, if in that area there are people aligned with the Marxist sectors, the family members could lie," he told the *New York Times*.[26] As one writer noted in 1986, "Duarte has put aside his Christian Democratic principles as well as his rhetoric about being caught between the left and right. He now speaks of unifying the right and the center for an all-out war on the left. And the left is effectively defined, not just as the guerrillas, but as those who are too outspoken in their demands that Duarte comply with his 1984 pledges."[27]

Duarte's participation in mounting regional peace efforts may have reflected nothing more than a desire to see his leftist neighbors, the Sandinistas in Nicaragua, forced into an accommodation with the U.S.-backed contras or eliminated altogether. Yet the signing of the Central American peace plan by five Central American presidents in August 1987 planted the seeds of significant political developments in El Salvador as well as in Nicaragua, some positive and some negative. The agreement called for steps toward democratization and national reconciliation in all countries in the isthmus, including dialogue with and amnesty for opposition forces, complete press freedom, political party pluralism, the lifting of states of emergency, and, in broad terms, respect for human rights. The peace plan also required governments to "give urgent attention" to the needs of refugees and the displaced.

Although the agreement did not lead to an overall improvement in the observance of human rights in El Salvador, it brought about a significant political opening in urban areas, allowing civilian politicians allied with the rebel FMLN to return in November 1987 and paving the way for their subsequent participation in the 1989 presidential elections, their first participation in more than a decade. The peace plan also made it politically difficult for the government to reimpose the state of emergency, which had been allowed to lapse in January 1987 because of a strike by right-wing members of the Legislative Assembly. At the same time, the call for aid to refugees and displaced persons provided important pressure for the military to allow civilians it had driven out in ground sweeps in the early years of the war to return to their original communities. Between 1987 and 1990, several thousand refugees returned en masse from camps in Honduras to repopulate communities in the northern departments of El Salvador, while many of the displaced—those forced out of their original homes or communities but still in El Salvador—also returned home (see chap. 7).

In spite of these encouraging developments under the Central American peace plan, Duarte moved further still from his campaign promise to prosecute human rights offenders by using the call for amnesty to enact a broad measure that effectively precluded prosecution of thousands of atrocities committed by the military and by death squads before October 1987 (see chap. 6). An increase in political killings in the months after the amnesty seemed at least partly related to their strengthened sense of impunity.[28]

In March 1988 parties of the right and center contested legislative and municipal offices, resulting in victories across the board for the right-wing ARENA party, due largely to public disenchantment with the corruption of the governing Christian Democrats and the deepening economic crisis. Although leftist leaders who returned to El Salvador in 1987 had joined forces with those remaining in the country, forming a new Democratic Convergence (CD), they did not participate in the elections, for several leaders were threatened and the structures of their political parties could not be quickly rebuilt after years of repression.[29]

Elections were held again in March 1989, this time for the presidency. The preceding months had brought much political maneuvering and sustained discussions about ending the war. The central element of debate was a January 1989 proposal by the FMLN to participate in an election for the first time and to abide by and respect the results, provided several conditions were met, including the postponement of the voting until September. The government and the guerrillas failed to agree on the proposal, and the elections went ahead that spring as scheduled. Even though the FMLN boycotted the polling and called a nationwide traffic stoppage to hinder voting, the Democratic Convergence, including political leaders loosely allied with the rebels, did participate, making this the first election since 1977 in which any party of the left had appeared on the ballot. Ungo, who had returned from exile in 1987, and Mario Reni Roldán, leader of the Social Democratic Party (PSD), ran as the presidential and vice presidential candidates of the Democratic Convergence.

The ARENA presidential candidate, Alfredo Cristiani, a moderate in the ARENA spectrum selected on the understanding that the United States would not allow a D'Aubuisson triumph, won a resounding victory from an electorate fed up with the unending war, economic deprivation, and the corruption of the Christian Democrats. The Democratic Convergence received only 3.8 percent of the vote, perhaps because the guerrillas discouraged voting and undoubtedly because a decade of terror had decimated the left in El Salvador.

The ARENA government faced a major challenge in November 1989 when the FMLN launched an urban offensive that appeared to threaten the army's hold on San Salvador. Rebel units occupied sections of most major cities in the first few hours of the offensive, holding many positions for the next ten days;[30] fighting lasted for about three weeks, into the first week of December. In launching their attack on the government forces from the poor barrios that ring the capital and later from positions in wealthy neighborhoods, the rebels proved their ability to infiltrate even the areas most hostile to them and attack the army from almost anywhere. Although clearly demonstrating the rebels' well-developed urban infrastructure, the offensive failed to incite the broad insurrection that the guerrillas hoped for, illustrating the limits to their popular support. The onslaught impressed the military and its backers with the rebels' fighting forces, but did not fundamentally alter the military stalemate.

The army's cold-blooded murder of six Jesuit priests, their housekeeper, and her daughter in the midst of the offensive brought a rain of criticism on the military and against Washington's decade-long policy. As Salvadoran authorities contrived to prevent examination of the role of senior officials in the massacre, the U.S. Congress in October 1990 approved a 50 percent reduction in military aid to El Salvador, the largest reduction in the entire decade.

Meanwhile, efforts to negotiate an end to the fighting proceeded in fits and starts. A series of talks were held in 1989, only to be broken off by the guerrillas after a bomb ripped apart the headquarters of the leftist National Federation of Salvadoran Workers (FENASTRAS) in October, killing ten unionists, including the FENASTRAS leader, Febe Elizabeth Velásquez. The FMLN justified its November offensive in part as retaliation for this act of terrorism.

In January 1990, when the fiercest fighting of the offensive had ended, the government and the guerrillas agreed to resume a dialogue. Several rounds of negotiations, held throughout the year with U.N. mediators, appeared to hold greater prospects for peace than any negotiations held previously. During the July 20–26 meeting in San José, Costa Rica, the U.N. mediator Alvaro de Soto broke a deadlock by guiding the parties to a discussion of human rights. The final agreement included commitments to respect fundamental rights of life, liberty, and freedom of expression and association and called for an immediate end to disappearances and kidnappings. It also reaffirmed important rights of detainees and prohibited nighttime arrests, political detention, and the use of detention as a means of intimidation. Initially, the agreement provided for verification by a U.N. mission once a cease-fire was in place, at one time contemplated for September. As 1990 drew to an end, the talks remained at a standstill, primarily owing to disagreement over the central issue of military reform. With a cease-fire nowhere in sight, the United Nations agreed to play a more active mediating role, coming up with its own proposal for presentation to both sides, and to initiate its unprecedented verification work on the human rights accord in the early part of 1991, a decision that could have a significant positive impact on human rights practices in El Salvador.

Opinion in Washington had, by the end of 1990, also shifted in the direction of support for negotiations: besides halving military aid to protest the murder of the Jesuits and their attendants, the legislation passed by the U.S. Congress in October explicitly seeks to promote a negotiated settlement by penalizing the government with greater aid reductions if it does not bargain in good faith or by restoring aid if the rebels leave the negotiating table or launch another major offensive. That the Bush administration has now made a negotiated settlement a central goal of U.S. policy is a momentous shift from the Reagan years. That both sides in the conflict remain open to further negotiations provides one of the very few rays of light as ten years of carnage draw to a close.

2

THE ASSAULT ON CIVIL SOCIETY

Through much of the twentieth century Salvadorans have joined forces in independent social groups—unions and peasant leagues, community organizations, churches, schools, and political parties—to seek a better existence within a political system dominated by a tiny oligarchy and its powerful military allies. Facing an array of legal constraints and overt displays of force—from the outlawing of unions to the murder of outspoken activists—these institutions have been crushed repeatedly, only to rise again when the desire for change has overcome the fear of repression. Since the outbreak of civil war in the late 1970s, military forces and death squads, equipped with modern U.S. technology, have sought systematically to exterminate the newest generation of popular leaders.

Peasant and union leaders, students and teachers, human rights activists, and journalists have borne the brunt of state violence in the 1980s. Murder, disappearance, arbitrary arrest, and torture have served not only to eliminate political opponents but also to drive home the dangers of openly expressing dissent. Adding to the terror has been the murder of thousands of civilians who had no apparent involvement in political activity. The continued practice of terror, combined with the failure to prosecute a single army officer for a human rights violation, has maintained and entrenched military authority (see chap. 6).

U.S. officials and other defenders of the Salvadoran government, noting a marked decrease in the number and frequency of human rights violations over the course of the decade, have concluded that human rights conditions are much improved. Certainly the carnage of the early part of the decade has not been sustained, but for a number of reasons that view appears to be overdrawn. First, although the numbers of people who have been murdered and who have disappeared remain far below the levels in 1980–83, the decline has not been steady; indeed, there have been some increases in recent years. Targeted killings registered in the thousands in the early 1980s.[1] Month after month the death toll of "political opponents" mounted. In response to belated U.S. pressure, targeted violence declined during the early years of the Duarte presidency. By the end of the decade, however, it was on the rise again. According to Tutela Legal, the human rights office of the Catholic Archdiocese of San Salvador, targeted government and death squad killings increased from 96 in 1987 to 152 in 1988. This suggests that the temporary numerical decline was based not on structural change—the criminal punishment and removal from positions of power of the killers—but on an ephemeral shift in policy, whereby the perpetrators apparently decided for a time to kill fewer people, remaining free to reverse that policy whenever they saw fit.

The use of severe forms of torture also declined in the mid-1980s, only to reemerge toward the end of the decade. From 1980 to 1983 detainees were systematically tortured by all units of the security forces. The most frequent types of torture reported were severe beatings, death threats, choking, electric shock, smothering with a hood, drugging, sexual violence, submersion in water, burning with cigarettes, and mock executions. During the second half of 1984, there was a sharp decline in the use of torture by the security forces, which stayed at that lower level for several years. Strong pressure by human rights groups—both governmental and independent—and by U.S. officials apparently contributed to the reduced frequency of torture. Instead, the security forces came to rely on more subtle forms of coercion: prolonged forced standing or exercise, threats, confinement in very cold or tiny rooms, and deprivation of food, water, and sleep. Then, in 1989, particularly after the right-wing ARENA party won the presidential elections in March, human rights organizations detected a resurgence of more drastic methods of torture on the part of all branches of the armed forces.[2]

Another reason that the decline in human rights violations represents no great improvement suggests itself. Even though it is true that the military and the death squads grew more selective in targeting victims of violence later in the decade, they may simply have needed to kill fewer in order to generate a commensurate level of terror. As the November 1989 murder of six Jesuit priests illustrates, the identity of the victims may be at least as important as their number in intimidating the population. If the army could kill such important religious figures, some of whom were of international renown and one of whom was on friendly terms with President Cristiani, who could be safe?

Finally, there is little indication that the authorities' attitude toward political opponents, unionists, human rights monitors, or church workers has changed over the last decade. In November 1989, in response to the most robust guerrilla offensive in years, government and military officials launched a series of rhetorical and physical attacks against religious leaders, opposition politicians, and other members of the peaceful opposition. The best-known attack, the massacre of the Jesuits, was by no means a singular event. The government-controlled radio station broadcast death threats against prominent Jesuits and Catholic Church officials, sometimes cloaking the threats in concern over the targets' safety, as in Attorney General Mauricio Colorado's letter to Pope John Paul II, made public on November 18, two days after the Jesuits were killed, asking the pope to recall El Salvador's Catholic bishops, purportedly for their safety, and the attorney general's statement later that month that he would hold the rebel FMLN to blame for "any nefarious act" that might befall Archbishop Rivera Damas and Auxiliary Archbishop Gregorio Rosa Chávez.[3]

The government-controlled radio station also broadcast death threats against Rubén Zamora and Guillermo Manuel Ungo, leaders of the opposition coalition, the Democratic Convergence. On November 22 it broadcast an interview with Roberto D'Aubuisson, ARENA party leader and legislative assemblyman, in which he described the guerrilla offensive as a joint action of the FMLN and the Democratic Convergence; the involvement of the convergence, he argued, provided the "moral justification to annihilate" it. Government forces searched the offices and homes of Democratic Convergence officials on several occasions toward the end of 1989. The Treasury Police arrested and beat a leader of the group, Jorge Villacorta, on December 6, 1989. On January 12, 1990, Héctor Oquelí Colindres, another convergence leader, was kidnapped and murdered in Guatemala, raising the specter of ongoing cooperation between death squads and security forces in both countries.[4]

It has been reported that the Jesuit murders may have been part of a broader army Plan Djakarta to wipe out opposition leaders from religious, labor, and other communities,[5] reflecting the traditional and continuing tendency of high army officials—fully supported by their U.S. counterparts—to link the armed with the peaceful opposition, thereby justifying attacks against both. Of course, international humanitarian law requires that a party to a civil war distinguish between civilians and combatants and expressly prohibits targeted violence against civilians. Statements by the head of the human rights office established by the army in 1990 to demonstrate its good intentions revealed the prevailing military views.[6] Months after President Cristiani had publicly acknowledged army responsibility for the Jesuits' murders, Maj. Roberto Molina, head of the new office, was blaming anyone but the army for the crime. Asked by an American reporter, "Who killed the Jesuits?" Molina replied: "Foreigners, dark forces of the United States bent on breaking the armed forces as an institution. It was the Trilateral Commission, the Society of the Skull, groups where just to mention their names risks your life."[7] Molina even blames the Jesuits. He told Americas Watch in July 1990, "The Jesuits have been expelled from many countries. They have created problems for many governments. In fact, the Vatican is now having many problems with them."

THE PERPETRATORS OF TARGETED VIOLENCE

The Armed Forces

The Armed Forces of El Salvador currently total fifty-six thousand—almost four times their size in 1981; the figure includes the 11,500 members of the three security forces.[8] These institutions—the army, the air force, the National Police, the Treasury Police, and the National Guard—have been responsible for the greatest portion of political violence during the past decade. In early 1982, when public concern about the gross misconduct of these forces was growing, the Reagan administration explained the U.S. role in El Salvador as in part an effort to improve the human rights performance of the Salvadoran military:

> One of the principal missions of our military trainers in El Salvador is to increase the professionalism of the armed forces and improve the system of military discipline and command and control, thus reducing the abuses suffered in the past by the civilian population at the hands of the armed forces. To the extent that members of the armed forces see themselves first as military professionals, they are less likely to take action on behalf of partisan political causes or private interests. Discipline in the army and sensitivity to the problem of military abuse of civilians have improved and should improve further through professional training programs, such as those we are instituting for Salvadoran officers and infantrymen in the United States.[9]

Whether or not reducing abuses was a principal mission of U.S. military trainers, the Salvadoran Armed Forces have shown themselves to be stubbornly resistant to reform. The unit most closely associated with U.S. training, the elite Atlacatl Battalion, remains perhaps the most appalling violator of human rights in El Salvador.[10] Just three days before its troops massacred the Jesuits, their housekeeper, and her daughter in November 1989, the battalion was undergoing training by U.S. Special Forces from Fort Bragg, North Carolina.[11] Yet the Atlacatl Battalion and its commanders are not alone in the ranks of military human rights abusers. A report by the Arms Control and Foreign Policy Caucus of the U.S. Congress found that fourteen of the fifteen highest-ranking army officers in May 1990 had commanded troops responsible for atrocities at some point during their careers.[12] Even after a highly publicized reshuffling of the high command in September 1990, the overwhelming majority of senior positions were filled by officers linked to human rights violations.

In spite of the goal of professionalization, the promotion of human rights abusers has been standard practice in El Salvador, because graduating class, not merit, remains the chief criterion for advancement. The Salvadoran army has traditionally promoted everyone in a particular graduating class at the Military School at regular intervals. The seniority system promotes insularity and uncritical class loyalty and surrounds accused human rights abusers with an unbreachable wall of fraternal silence. The history of gross abuses committed by the army over the years has only reinforced officers' perception of the need for solidarity. As the Arms Control and Foreign Policy Caucus concluded, "Of the 15 primary commanders, 12 are members of the *Tandona,* the 'big class' that graduated from the Salvadoran Military School in 1966 and that is resisting pressures to reform. This unprecedented concentration of power permits the *Tandona* to protect its members from removal for corruption, abuses or incompetence. The *Tandona* at times shows more loyalty to its members than to the rule of law or even to the President." A 1988 study by four U.S. military advisers concluded that "the *tanda* system, a sort of West Point Protective Association gone berserk, remains today the chief barrier to a competent officer corps."[13]

An analysis in the *New York Times Magazine* in 1989 said that the armed forces have used the exorbitant sums bestowed upon them in recent years in substantial measure to line their own pockets and enhance their own power: "One billion dollars in American military aid seems to have bought an army big enough to survive its own mistakes, and powerful enough to resist any effort to reform it—to end pervasive corruption or weed out corrupt officers. Instead of fostering reform, the American money has been absorbed into a network of corruption and patronage that has grown up over half a century, and has made the Salvadoran military an empire unto itself."[14]

The Death Squads

The chilling term *death squad* achieved its greatest notoriety in Central America in the 1980s, nowhere more so than in El Salvador, where the victims of these units number in the thousands. The term is necessarily imprecise, for it describes above all a style of abduction and murder that seeks to preserve deniability for the perpetrators.

Death squads generally are plainclothes units of the armed forces that avoid accountability by such means as using vehicles with smoked-glass windows and without numbered license plates. Death squad victims are often seized, interrogated, and tortured before being killed, their mutilated bodies being left by the sides of roads or in "body dumps," such as the notorious lava bed north of the capital known as El Playón, where more than 250 homicide victims were found in 1982 alone.[15] In other cases, death squad victims are gunned down in broad daylight on the street or in their offices, as if the squads were flaunting their impunity. Particularly in the early 1980s, death squads frequently claimed "credit" for their killings.

Intending not only to eliminate people with undesirable political views but also to terrorize the survivors, Salvadoran death squads have adopted such theatrics as publishing lists of future victims, sending their targets invitations to their own funerals, and delivering coffins to their doorsteps. The mutilation of bodies helps maximize the horror. The former *Washington Post* reporter Christopher Dickey recalled that the first death squad victims he ever saw in San Salvador were two young men shot in the heads as they drove home from work. On a wall near the murder scene, a crude skull had been painted, with a handful of the victims' brains thrown in the middle as a "signature."[16]

What intimidation is not accomplished by murder, is achieved by threats. Letters, phone calls, and paid communiqués in the press denounce individuals as subversives and promise their elimination. One member of the Constituent Assembly was addressing the legislature on the subject of land reform in October 1983 when the phone in front of him rang. The caller warned that if he did not shut up, something serious would happen to his family.[17]

It has been well established over the decade that from the late 1960s until the mid-1980s the death squads were simply plainclothes paramilitary units run by the armed forces.[18] To what extent this remains true is a subject of debate. In some cases death squads may be composed of individuals settling private disputes or compensating for what they view to be the army's inadequate efforts to eliminate the guerrillas and their supporters. The heavily armed plainclothesmen seen nabbing victims in the streets and dumping corpses in ravines or on roadsides, however, operate day and night without interference from the security forces, a fact showing, at a minimum, the complicity of those forces.

As Amnesty International noted in a recent report on death squads in El Salvador, their actions allow the government to maintain deniability for political murders:

The use of the "death squad" strategy—murder through domestic covert action—serves as a short-term solution to both peaceful dissidence and armed opposition, while allowing governments to avoid accountability for criminal acts. Once established, however, as the persistence of the "death squad" option in Central America since the late 1960s has shown, the formula is rarely abandoned. Even after an insurgency appears to have been controlled, "death squad" killings may become a permanent feature of a security system. The elimination of real or perceived government opponents, even when not ordered by the armed forces high command, is often allowed by discretionary powers delegated to the lower ranks and so will rarely be the subject of judicial investigation or prosecution.[19]

For the first few years of the decade, death squad killings, like killings by uniformed government forces, were a daily occurrence. Groups with names like the White Hand, the Secret Anticommunist Army (ESA), and the Maximiliano Hernández Martínez Anticommunist Brigade—named after the general who wiped out thirty thousand peasants to avenge a brief uprising almost sixty years ago—selected their victims from among prominent university, labor, and political figures and publicized their activities by threatening to bomb radio stations that refused to read their communiqués.[20]

A sharp decline in death squad crimes began in November 1983 and continued through 1984, attributable largely to pressure exerted by the Reagan administration and particularly to a December 1983 visit to San Salvador by then Vice President George Bush, who reportedly demanded the removal of several officers linked to the death squads (see chap. 7).[21] Yet a resurgence of paramilitary killings came in the first half of 1985, not reaching the levels of 1979–1983 but more than double the level in the latter half of 1984. More importantly, even when the number of killings decreased again later in 1985 and in 1986, the pattern of death squad activity did not change, nor was any death squad member ever prosecuted.

Three new death squads published communiqués announcing their existence in 1985. The Protective Salvadoran Army (EPS) appeared in October to "bring justice to all those who participate in the theft of children." In December the Protective Army of Santa Ana (EPSA) promised to compensate for "the incapacity and negligence and possible corruption of the authorities in charge of applying the law to delinquents." A third squad, the Ghost Busters Commando (COCAFAN), condemned "terrorist groups that try to bury the country and destroy the sectors that work honestly to save the country from chaos. Those groups . . . will be overthrown by the army with the help of men who love the nation and will not permit communists, criminals, and enemies of the people, who want peace, democracy, liberty, and justice to convert it into a Cuba or a Nicaragua."[22]

Death squads maintained a lower profile over the next two years, though on June 15, 1987, the Maximiliano Hernández Martínez Anticommunist Brigade reappeared, issuing death threats to fourteen students and teachers at the National University in San Salvador (also called the University of El Salvador).[23] Then, in 1989, death squads adopted a higher profile, showing that they were still free to operate openly without fear of apprehension or prosecution. Nine death squads issued communiqués that year, including older groups, such as the Maximiliano Hernández Martínez Anticommunist Brigade and the Ghost Busters Commando, and new organizations, such as the Central American Anticommunist Hand (MACA), the Eastern Solidarity Committee (COSOR), and the Democratic Defense Commands (CDD).[24]

In the early 1980s, U.S. officials insisted that the death squads were independent rogue bands, unaffiliated with the armed forces, for whom the government of El Salvador bore no responsibility. By the end of the decade they admitted that "in the early 1980s, members of the security forces repeatedly violated the human rights of their fellow citizens and were unquestionably involved in widespread death squad activities." With respect to ongoing violations, the Bush administration contends that they "are likely the result of individual acts of right-wing vigilantism rather than of organized paramilitary death squads as existed before 1984."[25] But the evidence suggests this recent statement is almost as disingenuous as the first.

Certainly the links between the death squads and the armed forces during the 1970s and early 1980s are incontrovertible. The dramatic reduction in death squad killings after Vice President Bush's highly publicized visit to El Salvador in December 1983 speaks volumes about the intimate relations between death squads and the armed forces. If a whisper in the ear of the right military officer could so greatly reduce the flow of blood spilled by the death squads, there can be little doubt as to where the murderers got their orders.

The continued functioning of the death squads and their persistent links to the armed forces are revealed by numerous recent abductions: men in civilian clothes have taken victims who later appeared in security force detention centers. In 1983 the head of the National Police, Col. Carlos Reynaldo López Nuila, defended this practice, saying it was necessary to surprise subversives.[26] Even more persuasive evidence is found where the detention of an individual by the armed forces follows directly on the heels of public death squad threats against the victim. On September 7, 1989, the Revolutionary Action for Extermination (ARDE) issued a death threat over Radio Chaparrastique in San Miguel against several people, including Inmar Rolando Reyes Flores, treasurer of the Association of Treasury Ministry Employees (AGEMHA). Eight days later, Reyes was captured by Cavalry Regiment soldiers and brought to the Third Brigade barracks, where he was tortured before being released. In another case, armed plainclothesmen and a man in a black uniform seized two university students from their house in Santa Ana on January 15, 1989. The students were taken first to the Second Brigade barracks in Santa Ana and later to Treasury Police headquarters. Although the military acknowledged custody of the students two days after their capture, two local radio stations broadcast a communiqué from ARDE stating that the death squad was holding them and might kill them.[27]

In August 1988 the *Washington Post* published a series of articles based on the accounts of two young men who had participated in death squads operating out of the Constituent Assembly building (now the Legislative Assembly building) in the early 1980s. They said the paramilitary units were run by Roberto D'Aubuisson, the leader of ARENA, and the dentist Héctor Antonio Regalado, and were being reactivated and rearmed in 1988, using as a launching pad the assembly, which ARENA controlled in 1988, and the five-thousand-member Municipal Police, under the jurisdiction of the mayors of the nation, most of whom belonged to ARENA. One of the informants, former death squad member Hernán Torres Cortez, attended several meetings in the assembly building in 1988 at which the reorganization and rearming of the death squads was discussed. He said ARENA had hired sixteen new security agents at the assembly, presumably to act as death squad operatives, like their predecessors in 1982 and 1983.[28]

Finally, recent allegations by a deserter from the First Brigade appear to support prior reports of death squads operating out of the intelligence sections within the armed forces and suggest that such activities were continuing as recently as 1989.[29] Although difficult to corroborate, the defector's detailed descriptions of the inner workings of military assassination units merit close examination. Particularly significant for U.S. policy are his assertions that U.S. advisers work closely with the First Brigade's intelligence unit—the very unit he charges with systematic killings of civilians—pay for some of its operations, and review photocopies of its arrest reports. U.S. officials have denied knowledge of torture or killings by the unit but have not contradicted other aspects of the story. A U.S. Embassy statement issued in response to the soldier's claims said the embassy "exchanges information with the Salvadoran armed forces on a regular basis, but does not regularly or systematically receive photocopies of military reports on captured guerrillas." The embassy acknowledged that it does not routinely follow up on arrest cases it has been informed of but asserted that it "does of course follow up any specific reports of human rights abuses by either civilian or military authorities."[30]

The deserter, César Vielman Joya Martínez, left El Salvador in 1989 and applied for political asylum in the United States. He did this, he said, after learning that his superiors planned to kill him, apparently having decided he could no longer be trusted. His flight also followed action by a court in Quezaltepeque charging him and another soldier with the murder of two suspected guerrillas in a joint action by the First Brigade and the Atlacatl Battalion. After the *Washington Post* and other international media published Joya Martínez's allegations that the First Brigade intelligence unit ran a clandestine death squad, Salvadoran authorities released his codefendant, Cpl. Alcides Gómez Gómez of the Atlacatl Battalion, from prison. In September 1990, Joya Martínez was convicted in a U.S. federal court of having illegally entered the country after a previous deportation.[31]

Americas Watch interviewed Joya Martínez in the United States and sought to corroborate details of several murders that he claimed to have participated in under orders from superiors in the First Brigade. The results of our investigation were mixed. Part of the difficulty derives from the nature of the underworld activities he has described, whose continuance depends on clandestine methods. In many of the murders, the body was never found, and in most cases, Joya Martínez did not even know the name of his victim. In one case in which he knew his victim by name, we were able to verify that the victim's death occurred in the manner Joya Martínez described; that it was not a publicized case lends credibility to his account. In another case we were unable to verify the event. Although his testimony contained some inconsistencies, it has the ring of truth.

Joya Martínez said he entered the First Brigade in August 1987 and, after completing a three-month training program, started working as a case officer in Section 2, Intelligence. His activities fell into two broad categories: the official and the covert. His official functions were principally surveillance and information gathering. As part of his surveillance duties, Joya Martínez said, he managed operatives and informers in the Nejapa and Apopa areas, north of the capital, using information from them and other army investigators to verify the location of individuals under suspicion. He was responsible for keeping tabs on members of unions and other popular organizations in his geographical area, preparing reports indicating where suspects could be found.

His unofficial activities, which included assassinating victims handed over to his small group by superiors who instructed that they be executed and their bodies disposed of, were not widely known within the First Brigade but were known to a tight circle of ranking officers. His victims were selected on the basis of reports from the intelligence department of the Armed Forces General Staff, reports that were passed first to the commander of the First Brigade and then to the head of the brigade's intelligence unit. In some cases, suspects were questioned by an interrogation department and then turned over to Joya Martínez's "special forces" group, which took them away in a van to kill them. In other cases, the victims were killed without interrogation. Joya Martínez said his instructions included the type of weapon to be used against the victim: one victim's throat was slit, another was shot with a forty-five-caliber pistol, another with a nine-millimeter weapon. One killing, which he described as an "experiment," involved injecting a man with sulfuric acid provided by the head of First Brigade intelligence. Another victim had his body blown apart by TNT after his throat was cut. Usually, identification documents were removed before the bodies were discarded. In several cases, bodies were dumped in the ocean. When the death van returned to the brigade, a special unit was charged with cleaning up the blood.

Often Joya Martínez knew little or nothing about a victim turned over to him for execution; on one occasion, the victims were hooded, and his supervisor warned him not to speak to them. One of his superiors threatened to kill him if he ever talked about the murders.

Fear provides a constant backdrop to Joya Martínez's netherworld of spy and counterspy. Although he recounted the murder of a businessman and a student, several of his victims were informers for the army who had ceased providing information or who were suspected of being double agents. The brigade's department of counterintelligence followed every step Joya Martínez's unit took, he said, and he believes it was responsible for the murder of one of his own informers. Although Salvadoran officials have claimed that Joya Martínez fled from El Salvador to escape criminal prosecution for murdering prisoners, he insisted that he fled when he learned that his unit was preparing to kill him.

TARGETED SECTORS OF THE PEACEFUL OPPOSITION

Labor and Peasant Organizations

The Salvadoran conflict stems, to a great extent, from the persistent denial of basic socioeconomic rights to the peasant majority. Throughout the past decade systematic violence has befallen not just peasants protesting the lack of land and the means to a decent existence but, in a steadily widening circle, individuals and institutions who have espoused the cause of the peasants and decried their fate: labor leaders, priests and nuns, political leaders, journalists, teachers and students, health workers, and human rights monitors.

Salvadoran law prohibits the majority of the labor force—agricultural workers and public employees—from organizing unions, entering into collective-bargaining agreements, and holding strikes. Less than half the population—nonagricultural workers in the private sector and employees of autonomous institutions—enjoys these rights. Agricultural workers, approximately half the work force, are not entitled to written contracts. And most farm workers—those who work only during seasonal harvest periods—have no right to stability in employment. They may be discharged at any time, for any reason or no reason at all, without compensation.[32]

In practice, virtually all labor activity was eviscerated by the slaughter of union organizers during the early 1980s. Following the 1984 election of President Duarte and the tentative opening of political space, organizational and strike activity intensified, and as workers pushed to expand the limits of the freedom they were granted, unions that had been underground opened offices. Agricultural cooperatives in rural areas proliferated, although their members have been more frequently subjected to violence than their industrial or public employee counterparts.

Salvadoran authorities have long suspected unionists of guerrilla ties, and U.S. officials have largely reinforced these prejudices. U.S. State Department and embassy officials have consistently referred to opposition unions, including the militant FENASTRAS and National Unity of Salvadoran Workers (UNTS) federations and the Coffee Industry Union (SICAFE), as FMLN front groups or FMLN affiliates. Such open disparagement by the U.S. government undermines the already-precarious position of these organizations and legitimizes attacks against them or their members, as well as impedes the expansion of political space, which U.S. policy officially supports. Regardless of their political orientation, the unions and labor confederations most maligned by U.S. and Salvadoran officials are genuine, legally recognized labor organizations engaged in traditional union activities.[33]

Although there are no overall figures for the killings and disappearances of labor and peasant activists, clusters of incidents give a general idea of the scale of the repression, particularly during 1980 and 1981. One example illustrates the extent to which repression by the military forces and the death squads enfeebled the reforms promoted by civilian members of the first junta after the 1979 overthrow of General Romero: the murder of forty employees of the office charged with implementing the agrarian reform, the Salvadoran Institute for Agricultural Transformation (ISTA), between March 1980, when the agency was founded, and September 1981. One of those killings, the January 3, 1981, murder by National Guardsmen of the ISTA president José Rodolfo Viera and his two dining companions in the coffee shop of the Sheraton Hotel in San Salvador, achieved international notoriety because of the identity and nationality of his companions, Mark David Pearlman and Michael Hammer, both U.S. citizens who worked for the American Institute for Free Labor Development, a U.S.-funded agency closely associated with the agrarian reform program (see chap. 6).[34]

In December 1981 the Salvadoran Communal Union reported that eighty-three of its promoters and members were murdered by army troops, security force personnel, or death squads in 1980 and 1981. Another nine were killed by unknown assassins, believed to be of the right.[35] Although the pattern in later years has been one of targeted, rather than mass, killings, there have been significant deviations, such as the killing of ten people, eight of them members of FENASTRAS, in an October 1989 bomb attack on the union headquarters.

The following incidents represent a small sample of the military and death squad attacks against workers and their organizations over the course of the decade.

· On October 16, 1979, the day after a military coup overthrew the regime of Gen. Carlos Humberto Romero, government forces ousted striking workers from several factories in San Salvador, killing eighteen, arresting seventy-eight, and torturing many of those arrested. Within a week of the coup, according to Amnesty International, the

government had killed more than a hundred demonstrators and striking workers who had been occupying farms and factories.[36]
· On November 20, 1982, armed, uniformed members of the army abducted seven members of the agrarian cooperative on La Florida
farm. Their bodies, bearing signs of torture, were found nearby on
November 22.[37]
· Between 4:00 and 5:00 A.M. on November 7, 1983, heavily armed
men, some in military uniform, arrived at El Cauca and Riveras del
Mar cooperatives in La Paz Department, both affiliated with the Salvadoran Communal Union, and dragged three peasants from their
homes. Two days later, the bodies of the three men—Miguel Angel
Leiva, Gustavo Rivas, and José Francisco Merino López—were
found stuffed into grain sacks in the town of Zaragoza, along with six
other bodies, including two pregnant women. All showed signs of
torture and strangulation. According to Cristobal Alemán Alas, a UCS
leader and member of the governmental Human Rights Commission
(CDH), the three peasants kidnapped from the agrarian reform co-ops
"died for attending UCS meetings."[38]
· Nine people associated with the San Carlos cooperative in La Paz
were attacked on April 8, 1987. The treasurer, Daniel Ortiz, and
three others were killed, and five others were wounded when armed
men in civilian clothes threw a grenade into Ortiz's house. The same
men later raped four young girls from the cooperative. Before these
attacks, the cooperative had suffered official harassment: the government temporarily detained twelve co-op officials and members, it
pressured the co-op to cede its land, and the army accused Ortiz of
working for the guerrillas. The army arrested two suspects in the attack, reportedly an ex-soldier and an ex–National Guardsman. The
latter was promptly released.[39]
· In the first half of 1988, army soldiers terrorized members of the Fifteenth of September cooperative, who were also members of the Salvadoran Association of Democratic Indians (ASID), in Tepemechín,
Morazán, through a string of captures and brutal murders followed by
weeks of surveillance and patrolling. On February 25, soldiers captured Felix Antonio Rivera, the twenty-five-year-old co-op leader,
along with sixteen-year-old Mario Cruz Rivera and eighteen-year-old
Sebastián Gutiérrez, and forced them to march to a nearby hamlet, El
Tablón. There the soldiers made them run barefoot through a burning
field with their hands tied, then took them to a washstand out of
sight, from which their cries of pain could be heard, followed by
shots. The soldiers left with Sebastián Gutiérrez still in custody. The

bodies of Felix Antonio Rivera and Mario Cruz Rivera were found by the washstand with their ears, noses, thumbs, and ring fingers cut off, according to witnesses. Their feet, calves, and legs were covered with blisters and burns. Cruz's body had several knife wounds and signs of heavy blows. Rivera's skull had been broken, and the skin was cut away from part of his face. His right knee was also broken.

A few days after the incident, Rivera's father, Santos González, died of a heart attack. The soldiers had beaten him when they came for his son.

Asked about the incident several months later, Col. René Emilio Ponce, then commander of the Third Brigade (now minister of defense), told reporters that two "subversives" had been killed in a firefight, and showed no interest in pursuing the allegations of atrocities committed by soldiers under his command.[40]

In another incident in Tepemechín, on April 5, soldiers of the Fourth Military Detachment captured Eleutherio Gómez at his house and killed him when he tried to escape. The previous day soldiers had captured José Telesforo González, another Fifteenth of September cooperative member; they tortured him before a judge ordered his release on April 11.[41]

· On July 12, 1988, three armed, masked men in civilian clothes abducted Eliseo Córdova Aguilar, member and former secretary of the Salvadoran Social Security Institute Workers' Union (STISSS), along with his nephew and a neighbor. The masked men handcuffed and blindfolded the three captives and drove them in Córdova's car to a spot near Lake Ilopango. Córdova was interrogated for a half hour a short distance away from the car, during which time the union and salaries were mentioned. His captors then drove him away in another vehicle, and he has never since been seen. The other two captives were released. Americas Watch received allegations that the Treasury Police was responsible for Cordova's disappearance.[42]

· Four armed plainclothesmen seized José Tomás Mazariego, a member of the executive committee of the Association of Telecommunications Workers (ASTTEL) and secretary of relations of the Federation of Independent Associations and Unions of El Salvador (FEASIES), in downtown San Salvador on June 12. Mazariego was taken to Treasury Police headquarters, where he was accused of belonging to the FMLN and tortured during three days of interrogation. He was beaten and slapped; a hood was placed over his head three times to temporarily suffocate him; and acid was placed on his knees. He was released on

June 15 without charge.[43] (Mazariego subsequently died in an automobile accident.)

On July 29, 1989, uniformed soldiers of the Fourth Brigade seized María Magdalena Penate de Leiva, a member of the social security workers' union, along with her husband, from a bus in El Tule, Cuscatlán. The soldiers are said to have accused Penate of being a guerrilla because she belonged to the union. With the captives in tow, the soldiers searched their house and burned it and then held them in separate rooms in a private house. Days later, soldiers took them away from the house in a vehicle and pushed Mr. Leiva from the moving vehicle onto the ground and shot him in the stomach. They left him unconscious in the area of Ingenio San Francisco, San Salvador, where he was found and taken to a medical center. His wife, who was in her fourth month of pregnancy, has not been seen since.[44]

· On August 19, 1989, Juan Francisco Massín, a member of the bakery union at the Pan Lido factory, and Sari Cristiani Chan-Chan, a photographer for FENASTRAS, disappeared after their capture by air force soldiers. Neither has been seen since.[45]

· On the night of September 17 and in the early morning of September 18, 1989, National Guardsmen raided four houses and the Santa Mercedes textile factory in Ilopango and arrested ten persons associated with FENASTRAS. The next afternoon, FENASTRAS held a march to protest the arrests. The marchers obstructed traffic and burned two buses, and National Policemen arrested sixty-four people, most of them members of FENASTRAS-affiliated unions. Most were released within seventy-two hours; many were physically mistreated while in custody. Of thirty-seven detainees examined by the forensic physician of the First Criminal Court on September 21, nineteen exhibited marks or bruises indicating they had been beaten. Several detainees contended they had been raped while in detention. One rape—that of Julia Tatiana Mendoza Aguirre—was confirmed by the court physician.

At 12:30 P.M. on October 31, 1989, a powerful bomb destroyed the FENASTRAS headquarters, killing ten and wounding more than thirty. Eight of the dead were affiliated with FENASTRAS, including Febe Elizabeth Velásquez, a member of the executive committees of both FENASTRAS and UNTS, and Julia Tatiana Mendoza Aguirre, who had been detained the previous month. The bomb was apparently timed to cause maximum casualties while FENASTRAS members lunched inside the offices. The bombing marked a qualitative escalation in the use of political violence in urban areas and served as the catalyst for the FMLN offensive launched eleven days afterward. Almost a year later, the investigation into the bombing had produced no known evidence leading to an identification of the perpetrators.

· The coffee workers' union (SICAFE) has been a frequent target of repression. Two members of the union—Edwin Ernesto Vargas Aguilar and Julio Ernesto García Lucero—and Luis Armando Lemus Urrutia, a baker, disappeared on May 1, 1987, after attending the May Day demonstration at a park in Santa Ana. The victims were at the bus terminal after the demonstration when a white jeep with tinted glass windows pulled up; from it emerged two armed men in civilian clothes who seized them and sped away. A witness reportedly recognized the abductors as employees of the intelligence section of the Second Brigade in Santa Ana, although the authorities denied having the coffee workers or the baker in their custody.[46] The three are still missing.

Between November 1988 and late 1989 death squads murdered two SICAFE leaders in Santa Ana and wounded two other local union members. On November 16, 1988, an armed plainclothesman fatally shot Sonia Elizabeth Flores Martínez, secretary of assistance and social planning of the Santa Ana local, as she left work at the National Coffee Institute (INCAFE) coffee-processing plant in Santa Ana. Flores had previously been threatened regarding her union work. Two young men shot and killed Pablo Obdulio Vargas Carcamo, secretary of organization, on May 11, 1989, on a street corner in Chalchuapa. Vargas had previously received threats concerning his union activity. On the same day, Manuel Antonio Pérez, press secretary, was shot and injured in front of the same INCAFE processing plant where Flores was killed earlier. Finally, on December 5, 1989, Mario Roberto Alvarez, secretary general of the Santa Ana local, was shot six times by a man in plainclothes who first demanded to see his identification. He survived and left the country shortly afterward.

· In December 1989 six members of the San Cayetano El Rosario cooperative, in Llano de la Laguna, a hamlet in Ahuachapán Department, disappeared after their abduction by soldiers in two separate incidents. Soldiers seized Julio César Juárez Vásquez and his brother Juan Antonio on December 5 and, on December 29, captured the co-op president, Gerardo Saldana Salazar; the treasurer, Leonardo Pérez Núñez; the secretary, Juan Saldana Salazar; and the driver, José Eladio Saldana Salazar. The commander of the Seventh Military Detachment, which had responsibility for the area at the time, was Col.

Roberto Mauricio Staben, a tandona member with a notorious human rights record.

Church Officials and Religious Workers

Long one of the central institutions in Salvadoran life, the Catholic Church has been at the forefront of the social transformation that has swept across much of Latin America over the past two decades. The doctrines that evolved out of bishops' conferences at Medellín in 1968 and Puebla in 1979 fundamentally altered the church's traditional relation to society, for priests and nuns became leading voices for change and consequently targets of official violence. As the dominant religious institution in El Salvador, the Catholic Church has experienced the brunt of the repression against religious institutions, but representatives of other faiths have not been exempt.

It is no coincidence that the two most notorious crimes of the decade were the 1980 murder of an archbishop and the 1989 slaying of six Jesuit priests. These were only the most prominent of many religious figures bitterly resented by powerful segments of Salvadoran society for their refusal to remain silent in the face of injustice. By using the pulpit to speak of politics, by helping the poor organize to defend their rights, and by standing behind their protests, the Catholic Church has, in the view of some, abandoned its role as upholder of a traditional moral order. Maj. Roberto Molina, head of the human rights office of the army, spoke for many on the Salvadoran right when he told Americas Watch in July 1990 that "the progressive clerics bear a great responsibility for what has happened to this country. They have launched the class struggle—black against white, poor against rich, small against big." Archbishop Oscar Arnulfo Romero explained the persecution this way, shortly before his death:

> While it is clear that our Church has been the victim of persecution during the last three years, it is even more important to observe the reason for the persecution. It is not that just any priest or just any institution has been persecuted. It is the segment of the Church which is on the side of the poor and has come out in their defense that has been persecuted and attacked. Here we once again encounter the key to understanding the persecution of the Church: the poor. It is again the poor who permit us to understand what has happened. That is why the Church has come to understand what persecution of the poor is. The persecution comes about because of the Church's defense of the poor, for assuming the destiny of the poor.[47]

Eighteen Catholic priests, one Lutheran minister, three American nuns, and a lay American church worker have been murdered or have disappeared in El

Salvador since 1972. Most cases have received little international concern. Some are described below.[48]

International attention was riveted to El Salvador on March 24, 1980, when Archbishop Romero was killed by a bullet to the heart while saying mass in the chapel at the Divine Providence cancer hospital. The unidentified assassin fired from the direction of the entrance to the chapel and fled in a waiting getaway car.

Romero had been repeatedly threatened as a result of his forthright sermons; in the months preceding his assassination, he had become the most outspoken and influential opponent of the military's merciless campaign against its perceived enemies. His homilies were a weekly catalogue of carnage by government troops. A month before he was killed, Romero wrote an open letter to President Jimmy Carter pleading in vain for a halt to U.S. military aid to El Salvador. The day before he was slain, he ended a nationally broadcast homily in the National Cathedral with a plaintive appeal to members of the military and police to disobey orders to kill civilians.

A serious investigation into the slaying of the archbishop was not begun until six years after his death, and even that effort was ultimately suppressed by the ARENA-dominated Supreme Court (see chap. 6). Ten years after his death, the case is collecting dust in the files of the Fourth Criminal Court in San Salvador.

Equally brazen, though little noticed outside El Salvador, was the assassination of Father Manuel Antonio Reyes Monico, a priest of the Archdiocese of San Salvador. National Police agents arrested Reyes on October 6, 1980; his body was found the next day on the outskirts of the capital, with a bullet wound in the mouth and another in the chest.

Sometimes just being related to a priest can bring death. Father José Ernesto Abrego, a parish priest of San Benito, San Salvador, disappeared along with three relatives on November 23, 1980, while driving from Guatemala City to San Salvador. Two other relatives left San Salvador for Guatemala City on November 29 to search for the missing cleric and his companions, only to disappear themselves; their bodies were later found in Juayua, Sonsonate, forty-four miles west of San Salvador. Another relative of the priest's, Carlos Abrego, also disappeared after receiving a telephone call in Guatemala City offering information regarding the whereabouts of the priest. Father Abrego's tortured body was found later that month, but neither Carlos Abrego nor the three relatives who had been traveling with him at the time of his disappearance were ever found.

At about the same time, on November 28, 1980, five National Guardsmen abducted Father Marcial Serrano, the parish priest of Olocuilta, La Paz, as he left Chaltipa, a hamlet in the department of San Salvador, after celebrating mass there. His vehicle was later found in the National Guard garrison with the license plates changed. Although the National Guard contended that the pickup was abandoned when recovered, witnesses disputed this account. Serrano's body, reportedly tossed into Lake Ilopango near San Salvador, was never recovered.

And on December 2, 1980, five National Guardsmen raped and murdered four U.S. churchwomen—the nuns Ita Ford, Maura Clarke, and Dorothy Kazel and the lay missionary Jean Donovan—on the road from the international airport to San Salvador. The women's bodies were found the next day in Santiago Nonualco, La Paz. The guardsmen were eventually convicted in the case, the first known conviction of government forces for political killings, but higher-up involvement was never investigated (see chap. 6).[49]

Given the international notoriety of this next case, a few more details will be given here. In the early morning hours of November 16, 1989, uniformed Salvadoran army soldiers entered the campus of the Central American University, José Simeón Cañas (UCA) and murdered six Jesuit priests—Ignacio Ellacuría, fifty-nine, rector of the university; Ignacio Martín-Baró, forty-seven, vice rector; Segundo Montes, fifty-six, director of the Human Rights Institute; Juan Ramón Moreno, fifty-six; Amando López Quintana, fifty-three; and Joaquín López y López, seventy-one. Soldiers also killed the priests' housekeeper, Julia Elba Ramos, forty-two, and her daughter, Celina Mariceth Ramos, fifteen. The victims included some of El Salvador's most prominent intellectuals. Ignacio Ellacuría, a theologian and philosopher, was perhaps the leading proponent of a negotiated solution to the war who had the ears both of the FMLN and President Cristiani, with whom he enjoyed a personal friendship. Ignacio Martín-Baró, a psychologist, was, like Ellacuría, a respected analyst of the Salvadoran situation. In addition to supporting the efforts of psychologists in El Salvador who treated people traumatized by the war, he headed the Public Opinion Institute at the university, which conducted public opinion polls on the crucial issues facing the country. The sociologist Segundo Montes was El Salvador's leading academic expert on the problem of refugees and the displaced and ran the UCA's respected Human Rights Institute, founded in 1985.

The Jesuit order and the Jesuit-run UCA have long been favorite targets of the right in El Salvador because of their outspokenness. As Father Ellacuría wrote in a letter to the *Boston Globe* three years before his death: "We have endured a great deal during these recent years; one of us, Rev. Rutilio Grande, was murdered, and the rest of us have received an ultimatum: Get out of the country or be killed. We decided to stay. Since then our home and our university have been bombed 14 times."[50]

In testimony given in a federal court in Los Angeles, California, in January

1987, in a case involving the rights of Salvadoran refugees in the United States, (*Orantes-Hernández v. Meese*), Father Montes also told of the persecution against the Jesuits in El Salvador:

> In 1977 I believe they gave us one month, to the Jesuits of El Salvador, to leave the country or be murdered. And you could see slogans throughout the city saying "promote the country, kill a priest."
>
> In 1980 they strafed our house, machine-gunned our house. Afterwards bombs exploded on two occasions in that same year of 1980. One of the bombs exploded at the wall to my room and it opened up a three-foot diameter hole at the foot of the bed where I was.
>
> In 1983 when we returned after two and a half years of having had to be relocated in another house, again they exploded another bomb on us in September and they left some literature in which they accused us of being traitors to the country because we supported . . . dialogue.
>
> At the university they have set bombs on us more than 12 times. Continuously in the papers there are attacks and threats against us.
>
> There are lists of people who can be eliminated and we're on those lists, several of us, and I am personally.[51]

The UCA's principal publications, *Proceso,* a weekly summary of news developments, and *Estudios Centroamericanos,* a monthly journal of analysis, have consistently printed articles critical of the government. Although they have also faulted the FMLN for actions or strategies that conflicted with the UCA's sense of justice or human rights, they have placed the brunt of the responsibility for Salvadoran violence on the government and its supporters. So great was the animosity of the authorities toward the Jesuits that a group of army officers meeting at the National Intelligence Directorate (DNI) the morning after the massacre at the UCA reportedly cheered when told that Father Ellacuría had been killed.[52] A U.S. congressional task force monitoring the Salvadoran government's investigation into the killings reported in April 1990 that senior military officials in El Salvador described the massacre as "stupid," "self-defeating," and "dumb"—but never wrong.[53]

Although the troops who carried out the massacre tried to blame it on the guerrillas, faking a firefight and leaving behind a crude sign claiming credit on the rebels' part, on January 13, 1990, President Cristiani identified nine military men, including the tandona member Col. Guillermo Alfredo Benavides Moreno, as responsible for the crimes. Eight of the nine were provisionally detained; one remains at large. In late June 1990, after evidence of an army cover-up had accumulated, a lieutenant colonel was indicted for destruction of evidence, and later in the year, three Atlacatl Battalion soldiers were charged with perjury.[54] At this writing, hopes for prosecuting the authors of the crime are fading because of resistance from the military high command (see chap. 6).

Members of Political Parties

The wholesale slaughter of political opponents in the late 1970s and early 1980s fueled an insurgency against a regime that appeared to offer no peaceful path to change. By the early 1980s virtually every major opposition politician not yet killed had left the country for fear of losing his or her life. Throughout much of the decade the only parties to participate in elections were the centrist Christian Democrats and groups to their right. Not until late 1987 did the opposition leaders Guillermo Ungo and Rubén Zamora return to take part in politics and, under the umbrella of the Democratic Convergence, to participate in the 1989 presidential elections. Although these center-to-right parties were largely free to campaign in major urban centers, their activities were strictly limited in rural areas by a hostile military presence. Some of the more prominent attacks on leftist politicians through the course of the decade follow.

· Six members of the executive committee of the FDR opposition coalition were kidnapped on November 27, 1980, while preparing for a news conference at the San José High School in San Salvador. Their mutilated bodies were found east of the capital. Heavily armed men in civilian clothing carried out the abduction. According to Socorro Jurídico, the vehicles used in the abduction belonged to the security forces.[55]

· On October 7, 1983, Víctor Manuel Quintanilla Ramos, the highest-ranking FDR spokesperson remaining in El Salvador, was found strangled along with three others: Santiago Hernández of the United Federation of Salvadoran Unions (FUSS), the chemistry professor Dora Muñoz Castillo, and José Antonio García Vásquez, a member of the FDR-affiliated Independent Movement of Professionals and Technicians of El Salvador (MIPTES). The Maximiliano Hernández Martínez Anticommunist Brigade claimed responsibility for the murders. Before the bodies were found, Salvadoran television stations played a videotaped "confession" in which the victims "admitted" membership in the Communist party.[56]

· In November 1987, just days before the two principal leaders of the FDR were to return to El Salvador for the first time since the early 1980s, the bodies of two young men were found on the road from La Libertad to San Salvador. One had a broken neck; the other had been shot through the head and stabbed in the cheek. The letters FDR had been scrawled in red ink on the chests of both bodies. The victims, Roberto Antonio Cruz and Moisés Reyes Castro, had been captured by soldiers on the night of November 6, and their bodies were dumped shortly after midnight on November 8. Their murders were widely interpreted as a warning about the limits of the political opening brought about by the Central American peace plan of August 1987.[57]

· On October 19, 1989, a powerful bomb damaged the home of Rubén Zamora, injuring two of his personal security guards. Seconds earlier, three grenades were thrown into the house of Zamora's sister-in-law, Aronette Díaz, leader of the opposition Nationalist Democratic Union UDN). She and her two children were unharmed.[58]

The Christian Democrats have also been persecuted by the security forces, including high-ranking officeholders. On February 23, 1980, Attorney General Mario Zamora Rivas, a leading Christian Democrat, was killed by masked gunmen who crawled over the roof and lowered themselves onto the patio of his home while he was having a party. Forcing everyone to lie on the floor, the masked men asked, "Which is Mario?" and then shot him dead. The murder came a few days after Roberto D'Aubuisson appeared on television to denounce Zamora and his brother Rubén as guerrillas.[59] And on September 20, 1983, the Foreign Ministry official Amílcar Martínez Arguera was abducted. Both the Secret Anticommunist Army and the Maximiliano Hernández Martínez Anticommunist Brigade claimed credit for the kidnapping. A brigade communiqué accused the victim of "having an extensive communist background" and being a "traitor to the fatherland." He did not reappear.[60]

A September 1982 statement by the party alleged that thirty-five Christian Democratic mayors had been murdered, nine of them that year. In April 1983, security forces reportedly murdered the Christian Democratic mayor of El Carmen, Cuscatlán. A Christian Democratic spokesman interviewed by the *Los Angeles Times* in May 1983 recalled a string of incidents in the rural town of Chinamequita, where first one Christian Democratic mayor was murdered and then a second. He said, "The city council came here to San Salvador to name a woman the third mayor. She was murdered that afternoon."[61]

Not just cabinet members and mayors are at risk. On May 6, 1983, the corpse of a young man who had been strangled and shot in the head was dumped in the parking lot of the Camino Real Hotel in San Salvador, where most foreign journalists stay. A press release from a death squad that took credit for the murder was found in one of the victim's pockets. It warned Mauricio Armando Mazier Andino, a Christian Democratic member of the Constituent Assembly, that the same fate awaited him. Mazier Andino had given a speech in the assembly two days earlier calling for a crackdown on death squads.[62]

Just seven weeks later, on June 29, 1983, plainclothesmen abducted two Christian Democratic party activists—Joel Herrera Ochoa and his wife, Gloria Elizabeth Machón—at a bus stop in San Salvador. Their corpses were later found in the parking lot of the Siesta Hotel in San Salvador, with a note from the "Jorge Alvarez Command" of the Secret Anticommunist Army claiming responsibility for killing the two, whom it described as FMLN members. In response to the FMLN murder one day earlier of an ARENA assemblyman, the ESA had gone into a "state of maximum alert," vowing to execute ten guerrillas for each "good Salvadoran they kill."[63]

Although far fewer such cases were reported during the latter half of the decade, a reminder of the early 1980s came on December 12, 1988, when agents of the municipal police of Soyapango, a suburb of San Salvador, shot dead the Christian Democratic organizer Francisco Eduardo Bonilla Campos during a voter registration drive. Bonilla and eight other organizers had stopped at a Shell gas station when the ARENA mayor of Soyapango, Antonio Vásquez Corena, and several municipal police agents under his direction drove up in a gray van with darkened windows. The police made the organizers put their hands up and began to beat the coordinator of the group, Rufino Landaverde Alfaro. Bonilla intervened to try to protect Landaverde and was promptly shot by one of the police agents. He died in the hospital a few hours later.[64]

The Press

More than three dozen journalists have been killed or have disappeared in El Salvador in the past decade.[65] Bombings, threats, and assassinations drove all independent press organs out of existence in the early 1980s and forced the radio station of the Archdiocese of San Salvador, YSAX, off the air for several years. Throughout much of the decade the press generally supported the government or criticized it from a right-wing perspective. During the latter years of President Duarte's administration news programs on television and to a lesser extent radio offered a far broader range of views. Since 1989 a revamped afternoon daily newspaper, *Diario Latino,* has provided the point of view of the left and center left.

Even though *Diario Latino* represents a voice not heard in El Salvador since the onset of the war, its existence alone does not indicate that the press can now publish freely. On the contrary, substantial sectors of the military and the government still apparently equate public criticism with treason. The killing of two journalists by soldiers in March 1989 and army intimidation of the jury

hearing one of the cases indicate how far El Salvador still has to go in inculcat-
ing respect for a free and independent press (see chap. 6).

The following incidents were among the most serious human rights violations directed against members of the press in the past decade.

· In 1980 the premises of *El Independiente* were repeatedly bombed
  and fired on; in one incident, a fourteen-year-old newsboy was shot
  dead while standing in a doorway. Jorge Pinto, the editor, was the target of three assassination attempts in the course of two months alone.
  On January 15, 1981, army tanks and trucks surrounded the newspaper offices and occupied Pinto's home. Several days later, eight
  employees of *El Independiente* were arrested. The newspaper closed
  permanently that month.[66]
· The managing editor and a photographer for *La Crónica del Pueblo,*
  the only other paper that did not practice self-censorship, were abducted on July 11, 1980, and their mutilated bodies were found the
  day after, forcing that paper to cease publication, too.[67]
· On March 17, 1982, in what may have been an army ambush, four
  Dutch journalists—Jacobus Andries Koster, Jan Kuiper, Hanster
  Laan, and Johannes Willemsen—were killed. All four had been
  working for a religious television network in Holland and had jour-
  neyed to Chalatenango Department to film in an FMLN-controlled
  zone. Their bodies had multiple bullet wounds and showed signs of
  brutal mistreatment. Three of them had massive head wounds. One
  was shot through both knees, one in the hand. The men's pants had
  been partially or fully removed and their genitals were bloody.
  The journalists were apparently making contact with the FMLN at
  the time of their death. Military authorities claimed that they were
  killed in cross fire. Dutch government investigators termed parts of
  the official Salvadoran account "unbelievable." They found that Salvadoran authorities were watching the team of journalists closely
  prior to the killings, that elements of the army's firefight story were
  not consistent with the accounts of residents of the area, and that initial official descriptions of the incident were later altered.[68]
  Koster had been taken to Treasury Police headquarters for questioning six days before he was killed. On the next day, March 12, *El Diario de Hoy* published a picture of all four journalists with the
  headline "Foreign Journalist Contact of Subversives."[69]
· In July 1985 Salvadoran troops fired on the reporter Jon Lee Anderson, the Reuters photographer Nancy McGurr, and the Pacific News

Service correspondent Mary Jo McConahay, subsequently claiming to have mistaken them for "gringo terrorists." The three unarmed journalists were attacked as they were wading across a river; the shooting continued after their hands were raised and they identified themselves in Spanish as journalists. An army colonel filed a written report on the incident, saying, "It is my belief that the three journalists planned to have a meeting with terrorists."[70]

On March 18–19, 1989, the evening before and day of the presidential elections—within a period of less than twenty-four hours—members of the Salvadoran Armed Forces were involved in the unprovoked shooting deaths of two journalists, Roberto Navas Alvarez, a Reuters photographer, and Mauricio Pineda DeLeón, a television soundman with Salvadoran Channel 12, and the wounding of a third, Reuters photographer Luis Galdámez. When the Dutch cameraman Cornel Lagrouw was gravely injured in cross fire on March 19, an air force plane and helicopter strafed and fired rockets at the press vehicle attempting to take him to the hospital, forcing it off the road and delaying his arrival at the hospital.[71] A jury acquitted the only person tried for any of these crimes—an Arce Battalion corporal implicated in the shooting of Pineda—in June 1990 after thirty soldiers entered the courtroom to watch the proceedings (see chap. 6).

Students and Teachers

Schools and universities have been highly controversial in El Salvador; institutions of higher learning in particular have been suspect for criticizing the status quo through the teachings of professors and the publication of scholarly articles and books. Several of the Jesuit priests murdered in November 1989—the rector and the vice rector of the Central American University among them— were frequently attacked for their role in disseminating "subversive" doctrines among the nation's youth. The army has regularly accused the FMLN of using the National University as a recruiting ground, a training center, and a weapons depot. The university was closed several times during the 1970s and from 1980 to 1984, seriously disrupting higher education for students who could not afford to attend private institutions. Amnesty International reported that ninety primary-school teachers were killed between January and October 1980, and 156 teachers of various levels were killed between January and mid-March 1981.[72] A total of thirteen university faculty members, students, and workers were killed in 1989, most of them by members of the armed forces.[73]

The following is a sampling of the violence experienced by Salvadoran students and teachers.

- On January 27, 1980, National Guardsmen detained the schoolteacher Alvaro Rafael Rodríguez Olmedo in the hamlet of Quitazol, Tejutla. In the presence of his mother, the guardsmen ransacked his house, then took Rodríguez into the street, where they beat and shot him. He died in the hospital the same day.[74]
- On April 19, 1980, National Guardsmen murdered a teacher, Mauricio Vladimir Hernández, in front of 40 seven-year-old students in Tecapán, in Usulután Department.
- On April 19, 1980, National Guardsmen shot and wounded Angel Erasmo Figueroa, a professor at the National University, in Armenia, Sonsonate. When Figueroa was about to be operated on at the San Rafael Hospital in Santa Tecla, National Guardsmen surrounded the hospital; five of them entered the operating room and machine-gunned Figueroa to death as he lay unconscious on the operating table.
- On June 26, 1980, following a two-day national strike, combined forces of the army and the National Guard attacked the National University while five thousand students were inside. Between twenty-two and forty students were killed. Many students, professors, and employees of the university were beaten, abused, and forced to submit to strip searches. The buildings were ransacked: soldiers shot at computers, burned books, and sold university microscopes on the street to passing motorists. The damage was estimated at over eight million dollars.[75]
- Following raids on the National Teachers' Association (ANDES) headquarters in San Salvador, Professor Lionel Menéndez, a union leader, was shot and wounded in May 1980. National Police and National Guard vehicles surrounded the Rosales Hospital, soldiers abducted Menéndez from the operating room, and he disappeared.
- Felix Ulloa, rector of the National University and international president of the World University Service, was killed by machine-gun fire on October 28, 1980.
- On May 14, 1982, according to Amnesty International, security forces captured Raul Beltrán Navarrete, an agricultural engineer and lecturer at the National University. He remains disappeared.[76]
- Hugo Francisco Carrillo, a professor of international relations in the law faculty of the National University, was abducted on September 14, 1983, by heavily armed men in civilian dress. He did not reappear. His kidnapping was claimed by the Anticommunist Command for Salvation of the University (CASU).[77]
- On July 12, 1985, the Secret Anticommunist Army named eleven

teachers, students, campus union leaders, and employees of the National University as subversives and gave them twenty days to leave the country or be killed. The communiqué said that after executing them, the ESA would continue to monitor the university community until all the communists who were taking over the university were eradicated. Nine of those named left the country.[78]

· Mario Antonio Flores Cubas, an economics student at the National University, and José Gerardo Gómez, an agricultural worker, were detained by uniformed soldiers on February 2, 1989. Their bodies were found the next day in a ravine over 160 miles from the place of capture.[79]

· María Cristina Gómez González, a teacher, women's rights activist, and member of ANDES, was abducted by two heavily armed men in civilian clothes on April 5, 1989, as she was leaving the John F. Kennedy Elementary School in Ilopango, on the outskirts of San Salvador. In front of a multitude of students and teachers, Gómez was pushed into a gray Cherokee jeep with polarized windows, which sped away. An hour later, on the opposite side of town, she was tossed from the same car and shot dead in the back and head.

· On August 22, 1989, Miguel Ernesto Miranda Reina, a seventeen-year-old high school student, was shot dead by a soldier of the Atlacatl Battalion for allegedly resisting detention.

· Yuri Edson Aparicio Campos, twenty-three, a student at the National University, died in the Rosales Hospital on November 25, 1989, as a result of beatings by the National Police.

Health Workers

International humanitarian law seeks to ensure that the wounded and sick are cared for during an armed conflict. To effectuate this aim, the rules of war expressly protect medical personnel from attack or punishment regardless of the side to which they are ministering.[80] In El Salvador, doctors, nurses, and other health workers have been frequently branded as "guerrillas" and subjected to threats and unlawful violence for carrying out their medical duties. Several important cases of violence are described in chapters 3 and 6. Others follow.

· On November 12, 1989, soldiers of the Transmission Instruction Center of the Armed Forces (CITFA) captured Norma Guirola de Herrera, director of a women's institute; Mario Gálvez; and three other people from the Santa María neighborhood of San Marcos, department of San Salvador, where they were working to form a community health committee. All five were taken to the Zapote barracks, where they were accused of being FMLN combatants. That evening soldiers shot and killed Guirola and Gálvez. The fate of the other three prisoners is unknown.[81]

· On November 19, 1989, First Brigade soldiers captured five health workers from a Catholic clinic at the Church of San Francisco de Asis, in Mejicanos, San Salvador. Four were released two days later, but the fifth, David Hernández, has not reappeared.[82]

Human Rights Monitors

Human rights monitors in El Salvador have been routinely criticized and attacked for telling a story the authorities do not want to hear. By alleging that the reports of Salvadoran human rights groups are biased, U.S. and Salvadoran officials have sought to shift the focus of attention from the human rights situation in El Salvador to the qualities of those seeking to document it. In the process they have helped to legitimize the use of violence against men and women engaged in the difficult but necessary task of recording and disseminating evidence of violations. By investigating cases of abuse and publishing their findings year after year, Tutela Legal, Socorro Jurídico, the nongovernmental Human Rights Commission (CDHES-NG), and other organizations have performed a vital service in focusing the spotlight on human rights conditions in El Salvador.

These are some of the most serious cases of violence directed against members of human rights monitoring organizations in the past decade.

· On February 24, 1980, Roberto Castellanos, a sociologist working for Socorro Jurídico, and Annette Matthiessen, his Danish-born wife, were kidnapped from their house by the National Police. Their corpses were found three days later along the Pacific Coast highway. Castellanos appeared to have been tortured.[83]

· The CDHES-NG has suffered the most persistent persecution. On March 13, 1980, its office was bombed and its files confiscated by uniformed members of the National Police. Members of the group received telephoned and written death threats. On March 30, the names of a number of staff members appeared on a list of "traitors" published by the military press office. In September the CDHES-NG office was again bombed. After the blast, partially clothed, decapitated, burned bodies were placed in the office doorway. On October 3, María Magdalena Henríquez, CDHES-NG press secretary, was abducted by two members of the National Police while shopping with her son in San Salvador. She was found dead in a shallow grave near the port of La Libertad. She had been shot four times in the head and twice in the chest. On October 25, Ramón Valladares, an administrator with the CDHES-NG, was abducted and killed. The commission charged the National Police with responsibility for the murder.[84] On December 4, 1981, Carlos Eduardo Vides, director of the CDHES-NG statistics department, was abducted by army and security forces while traveling to San Vicente with two companions, who were also taken. One was an employee of the Archdiocese of San Salvador. In January 1982, Vides was reportedly seen in detention, but all three are believed to still be disappeared.[85] On August 20, 1982, Treasury Police agents kidnapped América Fernanda Perdomo, the public relations director, from a suburban home near the capital. Kidnapped with her were Saúl Villalta, a member of the FDR executive committee; María Adela Cornejo de Recinos, wife of an imprisoned labor leader; and her thirteen-year-old daughter, Ana Yanira. All four remain disappeared.[86] On February 23, 1983, Roberto Rivera Martelli, a gynecologist and founding member of the CDHES-NG who served on its governing board, was abducted from his clinic in a San Salvador suburb by several heavily armed men in civilian clothes. The area in which his clinic was located was regularly patrolled by the Treasury Police. He was not seen again. On March 16, Marianela García Villas, the CDHES-NG president, was killed when an army patrol ambushed a group of refugees with whom she was traveling near the town of Suchitoto. In the aftermath of the incident, the army first referred to García Villas as a journalist. Subsequently, when the army realized her identity, it said she was a guerrilla leader who had died in combat.[87]

In 1986, after a former employee, Luz Janeth Alfaro Peña, publicly denounced the CDHES-NG as a guerrilla front, several members were arrested and jailed; many of them were abused or tortured and forced to sign statements, which they later repudiated. Among those arrested and mistreated were Rafael Antonio Terrezón Ramos, Miguel Angel Montenegro, and Herbert Ernesto Anaya Sanabría. All were released by February 1987.[88]

Herbert Anaya, president of the CDHES-NG, was murdered by unknown gunmen close to his house in San Salvador on October 26, 1987. On January 5, 1988, the government claimed to have solved the case, based on the confession of Jorge Miranda Arévalo, a nineteen-year-old high-school student, obtained while he was detained incommunicado for twelve days. On February 20, 1988, Miranda recanted his testimony before the judge, saying he had been threatened by the National Police into implicating himself in the killing.[89] The court, which found no evidence to link him with the Anaya murder, has since freed him. There have been no other arrests in the case.

· María Teresa Tula, of the Committee of Mothers and Families of the Detained, Disappeared, and Assassinated of El Salvador (COMADRES), was captured at a bus stop in San Salvador on May 6, 1986. The men took her to a house where they interrogated her about her membership in comadres, punched, stabbed, and raped her, and then sought to buy her collaboration. She was released on May 8, still bleeding where she had been cut in the side. On May 28, 1986, she was arrested by the Treasury Police and accused of belonging to the FMLN. Later that year, President Duarte ordered her release in a show of clemency.[90]

3

COMBAT-RELATED ABUSES BY
GOVERNMENT FORCES

During the first several years of the civil war, the Salvadoran armed forces made little attempt to distinguish between the guerrillas and civilians residing in areas where the FMLN was thought to enjoy popular support and where its forces were active. The scale of the killing was enormous—far greater than in the second half of the decade, when the practices of the armed forces were modified both by more sophisticated ideas about winning hearts and minds and by sustained pressure to respect human rights.

Another factor that eventually limited military attacks on civilians was an alteration in guerrilla strategy. During much of the first half of the decade, the guerrillas had striven to maintain control over as much territory as possible. Eventually this proved counterproductive, hurting them militarily and inviting attacks on their civilian supporters. The guerrillas had virtually no capacity to defend the territory they held against the growing air power of the armed forces. Their change in strategy presented the armed forces with a less clearly defined group of civilian targets.

From 1980 to 1983 most civilian deaths took place in ground sweeps by the armed forces; sometimes the sweeps were supported by aerial attacks on fleeing peasants. Several episodes stand out for their ferocity.

· Sumpul River, May 14, 1980. Several thousand peasants fled during
a military operation apparently intended to flush out guerrillas in the
area, and attempted to cross the river into Honduras. What happened
to them first became known when it was decried by the clergy of
Santa Rosa de Copán, Honduras. According to a declaration signed
by Msgr. José Carranza y Chávez and all the priests of the diocese,
the refugees were met by Honduran Army troops who had arrived in
the area the previous day. The soldiers shouted to to the peasants over
megaphones that it was forbidden to cross the border. According to
the declaration: "On the opposite bank at about seven in the morning,
in the Salvadoran hamlet of 'La Arada' and its vicinity the massacre

began. At least two helicopters, the Salvadoran National Guard, soldiers and the paramilitary organization ORDEN, began firing at the defenseless people. . . . Salvadorans who crossed the river were returned by Honduran soldiers to the area of the massacre. By mid-afternoon the genocide had ended, leaving a minimum of 600 dead." At least six hundred unburied corpses were prey for dogs and buzzards for several days. Others were lost in the waters of the river. A Honduran fisherman found the bodies of five children in his fish trap. The Sumpul River became contaminated from the decomposing bodies.

Both the Salvadoran and the Honduran governments denied the report. Hugh McCullum, editor of a Canadian publication, the *United Church Observer,* reported that President Duarte acknowledged that "an action did take place in the area of Río Sumpul" and that "about 300 were killed, all of them Communist guerrillas."[1]

· Lempa River, March 18, 1981. Ten months later another large group of Salvadoran peasants tried to reach Honduras by crossing the Lempa River. They were fleeing a military sweep in Cabañas Department. According to survivors, the Salvadoran air force dropped bombs on them, helicopters strafed them, and the army shelled and machine-gunned them. Twenty to thirty people were reportedly killed, and many more were missing.[2]

· Lempa River, October 20–29, 1981. According to the Salvadoran Armed Forces, 152 guerrillas were killed in another military sweep along the Lempa River in 1981—a response to the FMLN's destruction of a bridge, the Puente de Oro. The Atlacatl Battalion was reportedly involved. Socorro Jurídico said that 147 noncombatants were killed, including forty-four minors.[3]

· Cabañas, November 1981. The Atlacatl Battalion conducted a military sweep in Cabañas Department in November 1981. An American graduate student doing anthropological research in the area, Philippe Bourgois, was caught up in it; he testified before the Western Hemisphere Subcommittee of the House of Representatives about his experience:

The evacuation route for the civilian population to Honduras was blocked by the presence of Honduran soldiers along the banks of the Lempa River, where it delineates the border between the two countries. For the next fourteen days, I fled with the local population as we were subjected to aerial bombardment, artillery fire, helicopter strafing, and attack by Salvadoran foot soldiers. In retrospect it appears as if the Salvadoran government troops had wanted to annihilate all living creatures (human and animal) within the confines of the 30 square mile area. On the fourteenth day, when we learned that the Honduran soldiers had withdrawn from the Lempa River, I escaped with other noncombatants to the refugee camps in Honduras.

Bourgois estimated that about one thousand local residents fled and that at least fifty were killed, another fifty were wounded, and a hundred were missing by the time he got out of the area on November 25. The Salvadoran press quoted Defense Minister José Guillermo García as calling the operation one of the most successful of the war.[4]

· El Mozote, December 1981. The largest civilian death toll in a single episode of the war generated a heated controversy. Up to one thousand civilians in ten or so hamlets and villages in Morazán Department were killed by the Atlacatl Battalion over about ten days in December 1981 (accounts differ as to exactly which days). Ironically, many residents of the area were evangelicals who had tried to remain neutral in the conflict. Yet because the department where they lived was an FMLN stronghold, they were caught in a strategic anvil-and-hammer (*yunque y martillo*) operation. Survivors compiled a list of more than seven hundred people killed, but many bodies could not be identified.

The massacres came to international attention on January 27, 1982, when stories appeared on the front pages of the *New York Times* and the *Washington Post*. Raymond Bonner of the *Times* and Alma Guillermoprieto of the *Post* had crossed guerrilla lines to travel to the area; they saw the carnage and interviewed a woman who was apparently the lone survivor from the hamlet of El Mozote.[5] Their accounts aroused controversy when the Reagan administration, and in particular the assistant secretary of state for inter-American affairs, Thomas O. Enders, attempted to discredit them (see chap.8).

After the El Mozote episode, the scale of killings in ground sweeps by the armed forces declined considerably. Although the the controversy cast a pall over press reporting on human rights in El Salvador—produced when the *New York Times* withdrew Bonner from El Salvador later in 1982 and made thicker when he departed from the newspaper some time after that—it also heightened pressure on the Salvadoran Armed Forces to avoid mass killings. Many noncombatants continued to die in ground sweeps, but never again were many hundreds killed at one time.

· Las Hojas, February 22, 1983. No counterinsurgent purpose is evident for the massacre of more than seventy people at the Indian farming cooperative of Las Hojas. Las Hojas is near Sonsonate, in the western part of the country, a region where the FMLN was not active at the time. The massacre apparently grew out of a land dispute between a local landowner and the Indian members of the cooperative. The landowner, frustrated when the cooperative rejected his plan to build a road across its land, denounced the farmers to the army as subversives, according to one account.[6] The army commander of the garrison at Sonsonate, Col. Elmer González Araujo, whose troops committed the massacre, sought to justify the killings by claiming that they involved combat with subversives. This persuaded almost no one; neither the U.S. Embassy in El Salvador nor the Salvadoran military high command, ordinarily quick to see killings by the armed forces as combat related, was willing to do so in the case of the Las Hojas massacre.

It began in the early dawn hours of February 22, when masked informers, accompanied by soldiers, went from door to door fingering those to be killed. About two hundred soldiers were involved in the operation; over seventy people associated with the cooperative were killed. There was no combat; many corpses were found with hands tied and heads blown apart by high-powered weapons.[7]

· Copapayo, November 1983. The Atlacatl Battalion reportedly massacred more than one hundred people in the towns of Copapayo, San Nicolás, and La Escopeta near Lake Suchitlán, northeast of San Salvador. Journalists who visited the towns on November 16, 1983, were given a list of 117 victims; according to residents, twenty women and children were taken inside a house and shot, and at least thirty people were drowned when troops firing automatic weapons drove them into the lake. The U.S. ambassador, Thomas Pickering, although saying that the exact circumstances were unclear, told Americas Watch that "troops of the Atlacatl Battalion had actually been involved in a massacre." The army claimed the victims were rebels killed in a military operation.[8]

Subsequently, the boatman who took journalists across Lake Suchitlán to view the site was himself killed, apparently by the military. The armed men who took him from his home on November 29 reportedly told his wife it was a mistake to cooperate with journalists.[9]

The last two known cases in which the military killed more than a score of civilians in a ground sweep took place in mid-1984.

· Los Llanitos, July 17–22, 1984. The episode at Los Llanitos, Cabañas, became known internationally when the *New York Times*, the *Boston Globe* and the *Miami Herald* carried accounts of it on September 9, 1984. Journalists from the three papers had visited the area carrying a list, compiled by an investigator from Tutela Legal, naming sixty-eight people who had been killed there. As the *Boston Globe* reported:

Villagers of Los Llanitos, a hamlet of 185 residents, said government troops combed the area for guerrillas three times earlier this year. But in the July campaign, villagers said, the soldiers for the first time avoided open roads. Instead they scaled rocks and cut through bush and bramble to take to the hills above the hamlets before village lookouts spotted them. When word finally went out at dusk on July 18 that the "enemy" was nearby, nearly 1,000 peasants from seven hamlets grabbed their children and set out on a frantic march, stumbling in the darkness down ravines and over promontories, the villagers said. They hoped to reach the caves and gullies where they had hid safely during past incursions.

The *Globe* account went on to describe the machine-gunning of a group of thirty-six villagers and the soldiers' burning of many corpses.[10]

· Gualsinga River, August 28–30, 1984. The Atlacatl Battalion began a sweep on August 28 near Las Vueltas, Chalatenango, driving civilians from that village and the nearby villages of El Tamarindo, Haciendas and Leoneses. Four foreign journalists traveled to the scene a few days later. A Reuters dispatch reported:

The villagers said they fled so fast they managed to take only the few belongings they could carry, leaving behind most of their possessions, including pets and pack animals. "When they passed through the villages they killed the horses and the dogs," Mr. Cartagena [a villager] said of the soldiers.

The reporters observed a gaping hole in the roof of one house in El Tamarindo, reportedly caused by a mortar shell that residents said killed a young girl inside. They also saw the rotting remains of two horses in the village. The survivors said 300 to 400 peasants from the three villages grew weary from the six-mile walk up steep mountain passes and settled on the bank of the Gualsinga River, just outside the hamlet of Santa Lucía.

On the morning of August 30, troops of the Atlacatl Battalion moved in by helicopter and began to cordon off the area, the villagers said. They said that when they realized the army had surrounded them, they scattered in all directions. It was then, they said, that the shooting began.

Many people with no place to turn jumped into the rapidly flowing river. Some, like Mr. Cartagena survived. Many drowned.[11]

Tutela Legal said that at least fifty died in the Gualsinga River massacre and that thirty-one bodies were identified.[12] Just as Assistant Secretary of State Enders had sought to discredit accounts of the El Mozote massacres nearly three years earlier, his successor as head of the State Department's Bureau of Inter-American Affairs, Elliott Abrams, attempted to discredit accounts of the smaller-scale massacres at Los Llanitos and the Gualsinga River. Abrams discussed them on ABC television's Nightline several months after they occurred. A representative of Americas Watch, Aryeh Neier, also appeared on the broadcast.

Ted Koppel: Secretary Abrams, why was neither of those incidents reported [in the State Department's country report on El Salvador]?
Sec. Abrams: Because neither of them happened. Because it is a tactic of the guerrillas every time there is a battle and a significant number of people are killed to say that they're all victims of human rights abuses.
Aryeh Neier: That's why *The New York Times*—
Sec. Abrams: Ted, there's one very important point here.
Aryeh Neier: —and *The Boston Globe* and *The Miami Herald* and *The Christian Science Monitor* and Reuters and all the other reporters who went to the scene and looked at what took place, they were simply being propagandists for the guerrillas? Is that right?
Sec. Abrams: I'm telling you that there were no significant—there were no massacres in El Salvador in 1984.[13]

As the debate continued, Abrams claimed that the U.S. Embassy had investigated the reports of these massacres. Pressed on this, he backed away, saying, "My memory is that we did [investigate], but I don't want to swear to it because I'd have to go back to look at the cablegram." As it turned out, Abrams's reliance on an embassy investigation had even less basis than Enders's reliance on its investigation in the El Mozote case. Then, the embassy had at least tried to investigate; in the Los Llanitos and Gualsinga River cases, as the embassy subsequently informed Americas Watch, it had not even made an attempt.[14] Because the military sweeps took place in areas ordinarily contested by the FMLN and because the embassy did not permit its personnel to go into those areas, it was not surprising that investigations were not conducted.

Although the death toll in ground sweeps had abated by 1984, many civilians were still being killed in aerial attacks and some by long-distance shelling. The armed forces used both forms of attack indiscriminately; that is, they did not try hard to distinguish between military and civilian targets.

An episode that marked the increasing significance of air power in the war and the willingness of the armed forces to deploy air power against the civilian population was the bombing of Tenancingo on September 25, 1983. Located only twenty-one miles northeast of the capital, the town had been the scene of a confrontation between the Salvadoran army and the guerrillas. The bombing raid followed this confrontation. Many buildings in the center of town were leveled or partially destroyed during the attack. When residents began to flee, two relief workers from a Salvadoran agency, the Green Cross, formed a large group of them into a column and waved the Green Cross flag to signal to the planes. A plane dropped a bomb into the middle of this group. According to testimony obtained from townspeople by Tutela Legal a few days later, this bomb killed about thirty-five people. In all, the death toll was about seventy-five.[15] Tenancingo became a ghost town; its 2,500 residents fled, as did the nearly ten thousand people living in outlying hamlets. Several years later under the sponsorship of the Archdiocese of San Salvador, it became the first bombed-out town to be repopulated.[16]

In the months after the bombing, it became clear that the Salvadoran armed forces were deliberately using their aerial power to drive civilians out of areas in which the guerrillas were active and seemed to enjoy substantial peasant support. This strategy followed the famous Maoist dictum that in order to deny sustenance to the fish (the guerrillas), it was necessary to drain the sea (the civilian population in guerrilla-contested zones). Contributing to this conviction was a January 25, 1984, cable from the U.S. Embassy in San Salvador to the U.S. State Department, circulated to members of the Congress, that purported to explain the discrepancies between the number of civilian deaths tabulated by Tutela Legal and by the embassy. The cable, which apparently reflected the views of the Salvadoran Armed Forces, said many of the deaths reported by Tutela Legal actually involved supporters of the guerrillas who "were something other than innocent civilian bystanders." It called them *masas*, a term that the Salvadoran guerrillas used for their civilian supporters, and described them as persons who "live in close proximity of and travel in the company of armed guerrillas."[17]

In arguing that Tutela Legal had inappropriately labeled the deaths of such people as civilian casualties, the embassy was arguing that attacks on them were legitimate in the eyes of the U.S. government. But its position flew in the face of international agreements to which both the United States and El Salvador are parties.[18] These agreements require that every effort be made to protect noncombatants, regardless of who they support or where they live. It is no more legitimate for the Salvadoran Armed Forces to attack civilians who support the guerrillas and live in areas they control than for the guerrillas to attack civilians living in the cities who support the armed forces. Facing a hail of criticism, the embassy retreated, at least in public. In a July 1984 meeting with Americas Watch, the embassy claimed its position had been "misunderstood" and that indeed "*masas* are not an appropriate military target of and by themselves, only insofar as they may be part of a legitimate target of armed guerrillas."[19]

Public shift in position aside, interviews with displaced people and refugees throughout 1984 made it plain that aerial power was being used extensively to drive masas, or those designated in this way, from large sections of the country that were controlled by the guerrillas. The apparent purpose was to deprive the guerrillas of sources of food and information about troop movements. In the process, many hundreds of civilians were killed in aerial attacks, and many more were injured. Villages were laid waste, farm animals were killed, peasants left their homes, often without any possessions.[20] Some people went to camps for the displaced in El Salvador or refugee camps in Honduras; others entered the streams of refugees heading for the United States or settled in Mexico or in other Central American countries; still others flocked to the cities, particularly the capital, where they created sprawling slums that greatly swelled the urban population.

In June 1984, José Napoleón Duarte, who had served as president of a military-civilian junta from 1980 to 1982, took office as the elected civilian president of El Salvador. Faced with controversy in the United States over the continuing aerial attacks on civilians, Duarte issued an order in September 1984 establishing rules of engagement.[21] It limited aerial bombing to support for ground troops receiving hostile fire or to attacks on guerrilla columns moving supplies; it required that aerial bombing take place only in nonurban areas or areas without major thoroughfares; and it provided that requests for such aerial support be accompanied by a statement about the proximity of civilians and Red Cross activities. The order also permitted aerial bombing to defend fixed installations, such as military bases, when these came under guerrilla attack.

If these rules of engagement had been implemented, civilian casualties would have been sharply limited and the depopulation of areas in which the FMLN was active would have been substantially curbed. Testimony gathered in El Salvador in the year following the issuance of these rules indicated, however, that the Salvadoran air force disregarded the directive. One possible explanation is that it was not intended to be more than a public relations gesture to appease members of the Congress and others in the United States who were disturbed by the reports of the aerial attacks on civilians. Another possibility is that Duarte issued the directive in good faith but that the failure to comply with it reflected the limits on his authority. The Salvadoran air force in particular, under the command of Col. Juan Rafael Bustillo, seemed beyond Duarte's control during this period. Indeed, in July 1984 a high military officer regarded as a Duarte loyalist, Col. Carlos Reynaldo López Nuila, then the commander of the security forces and previously the commander of the National Police, complained to representatives of Americas Watch that the air force had failed to comply with the policies adopted by the high command regarding human rights.[22]

That the Salvadoran Armed Forces did not abide by the president's directive on aerial attacks was even evident in their press statements. For example, in January 1985 the armed forces engaged in one of their periodic efforts to dislodge the FMLN from an area long regarded as one of their strongholds: the Guazapa volcano near the capital, where thousands of civilians lived until the evacuation. According to a statement by the Press Office of the Armed Forces (COPREFA), the Guazapa operation was preceded by softening-up bombardments (*bombardeo de ablandamiento*) for several days.[23]

Later during 1985, the armed forces announced publicly that they were relocating civilians still living on the Guazapa volcano. The evacuations, which took place in April, May, and June involved at least several hundred civilians and probably as many as a thousand. Although these evacuations, unlike the one in January, did not involve bombing in advance for softening-up purposes, the armed forces did threaten residents with death if they refused to go. Even though civilians remained on the volcano after the evacuation, indiscriminate aerial bombardment resumed.[24]

The reluctance of the Reagan administration to condemn ongoing abuses by the air force during this period may have been related to the air force commander's cooperation in a covert operation that did not come to light for another two years. On October 5, 1986, Sandinista troops in Nicaragua downed a cargo plane carrying supplies for the contras and captured an American survivor, Eugene Hasenfus. The episode was crucial in uncovering the Iran-contra scandal and also led to the public disclosure that planes supplying the contras had been regularly using the Salvadoran air force base at Ilopango under General Bustillo's command (by the time of the Hasenfus episode, he had been promoted). Duarte reportedly wanted to fire the air force commander after these revelations but was overruled by the defense minister, Gen. Carlos Eugenio Vides Casanova, who raised the specter of an air force revolt.[25]

Aerial attacks on civilians continued throughout much of 1985. A typical account from a refugee who, along with forty-six others, fled to the Colomoncagua refugee camp in Honduras from Joateca in 1985, follows.[26]

M.P., 38, a farmer who lived in the hamlet of Paturla near Joateca, Morazán, described how on March 28 at about 3 p.m. he heard planes. He went to the door of his house and saw two planes pass over the hamlet; one dropped a bomb that landed in a well in the town. He and his 13-year-old brother dashed for cover in a ravine; in the confusion they did not see what happened to the other family members. Five more planes appeared from behind the hill. M.P. described some of the planes that came as "shooting fire." They hid in the ravine that night.

After the aerial bombing came a ground sweep. M.P. and his brother stayed in hiding for four days, though they thought they heard the soldiers pull out. When the boys returned to the village, they found that the rest of the family had been killed in their home, apparently by the bombing—though it was difficult to determine the cause of death, because the house was partially burned and the bodies had been chewed by animals, M.P.'s father, his grandmother, and three brothers were among the dead. Of seven houses in the immediate area, only one was intact. In one of the destroyed houses, he counted eight bodies, apparently killed by a bomb. He also saw several bodies of persons who were apparently shot to death. M.P. and the others who came with him walked at night to avoid soldiers and hid in the ravines by day, taking fourteen days to reach the Colomoncagua refugee camp.

Later in 1985, on November 6 and 7, representatives of Americas Watch visiting Colomoncagua interviewed members of a group of 134 refugees who had arrived at the camp on November 5. They had fled from La Tejera, another community near Joateca, and provided similar accounts about what had happened there and in nearby communities. Like the refugees interviewed earlier in the year, they had undertaken the arduous trek at night, hiding from the army in the daytime. Additional bombings of civilians, at La Joya, Morazán, (one of the hamlets affected by the December 1981 massacres at El Mozote), came to light when reporters from *Time* magazine went to this guerrilla-controlled area in January 1986. Residents of La Joya told them, they said, of a bombing and strafing attack on Christmas morning.[27]

An episode in January 1986 sparked more than the usual controversy over aerial bombing. The archbishop of San Salvador made a well-publicized pastoral visit to a guerrilla-controlled area, eastern Chalatenango—his first visit to the area, although it lies within the Archdiocese of San Salvador. When the air force conducted a bombing raid close to the spot where the archbishop was meeting with parishioners, he felt obliged to speak out. The next Sunday, January 12, a statement was read on his behalf in the National Cathedral in San Salvador and broadcast by the rebel Radio Venceremos. The statement described the bombing raid, then added: "I spent several hours talking with the civilian population, who told me their problems and hopes: the fear of indiscriminate bombings, the destruction of their houses and belongings in opera-

tions. . . . The greatest plea is that I advise that there is a large civilian population here. . . . The petition is clear: that I make myself the voice of all and
express to those who should hear that the bombings cease in areas inhabited by
the civilian population."[28]

The archbishop's insistence that a civilian population remained in the area
was a response to the armed forces' declaration that bombed guerrilla-
controlled areas had been depopulated and that anyone who remained was a
guerrilla. As the spokesman for the armed forces, Col. Carlos Armando Avilés,
put it: "The good people, the people not with the guerrillas, aren't there."[29] It
was a variation on the theme expressed a couple of years earlier in the State
Department cable—that the masas were other than innocent civilian bystanders. It also reflected the view of the armed forces that they had largely
succeeded by 1986 in their efforts to drain the sea—a view contradicted by the
accounts of journalists, who occasionally traveled to guerrilla-controlled areas,
and by local residents, who continued to leave them. In fact, the International
Committee of the Red Cross (ICRC) was providing food and health services to
approximately one hundred thousand civilians in guerrilla-controlled territory
each month in early 1986, though the military often blocked its vehicles as they
tried to cross into those areas.[30] Although these areas were not completely
depopulated, the size of the civilian population was greatly reduced, and the
population of refugees and internally displaced Salvadorans greatly swollen.
Eliminating the remaining civilians there apparently remained a goal of the
armed forces, but by the early part of 1986 the controversy over the bombings
had been sustained for too long in the United States and other countries to
permit continued heavy reliance on bombings and aerial attacks, nor did the
armed forces probably need to rely so heavily on such methods, because the
policy of depopulation had made such headway. The forcible evacuations from
the Guazapa volcano in 1985 had indicated that less violent means could also be
effective.

In January 1986 the armed forces launched Operation Phoenix in
Chalatenango. First the area was bombed—again, a softening-up operation—
then five thousand ground troops went in. The commander of the armed forces,
Gen. Adolfo Onecífero Blandón, enumerated the accomplishments of this operation: the destruction of 206 tatus (dugout air shelters), the destruction of
eighteen clandestine medical clinics, and the capture of 427 masas.[31] As the
Los Angeles Times summarized it, "During Phoenix, army officials said one of
the objectives was to clear out the guerrillas' civilian supporters to deprive the
rebels of food and other assistance."[32]

Thereafter, reports of civilian deaths during aerial attacks continued, but the
numbers were greatly reduced. In some cases, the aerial attacks resembled
those of 1984 and 1985 in being not only indiscriminate but even apparently

aimed at civilians. For example, on January 22, 1987, the Salvadoran air force killed seven civilians in an attack against the tiny hamlet of San Diego, San Miguel, near the Honduran border. Four of the victims were peasants fleeing on a road away from town. Although at least two guerrillas were in San Diego at the time of the attack, none were near the four peasants. Some witnesses thought the air force had deliberately attacked them. The three other civilians, Nicolasa Martínez and her two young children, died when their house was directly hit by a bomb. The *New York Times* reported that the armed forces tried to cover up the incident, but "as evidence of the air attack grew, the armed forces press office changed its account. Now it admits that there was an attack and that civilians 'might have been affected.'"[33]

Although aerial attacks continued sporadically, they were no longer the rule. Aside from pressure in the United States and elsewhere to protect human rights, probably the largest factor in their discontinuation was a shift in strategy by the guerrillas. They had controlled approximately one third of the country in the early years of the war, but from 1986 on—as a result of the air war—they were forced to de-emphasize control of territory. The forcible depopulation of guerrilla-controlled zones by the military made it difficult for the guerrillas to obtain adequate food supplies from the remaining civilian residents. They needed to procure supplies from other areas.

Their new strategy involved a greater reliance on the dispersal of their forces throughout the country. Small platoons of guerrillas operated in government-controlled areas, close to military bases and towns, circumstances that diminished the value of aerial attacks against them. They continued to obtain food from civilians in the areas in which they operated, whether by purchase, donation, or theft. Yet for the armed forces to bomb and strafe these civilians would have been counterproductive, because many were not supporters of the guerrillas and because such attacks in government-controlled areas, which were somewhat accessible to journalists and human rights monitors, would have raised a domestic and international outcry. Instead, the armed forces were forced to rely heavily on foot patrols to give chase to the guerrillas; this, in turn, spurred the guerrillas to sow land mines extensively in the paths that the foot patrols took, thereby deterring pursuit (see chap. 4).

With the reduction in aerial attacks on civilians, some in El Salvador began to think of repopulating communities that had been abandoned. The first such effort began in 1986 in Tenancingo, the town that had been abandoned after it was bombed in September 1983. Although progress was made on resettlement projects (see chap. 7), the armed forces resisted their establishment for fear that the returning civilians would once again provide a base of support for the guerrillas. When some communities were repopulated, they became renewed targets for the armed forces. As recently as February 11, 1990, for example, a

Salvadoran air force helicopter fired rockets at houses in the village of Corral de Piedra, Chalatenango. Two rockets hit a house in which twenty-one civilians had taken refuge: five were killed and sixteen wounded. Four of the dead were children between the ages of two and eleven. The dead adult was a thirty-year-old man whose two-year-old daughter was killed in his arms. Eleven of the wounded were children between four months and twelve years of age.[34]

The village of Corral de Piedra had been abandoned years earlier but was repopulated on October 29, 1989, less than five months before the attack, by 520 repatriates from the Mesa Grande refugee camp in Honduras. Soldiers had passed through several times since it was repatriated and had searched houses. Several hours before the bombing, combat between the Salvadoran army and the guerrillas had commenced outside the village. Several helicopters and fixed-wing planes showed up; then, when some guerrillas ran away through the village, bullets from the helicopters hit several houses besides the one in which twenty-one civilians were hiding.

The Salvadoran Armed Forces issued several conflicting statements about the episode, at one point labeling those killed as "terrorists," at another, lamenting the deaths of civilians and promising an investigation; they promised to indemnify the victims, then denounced Tutela Legal for demanding that those responsible be prosecuted, calling its exhortation a "malicious . . . effort to create a criminal case which does not exist against those who were complying with their duty."[35] Six months later, the air force retracted its promise to provide compensation (see chap. 6).

In spite of military hostility to resettlement in regions once controlled by the guerrillas, several thousand displaced persons and refugees went home between 1986 and 1990. Some episodes like the one at Corral de Piedra took place, but the massacres in ground sweeps of the early 1980s and the massive aerial attacks on civilians of the mid-1980s were not repeated.

MASSACRES

Still, the armed forces continued to abuse civilians sporadically but frequently in the course of combat (see chap. 2). Three massacres have occurred recently: at Los Palitos, San Francisco, and Cuscatancingo.

· Los Palitos, May 21, 1987. Soldiers of the Arce Battalion, then commanded by Col. Roberto Mauricio Staben, assassinated five young peasant men in the village of Los Palitos, in eastern San Miguel Department, apparently because the men had traveled with the guerrillas earlier in the month. According to relatives of the victims, the People's Revolutionary Army had come to the men's houses and demanded that they accompany them for three days to carry out an unspecified mission. In such cases the guerrillas usually give young peasants recruitment or political talks or assign them tasks, such as carrying food. Informants said the men were intercepted by Arce Battalion soldiers on May 20 as they returned, unarmed, from their mission. The soldiers took them to Los Palitos, where they held them overnight in a chapel known as the Hermitage. On the morning of May 21 the soldiers killed them and dumped their bodies in a well.

Family members learned of the killings a few days later and placed candles and crosses with the names of their loved ones around the well. When legal proceedings were initiated, the Arce Battalion moved into the area, threatening witnesses and residents if they testified against the government troops. Military spokesmen offered at least three different explanations for the killings, all of which excluded the possibility of military involvement and none of which comported with the available evidence.[36] In April 1988 the judge invoked the amnesty provision of the 1987 Central American peace plan to close the case without identifying the guilty parties (see chap. 6).

· San Francisco, September 21, 1988. Soldiers of the Jiboa Battalion, commanded by the head of military intelligence of the Fifth Brigade, Maj. Mauricio Beltrán Granados, massacred ten peasants in a hamlet in San Vicente Department, staging the executions to look like a guerrilla ambush. This case is striking in that pressure from the United States eventually forced the army to admit responsibility. The testimony of the participants, which Americas Watch reviewed in the court file in San Sebastián in June 1989, provides an unusual glimpse into army behavior in the field and the methodology of covering up for its crimes.

Acting under Major Beltrán's orders, soldiers blindfolded and bound seven men and three women and led them to a secluded spot; they detonated several captured guerrilla mines near the captives and then shot the wounded civilians at point-blank range to finish them off. Significantly, the killings were carried out over the protestations of Lt. Manuel de Jesús Gálvez Gálvez and several soldiers. According to the court record, Lieutenant Gálvez refused to participate in the murders for two reasons: first, killing the prisoners could get them in trouble, and second, "What if they came to where your family lived, they could do the same thing, kill them without investigating who they had captured." Six of the ten captives had not even been interrogated before they were slain. Gálvez's refusal to comply with the order to kill the peasants is the first publicly known instance in which a soldier has acted—some eight and a half years later—according to Archbishop Romero's plea to Salvadoran soldiers not to obey orders to kill civilians.

Unfortunately, other soldiers obeyed Major Beltrán's order. Even those who refused to participate in the crime felt powerless to prevent others from carrying out his demands. They, too, participated in the cover-up until the army high command showed that it wanted the truth to be revealed.

Major Beltrán had ordered one soldier to smear blood on his uniform and pretend he was wounded during a fictitious armed confrontation. The hands of the dead were untied and their blindfolds removed. Soldiers planted guerrilla arms and propaganda at the scene of the massacre to provide further evidence of a confrontation. The soldiers and officers rehearsed an elaborate cover-up story that the major mapped out on a blackboard in a classroom at the staff headquarters. It held that while evacuating eight peasant detainees to the Fifth Brigade barracks, the soldiers were ambushed by guerrillas. In the ensuing fight, all the captives and two guerrillas perished. A soldier wounded in an unrelated incident was recruited to pretend he had been hurt in the alleged ambush, and the troops were taken back to the scene of the massacre to rehearse the moves.

After an autopsy showed that the victims had been shot in the head and heart at close range, the army conducted an investigation whose conclusions reiterated the cover-up story. The head of the Fifth Brigade, Col. José Emilio Chávez Cáceres, claimed that guerrillas had returned at night after the ambush and shot the dead civilians at close range to make it look as if they had been executed by the army. The cover-up held until Vice President Dan Quayle of the United States visited El Salvador in February 1989 and indicated that military aid might be in peril if the case was not solved. This pressure eventually led the military to admit responsibility for the massacre and the cover-up (see chap. 6).[37]

· Cuscatancingo, November 18, 1989. In the midst of the FMLN urban offensive, soldiers shot dead seven unarmed young men in the San Luis section of Cuscatancingo, a northern suburb of San Salvador. Six of the victims were members of the neighborhood Olimpia soccer team. The seventh was a boy who was selling bread. The military, warning that it would soon attack by air, had ordered all residents to leave the area on the afternoon of November 17 and strafed the area the day before. The young men had stayed behind to guard their families' houses from looting. The guerrillas had all left the area by the morning of the massacre, and all the evidence indicates that a group of soldiers on patrol simply lined the youths up against a wall and shot them.[38]

Another grave violation added to the catalogue of horrors committed by the elite, U.S.-trained Atlacatl Battalion was the February 13, 1989, attack on an FMLN field hospital in the El Chupadero area of Los Encuentros, a hamlet in Chalatenango. An on-site investigation by Tutela Legal established that soldiers murdered ten people, including the Mexican physician Alejandra Bravo Betancourt Mancera, a fourteen-year-old Salvadoran nurse, three paramedics, and five wounded guerrillas. Tutela Legal investigators who examined the bodies believed that Dr. Bravo and the nurse were raped before being executed.[39]

A similar attack occurred on April 15, 1989, in San Ildefonso, San Vicente, when soldiers killed an Argentine doctor, a French nurse, a sixteen-year-old Salvadoran paramedic, a wounded guerrilla, and a schoolteacher after they were captured. Although the military claimed that the victims were killed in combat, an autopsy of the body of the French nurse performed in France indicated she had been tortured and most likely raped before being shot.[40]

During the powerful offensive launched by the guerrillas in November 1989, the authorities relied heavily on air power to hammer at guerrilla positions in poor barrios around San Salvador and in provincial capitals. Although the offensive left tremendous destruction in its wake, Americas Watch research in three heavily affected civilian neighborhoods—the Guadalupe and Santa Marta–Plan Piloto areas of Soyapango and Zacamil–Metrópolis—indicated that the bombing and strafing were aimed principally at guerrilla emplacements, though in some isolated cases the army attacked civilian buildings without first giving warning to evacuate, as required by the laws of war.[41] The guerrillas made a political point when they quietly withdrew from the poor neighborhoods of the capital and instead attacked the military from the heart of San Salvador's wealthy section. Needless to say, the air force did not bomb or strafe Escalón.

More than a decade after the onset of the war, killings, disappearances, and the torture of civilians taken into custody by the armed forces continue to be reported frequently, although the days in which the army slaughtered dozens of civilians in an afternoon are at an end, at least for now. The strategy now followed by the guerrillas does not provide military incentives to engage in mass killings of civilians; and the resumption of mass killings could have the effect of making El Salvador once again the focus of strong international pressure concerning human rights.

The Salvadoran Armed Forces continue to commit abuses against civilians in the course of their counterinsurgency campaigns, but the number and nature of the abuses stirs little active concern from the international community. Ironically, one reason for the relative silence is that when comparisons to the early 1980s are invoked, the current level of abuses seems low. This is known as improvement. In that respect, among others, the mass killings of the early 1980s still cause severe harm. Aside from the recurrent victimization of those who suffered themselves or lost families and friends at that time and the denial of justice to the victims, comparisons permit much of the world to see the current level of abuses as a tolerable human rights situation.

4

ABUSES BY THE GUERRILLAS

Like the government of El Salvador, the FMLN is bound by the provisions of Article 3, common to the Geneva Conventions of 1949 and to Protocol II, which was added to the Geneva Conventions in 1977. The principal violations of these international instruments by the guerrillas have been the use of summary executions and kidnappings for ransom. The kidnappings in the early years of the conflict consolidated rich Salvadorans against any compromise with the rebels and even today makes it hard to settle the war. In addition, the guerrillas have caused numerous civilian casualties through their use of land mines. Though in many cases not in technical violation of international law, specifically the U.N. Land Mines Protocol, the civilian toll resulting from the promiscuous use of this indiscriminate weapon has been tremendous.[1]

During the first half of the 1980s, virtually all reports of FMLN killings occurred under three kinds of circumstances: targeted assassinations, killings of civilian passengers of vehicles that failed to stop at guerrilla roadblocks, and executions of captured soldiers. The number of noncombatants killed by guerrillas was low in comparison with the number killed by the armed forces, according to Tutela Legal: in 1983, the first full year covered by reports on both sides, 5,142 killings of civilians were attributed to the Salvadoran Armed Forces and their allied death squads and 67 civilian killings to the guerrillas. Of the abductions during 1983 that had not been resolved by the end of the year, Tutela Legal attributed 43 to the guerrillas and 535 to the armed forces and the death squads.

Over time, the disparity between the number of abuses committed by the armed forces and allied paramilitary groups on the one hand and by the guerrillas on the other narrowed considerably. Pressure to respect human rights and changes in tactics to meet the exigencies of conflict reduced the number of noncombatants killed by government forces. The FMLN also came under pressure to respect human rights: human rights groups and the press disseminated reports on abuses committed by the FMLN, affecting its ability to obtain international support. Accordingly, FMLN spokespersons regularly sought out representatives of Americas Watch to try to justify the conduct of the guerrillas or to deny responsibility for particular abuses attributed to them. Nevertheless, the changing nature of the conflict did not reduce the strategic incentive for the FMLN to curb abuses.

In April and May 1984 the FMLN engaged in forced recruitment in at least two departments in El Salvador, San Miguel and Morazán. The International Committee of the Red Cross registered 1,570 newly arrived displaced persons in the town of San Miguel during those two months, and interviews with them indicated that most were fleeing from involuntary service in the FMLN. For example, Mauro A. told Americas Watch that he had lived in the border town of Sabanetas for eight years. On the morning of April 19, 1984, some armed guerrillas came to Sabanetas, rounded up people for a meeting in the center of town, which lasted from 5 A.M. to 3 P.M., and told their audience that they should not be neutral in the national conflict. If they did not "incorporate" into the guerrilla movement, they should leave town—within eight hours. Incorporation meant that children between the ages of six and twelve would go to the guerrillas' school; children between twelve and fifteen would undergo military training; people between sixteen and forty would serve in the military; and those over forty would work in production brigades. Some 370 residents decided to leave rather than incorporate.[2]

International law is largely silent on such practices, prohibiting only the recruitment of children under fifteen.[3] Both the guerrillas and the Salvadoran government have violated this provision, and both have used objectionable press-gang methods. In the view of Americas Watch, guerrilla forces cannot legitimately engage in forced recruitment in areas they do not control continuously; where they have continuous control, they in effect govern in the manner of a state and have a legal system capable of fairly handling objections to military service. Of course, the government has long used press-gang methods, exempting the children of the well-to-do. Abuses by one side do not justify the abuses by the other, however. Faced with criticism from human rights groups and disfavor within El Salvador, the guerrillas abandoned forced recruitment in September 1984.[4]

There were other episodes in 1984. A group calling itself the Clara Elizabeta Ramírez Front assassinated a number of right-wing civilian leaders.[5] The FMLN denied a connection to the Ramírez Brigade, which apparently represented a bona fide split from the organization.

Also, the guerrillas allegedly executed a group of captured civilians in Morazán: the mayor of Cacaopera, the village clerk, two municipal policemen, two truck drivers, and two other men—the first mass killing by the FMLN reported during the conflict. More than a year later, on December 29, 1985, the FMLN admitted in a broadcast on its clandestine radio station that it had committed this crime: "The Mayor and other members of enemy networks in that town, involved in criminal and repressive actions against the people, were put to death the day of their capture in the year 1984." The guerrillas and the government were involved at the time in negotiations for the release of Inés Guadalupe Duarte, daughter of the president, who had been kidnapped by the FMLN. The government simultaneously sought the release of others abducted by the guerrillas, including the nine people from Cacaopera, but the guerrillas said they could not release those from Cacaopera because they had already killed them. The FMLN also named a municipal official in another village whom they had executed in 1983.[6]

As it turned out, Inés Duarte and a friend, who were kidnapped on September 10, 1985 (her bodyguard and chauffeur were killed during the kidnapping), were released on October 24 in exchange for twenty-one prisoners held by the government. In addition, the FMLN released twenty-three municipal officials it had held hostage, and the government permitted ninety-six wounded FMLN combatants to leave the country for medical care. At the end of the year Tutela Legal reported that forty-five other noncombatants captured by the guerrillas had not been released. Some were municipal officials held because the FMLN claimed control of their communities and wanted to demonstrate that the government could not function there; others were being held for ransom in violation of the prohibition in the laws of war against hostage taking.[7]

In 1985 the FMLN killed ninety-seven noncombatants, according to Tutela Legal. The number included two massacres: the killing of civilians and members of the civil defense at Santa Cruz Loma, La Paz, on April 8, 1985, and the killing of a number of civilians and U.S. Marines at a restaurant in the Zona Rosa neighborhood of San Salvador on June 19, 1985. In the Santa Cruz Loma episode, one of the five groups making up the FMLN, the Popular Forces of Liberation, entered the village dressed as soldiers in an apparent effort to persuade unarmed members of the civil defense to accompany them. They executed six members of the civil defense, and another six civilians died in a battle in the village: a sixty-seven-year-old man, three women, and two children, when a rocket hit the house they were in, and a nine-year-old girl, who was shot when she ran from the house. In the Zona Rosa episode, another group that made up the FMLN, the Revolutionary Party of Central American Workers, attacked off-duty U.S. Marines sitting in a sidewalk café. Four died, along with nine civilian bystanders.[8]

By 1985 the guerrillas were frequently using land mines to deter army foot patrols from pursuing them. They were operating in small platoons in many parts of the country, and the mines were of great importance in helping them escape government patrols (see chap. 3). Yet in a small, densely populated country like El Salvador, the risk that civilians would accidentally detonate mines was very high, and the guerrillas did not take adequate precautions to avoid such civilian casualties. In 1985 thirty-one civilians died when they stepped on land mines, most planted by the FMLN, according to Tutela Legal. Many others lost limbs.[9]

The guerrillas used more land mines in 1986 than in the previous year as they deployed more forces in government-controlled areas of the country to evade aerial bombardment and became concerned about pursuit by army foot patrols. Fifty-four civilians were killed by mines in 1986. Of these, eight deaths were due to mines planted by the armed forces, according to the Tutela Legal; almost all the rest were caused by the guerrillas.

A typical injury took place near San Marcos Lempa, Usulután, on May 23, 1986, when María Encarnación López Vásquez, fourteen, the youngest in a family of ten children, went with four friends to pick mangoes. They were walking down a trail used by ox carts when she stepped on a mine that blew off her left leg. Interviewed thereafter by Americas Watch, she said that guerrillas frequented the area; they shot at soldiers and were trying to blow up a nearby bridge. There had been three previous land mine incidents nearby: a woman was injured, a boy lost both arms, and a man was killed just fifteen days before María López lost her leg.[10]

Aside from the land mine deaths, Tutela Legal attributed seven indiscriminate killings in 1986 to the guerrillas, all in traffic stoppages (paros); in a traffic stoppage the FMLN seeks to bring all moving vehicles to a halt and enforces its ban with violence. Two civilians were killed on December 8 when the FMLN attacked a bus traveling between Suchitoto and San Martín; an additional fifteen passengers were injured. During the same year Tutela Legal attributed forty-five targeted assassinations to the guerrillas. The majority were apparently killed because the FMLN considered them to be orejas, or informers, for the armed forces.[11]

The next year, 1987, Tutela Legal recorded fewer targeted killings by the guerrillas: thirty-one, among them a massacre of coffee pickers on a coffee plantation in Los Laureles, a hamlet on the slopes of the San Vicente volcano. The plantation belonged to Alfredo Cristiani, at the time head of the ARENA party and since 1989 president of El Salvador. The FMLN denied responsibility for the six deaths or for the disappearance of another man on January 19 in the same incident, but witnesses interviewed by Americas Watch identified the perpetrators as boys that they knew had been guerrillas in the area for several years.

Several coffee pickers saw the victims being taken into custody by the guerrillas, yet it did not occur to them that their coworkers would be killed, for the guerrillas had, so far as they knew, murdered no one in the area before. Minutes after they were told to leave, however, they heard gunshots. The next day, relatives returned to the site and found the bodies of the six who were killed; the seventh victim was never found. The guerrillas apparently believed the pickers were army orejas. Two of the dead and the missing man had been FMLN combatants, who had left the force two years earlier.[12]

The number of targeted killings by the guerrillas rose to forty-four in 1988, according to Tutela Legal, while civilian deaths from land mines planted by both sides rose from twenty-nine in 1987 to 65 in 1988.[13]

The guerrillas also continued to kidnap mayors who were organizing civil defense groups on the grounds that they were an integral part of the army's counterinsurgency effort. In some cases the mayors were mistreated in detention—kept blindfolded or kept for an extended period with their thumbs tied behind their backs—before being released. Over the years the guerrillas assassinated several mayors and other elected municipal officials, as many as eight between 1988 and early 1989.[14] To give an example: on April 15, 1988, Pedro Ventura, the ARENA party mayor of San Isidro, Morazán, was executed shortly after his election. The FMLN's Radio Venceremos announced that the FMLN took responsibility for the crime, saying that the mayor-elect had been repeatedly warned that central government authorities would not be permitted to operate in zones under FMLN control or in dispute because they formed part of the army's counterinsurgency strategy.[15]

In 1989 the FMLN carried out several assassinations of prominent right-wing civilians in the capital. Among them were the following cases.[16]

· Miguel Castellanos, editor of the journal *Análisis* and former FPL commander, was shot dead by guerrillas on February 16, 1989, as he was leaving his office at the Center for Studies of the National Reality (Centro para Estudios de la Realidad Nacional) in San Salvador. One of his bodyguards was seriously injured in the attack. The FMLN claimed credit, asserting that Castellanos had collaborated with the army and caused many deaths. His collaboration with the authorities is undeniable; he no doubt provided extensive intelligence on people and methods used by the guerrillas. Yet under international law he could not be considered a military target: he was not a member of the armed forces of a party to the conflict nor was he participating in hostilities at the time of the ambush.

· On March 15, 1989, a unit of the Armed Forces of Liberation, one of the member groups of the FMLN, shot Francisco Peccorini Letona, a seventy-two-year-old conservative intellectual, as he was driving toward the Deluxe Cinema in San Salvador. He died later in the Military Hospital. Peccorini, a dual U.S.-Salvadoran citizen and former Jesuit priest who had written numerous books, was professor emeritus in philosophy at California State University, Long Beach, and a member of the Committee for the Rescue of the University of El Salvador (Comité pro Rescate de la Universidad de El Salvador), a committee created to rid the university of communist influence. His assassination occurred only days after the March 10 attack on another member of that committee, also by the FAL.

· On April 19, 1989, Attorney General José Roberto García Alvarado was killed at an intersection in San Salvador when guerrillas placed a powerful explosive on top of his armored vehicle, just above the place where he was sitting. The explosion ripped through his body, killing him instantly. It was so precisely targeted that it only slightly injured his driver and his bodyguards. The FMLN privately admitted that the FAL was responsible.

· On November 28, 1989, Francisco José ("Chachi") Guerrero, former president of the Supreme Court, presidential candidate, and foreign minister, was shot in his car at an intersection in San Salvador. His bodyguard and a driver were wounded, as was one of the alleged attackers, Ernesto Erazo Cruz, from whom the police later took a statement implicating the FMLN. Eyewitness testimony suggested that this was a targeted assassination, but the FMLN contended that the killing resulted from an effort to requisition an automobile for military use.

Having faced criticism for these and similar executions over the years, the guerrillas began to assert that they had set up criminal courts in accordance with international humanitarian law. For example, on August 10, 1988, Comdr. Nidia Díaz, secretary of promotion and protection of human rights for the FMLN, wrote that the number of FMLN executions was rising because the Salvadoran Armed Forces relied increasingly on informers to gather intelligence and the informers' activities had caused "considerable" guerrilla casualties. Díaz's letter said: "The execution of the [death] sentence is preceded by an investigation whose results are judged by an impartial tribunal formed in accordance with the possibilities afforded by the zone [in which the guerrillas operate]. Most of the time we are obliged not to reveal the identity of the members of the tribunal and those defending the accused to avoid reprisals against them."[17]

Over a period of several years, Americas Watch held a number of meetings outside El Salvador with representatives of the FMLN debating this issue with them. We criticized their arguments in several reports, and eventually, in May 1990, published a report solely devoted to the question. The report, which reviewed twenty-nine killings committed by the FMLN between January 1988 and April 1990, concluded "that the organization of and procedural guarantees offered by the rebels' *ad hoc* courts flagrantly violate the non-derogable provisions of Common Article 3 [of the Geneva Conventions of 1949] and Article 6 of Protocol II [of 1977, which spells out restrictions on both parties to internal conflicts such as the war in El Salvador]."[18]

Whether criticism will affect the FMLN practice of assassination is not yet clear. What is clear is that the number of civilians killed by the FMLN continued to rise before its November 1989 offensive, and because the number committed by the armed forces and their allied paramilitary forces decreased, the disparity in the number of killings on each side was not very great. The guerrillas continued to use land mines; in just one episode, on May 22, 1989, nine civilians died when a mine exploded under a bus at El León Pintado, Santa Ana. In other indiscriminate attacks, the guerrillas launched catapult bombs, home-made devices that could not be targeted reliably and often misfired, killing civilians in the vicinity. Even though the FMLN announced a suspension of the use of these devices on February 27, 1989, it continued to use other types of explosives with a devastating effect on nearby civilians.[19]

During the November 1989 offensive, the FMLN engaged in numerous violations of international humanitarian law: committing summary executions, illegally using civilians as shields in isolated instances, attacking Red Cross vehicles, and misusing the Red Cross emblem on vehicles not employed primarily for medical purposes.[20] One of its most serious abuses during the offensive, and the only known multiple slaying of noncombatants, occurred during an attack on the National Center of Information (Centro Nacional de Información), a government press agency. The FMLN concedes that it killed six people. Five were government journalists, and it appears that they were not killed in combat but were captured and then executed.[21]

5

THE ADMINISTRATION OF JUSTICE

The administration of justice in El Salvador has been widely condemned as a misnomer: there is much injustice, but little justice, in Salvadoran courts. Lack of education and training, technical incompetence, insufficient funding, inadequate laws, and the low social prestige of judges all contribute to the weakness of the justice system. The primary reasons for the failings of the courts involve the military authorities—their lack of cooperation with, indeed, at times, the direct obstruction of, investigations of official culpability and their unwillingness to accept even minimal limits on the methods of detention and interrogation.

The refusal of the armed forces to submit to the rule of law has been expressed in a variety of ways, from the murder of judges and lawyers to the intimidation of witnesses to the covering up of crimes. Efforts to enhance the effectiveness of the justice system, in which the U.S. government has taken a leading role, have failed largely because their focus has been on questions of technical competence, to the virtual exclusion of the issue of military obstructionism. Increased funding for the courts and better training of judges, as much as they are needed, contribute little to improving the administration of justice when the source of the problem is a failure of political will.

DUE PROCESS

As noted in chapter 1, El Salvadorans have lived under a state of emergency for most of the past ten years; constitutional protections of basic liberties have been suspended. Each time a state of emergency was declared, the Salvadoran government promulgated special criminal procedures granting jurisdiction to military courts in cases of crimes against the state—that is, politically motivated crimes—and bestowing undue powers on police and army personnel with respect to criminal suspects.

Decree 507 of December 3, 1980, was enacted pursuant to the state of emergency of March 6, 1980, to amend the rules applicable in military courts to civilians charged with crimes against the state. Decree 507 and to a lesser extent its successor, Decree 50, so radically restricted due process rights in the course of modifying criminal procedure as to virtually eliminate them in practice.

Decree 507 permitted the authorities to hold a person for up to 195 days in incommunicado preventive detention; after fifteen days of detention the police were required to present the accused before a military judge, who then determined whether further detention was warranted. This extended period of detention constituted an open invitation to the security forces—National Police, Treasury Police, and National Guard—to arbitrarily detain, intimidate, and torture people and extract extrajudicial confessions with impunity.

The decree allowed the police and the examining judge to carry out the investigative phase of the proceedings in secrecy. The accused was denied the right to counsel throughout the period of administrative detention, and the police routinely ignored the provision that the military judge be notified within twenty-four hours of anyone's being detained. The decree authorized convictions based on uncorroborated confessions made in the presence of only police, army, or other security personnel. To establish a suspect's membership in a subversive association, the law required merely that the allegation be "confirmed" by national or international media, and it authorized a military judge of instruction to order that a person be held in "corrective detention" for 120 days even if no grounds were found for detention during the period of inquiry. Finally, the law applied its corrective measures to children under sixteen.

When the new Constitution of El Salvador was enacted in 1983, the assembly extended the effectiveness of Decree 507 until February 28, 1984. Four days prior to its lapse, on February 24, 1984, the assembly enacted Decree 50 to replace it. Decree 50, like Decree 507, granted military courts jurisdiction over civilian crimes against the state. These courts were under the direction of the Ministry of Defense and outside the control of the judiciary. Decree 50 provided for an investigative period of ninety days, that is, administrative pretrial detention without access to counsel for up to fifteen days, during which the security forces conducted an investigation, sixty days of investigation by a military judge of instruction, and fifteen days of further investigation by a military judge of first instance. Only after detainees were presented to a military judge were they entitled to legal assistance. By express reference to Decree 507, Decree 50 authorized the admission of extrajudicial confessions as long as two witnesses attested that no coercion was involved. Even if defendants failed to ratify their extrajudicial confessions in court, their statements could be rebutted by the security force members who witnessed the confession. Decree 50 also made reports by the Ministries of the Interior and Defense on the illegitimate or subversive nature of associations legally admissible and sufficient for the purposes of proof. All sentences by the military trial judge could be appealed to a newly created martial court, composed of one lawyer and two military officials, all appointed by the president.

Although Decree 50 sacrificed constitutional protections in the name of efficiency, in the months following its adoption there was no indication that prisoners were processed or brought to trial more rapidly than before. Decree 50 remained in force from 1984 to the beginning of 1987, with the exception of a brief interval preceding the March 1984 elections.

During each state of emergency the internal procedures of the army required that people be turned over to the security forces within seventy-two hours of arrest. This rule was frequently violated, partly because the army could not extract all the information it wanted from most detainees within seventy-two hours.

The end of the state of emergency in early 1987 meant that on February 28, 1987, Decree 50 lapsed by its own terms. The Armed Forces General Staff notified the military that no person should thereafter be detained longer than seventy-two hours without being charged, as mandated by the Constitution. In 1987 the government forces generally appeared to be obeying the order, though the right to consult an attorney during the seventy-two-hour period was consistently denied. By 1988 the army was once again repeatedly violating the seventy-two-hour limit, and many in the armed forces were publicly chafing at the bit for being asked to live within constitutional limits.[1]

Pursuant to the state of emergency declared in November 1989, individuals accused of crimes against the state—charged with acts of terrorism, sabotage, subversive association, or other politically motivated crimes—were tried in military courts while those in the military, as always, continued to be tried in civilian courts. From November 1989 through March 1990 state-of-emergency legislation suspended rights of due process, and procedural legislation approved by the Legislative Assembly on November 16 for the duration of the state of emergency once again extended the period of permitted incommunicado detention from seventy-two hours to fifteen days. Once the fifteen-day period of administrative detention was over, the detainee was guaranteed the right to counsel while giving a declaration, the right to know the identity of the detaining authority and the reasons for the detention, and the right to remain silent.[2]

Since March 1990 all constitutional rights of criminal defendants have, in theory, been in place.

In practice, arrests and detentions in El Salvador are carried out largely to intimidate, or "burn," suspected political opponents and to gather information, rather than to prosecute and convict violators of the criminal law. Salvadoran security forces frequently undertake arrests without any lawful cause, often alleging without evidentiary foundation that the detainee is somehow affiliated with, or assisting, the FMLN. Unionists, members of cooperatives, community organizers, church workers, and representatives of humanitarian agencies have all been subjected to arrest in this manner. Few have been convicted. Many prisoners have spent years in prison without trial. The small monetary remuneration that lawyers receive and the risk they run of being accused of having subversive connections if they represent prisoners accused of politically motivated crimes have kept low the number of defense counsels for political detainees. It is not uncommon for unrepresented detainees to remain in prison beyond the period of the potential sentence with no lawyer to call this to the court's attention.[3]

For much of the decade the security forces have made most of the arrests in urban areas, the army the majority in rural areas. The Defense Ministry has required since 1983 that family members, the governmental Human Rights Commission, and the International Committee of the Red Cross be notified of detentions within twenty-four hours. Compliance with these regulations, particularly by the army, has been inconsistent. For detainees to be transferred from one authority to another without notification is not uncommon, either. From 1982 through 1987 the Salvadoran government permitted the ICRC access to detained prisoners on the eighth day of detention. From 1987 to the present (except during the state of emergency in force from November 1989 through March 1990, when the eight-day rule again applied), the ICRC has been granted access after seventy-two hours.

From January 1987 until November 1989 and again since March 1990, when no state of emergency has been in effect, only the security forces—as distinguished from the army, air force, and navy—have had the authority to arrest anyone not caught within twenty-four hours of a crime. A great many arrests by the army have violated this provision. Even when no state of emergency has been in effect, detainees have rarely been advised of the reasons for their detention or the rights conferred upon them by law, although doing so is legally required.

The political purposes that to a great extent underlie these arbitrary arrest and interrogation procedures are evident in the authorities' proclivity for broadcasting extrajudicial confessions in a "trial by television" circus atmosphere that violate the fundamental norms of due process. For example, in August 1983 the Treasury Police arrested Pedro Daniel Alvarado Rivera and accused him of the May 1983 murder of Lt. Comdr. Albert A. Schaufelberger III, deputy commander of the U.S. Military Group in El Salvador. Shortly thereafter, Alvarado confessed to the crime on television in a presentation by the Treasury Police. Following an investigation, the U.S. State Department issued a statement saying that Alvarado "was not involved in the crime" and that his "confession was obtained under duress." In spite of express U.S. rejection of the methods by which Alvarado's confession was secured, the defendant remained imprisoned until April 1986 on the strength of that confession.[4]

In August 1985 the Salvadoran government announced having solved the case of the FMLN attack a month earlier, in which four U.S. Marines and nine civilians died. All three prisoners in the case were shown on television confessing to the crime and were also presented at a press conference. When transferred from the National Guard barracks to Mariona prison, they recanted their confessions, claiming that they had been subjected to physical and psychological torture and that they had been told what to say. The defendants were still in jail in 1990 and had yet to be tried.[5]

On November 8, 1985, Treasury Policemen arrested two students, José Vladimir Centeno and Jaime Ernesto Centeno and accused them of the October 26, 1985, kidnapping of Col. Omar Napoleón Avalos. They confessed while in incommunicado detention at Treasury Police headquarters. At a press conference held on the condition that the detainees not speak, the commander of the Treasury Police, Col. Rinaldo Golcher, announced that the police had discovered that the two brothers belonged to the Armed Forces of Liberation.

Their confessions were videotaped, given to the media, and played on the government-controlled television station. A full-page advertisement by the Ministry of Communications and Culture featured photographs of the brothers and another accused of the same crime, concluding that they were guilty of the kidnapping. Boldfaced capital letters stated, "Once More Justice Triumphs over Terrorism." The ad urged readers to "listen to their declarations for yourself on Radio El Salvador and on Channel 10-TV at 7 A.M., 8 A.M., and 12:30 P.M."

The Centeno brothers claimed that when they were finally sent to Mariona prison, they were tortured and were forced for several hours to rehearse the statements prepared for them. They gave their statements without the opportunity to consult counsel or family. But their confessions, whatever their legal admissibility, were taken not for court use but to condemn the detainees in the forum of public opinion. The Centenos remained in Mariona prison until November 1987, when they were released under a general amnesty.[6]

In a similar case, Treasury Police agents arrested six members of the Christian Committee for Displaced Persons of El Salvador (CRIPDES) and the National Coordinator for Repopulation (CNR), along with dozens of others, on April 19, 1989. Charged with possession of arms of war and sent to prison, they were released on August 8 for lack of evidence. While they were in prison, however, the army took out unsigned paid advertisements in the local press asserting that each of the six belonged to FMLN organizations. Under the title "S/He Is a Terrorist" there appeared a purported biography of each and the slogan "FMLN = CRIPDES."[7]

A second indication of the essentially political objectives of the judicial system is the enduring fact that people charged with politically motivated crimes in El Salvador rarely go to trial. At the end of 1982 over half the prisoners in Mariona, the prison for men, had been remanded between 1978 and 1981. Not one had been brought to trial. Of 650 prisoners arrested between September 1, 1984, and August 31, 1985, the military judge of first instance reached judgments on only thirty-four, absolving eighteen of charges against them. The Ministry of Justice reported that fewer than 10 percent of those in prison for all offenses at that time had been tried for any crime. Some had been incarcerated for as long as five years without trial.[8]

In the first part of the decade the number of prisoners held for politically motivated crimes in Mariona and Ilopango prisons was likely a fraction of the total held for political reasons throughout El Salvador. An undetermined number of others were held in unacknowledged detention in military barracks, security forces headquarters, and clandestine government detention centers.[9] As the disappearance of citizens declined in the mid-1980s, the number of acknowledged prisoners accused of politically motivated crimes probably more closely approximated the number of actual prisoners held for such crimes.

In January 1983 there were between six hundred and eight hundred acknowledged prisoners being held for politically motivated offenses under the auspices of the Ministry of Justice.[10] On May 4, 1983, the Constituent Assembly issued Decree 210, the Law of Amnesty and Citizen Rehabilitation, which declared an amnesty for certain politically motivated crimes committed by civilians, whether currently under prosecution or not. The military judge of first instance was empowered to determine which prisoners would benefit from the amnesty. By June 24, seven weeks later, 533 prisoners had been released. Fewer than two hundred of those confined before May remained in prison. Trade unionists linked to the National Federation of Salvadoran Workers and the Lempa River Hydroelectric Commission Workers' Union (STECEL) were formally denied amnesty, and they remained in prison.

The beneficial effect of the amnesty law was limited by the actions of the security forces a few days before the law was passed. On May 8 security forces arrested two prisoners accused of politically motivated crimes who had been released from Mariona prison after judicial dismissal of the charges against them, along with eight others. Eight of the ten—including the two former political prisoners, Manuel de Jesús Orellana Morán and Pedro Antonio Chamul Montano—were shot dead. Shortly thereafter, following the declaration of amnesty, many prisoners refused to leave Mariona and Ilopango without international observers being present.[11]

In the months after the amnesty, the number of acknowledged prisoners accused of politically motivated crimes climbed sharply. On January 10, 1984, there were 437 prisoners in Mariona and 54 prisoners in Ilopango, prisons for men and women respectively. The number of prisoners accused of politically motivated crimes continued to increase during the next year and a half. According to the governmental Human Rights Commission, there were 647 prisoners in Mariona and 63 in Ilopango in January 1986. The rate of arrests in political cases was substantially higher in 1986—averaging 340 per month—than in 1985, when it averaged 237 per month.[12]

The number of prisoners in the penitentiary system accused of politically motivated offenses (not including those detained by the security forces or at military headquarters or barracks) stood at 1,174 at the end of 1986—the largest number since the civil war began—but declined to 700 by May 1987. The decrease was attributable to fewer arrests (253 per month in the first four months of 1987), the addition of two new military judges of first instance to reduce the trial backlog, and, since January 1987, the trial of political cases before civilian judges, who appeared to be releasing prisoners faster than military judges.[13]

In 1988 and 1989 the number of prisoners held for politically motivated crimes and administrative detainees declined significantly; however, those detained were still frequently subjected to physical and psychological abuse. In early 1990 the number of prisoners in Salvadoran prisons was about six thousand, of whom 370 were accused of politically motivated crimes.[14]

ATTACKS ON JUDGES AND LAWYERS

Throughout the decade judges, lawyers, and court officials have been subjected to a variety of pressures, including offers of bribes, threats, and physical attack. The combined effect has been to perpetuate a system of justice incapable of rendering judgment in a fair and impartial manner.

- In February 1980 armed men shot and killed Mario Zamora Rivas, the Christian Democratic attorney general, in his home after a televised speech by former Maj. Roberto D'Aubuisson in which he urged security personnel to go beyond the law to combat subversion and named Zamora as one of many "subversives."[15]
- On March 27, 1980, three days after the assassination of Archbishop Oscar Romero, Judge Atilio Ramírez Amaya, who was responsible for investigating his death, was himself the object of an assassination

attempt that forced him to leave the country. On the two previous days Ramírez received death threats. Then at 10:30 P.M. on March 27 two men came to his house, posing as friends of a colleague, and shot at him, injuring his maid. The judge fired back at the attackers, who fled, but hit no one.[16] Shortly thereafter, Judge Ramírez left El Salvador.

· According to the Center for the Independence of Judges and Lawyers of the International Commission of Jurists (ICJ), five relatives of a judge in San Salvador were assassinated on April 14, 1981. The victims' heads were severed from their bodies and laid at the doorstep of the judge's home.[17]

· On October 9, 1981, the building housing the Supreme Court was bombed, and the president of the Supreme Court was seriously injured.[18]

· By early 1982 attorneys who had agreed to represent eleven STECEL unionists arrested in August 1980 for a strike action had withdrawn from the case after receiving death threats and, in some instances, being the objects of attempted kidnappings.[19]

· On May 16, 1985, the FMLN assassinated the military judge handling the cases of those accused of politically motivated crimes.[20]

· In early 1987 the home of Judge Miriam Artiaga Alvarez was machine-gunned twice. She was responsible for a portion of the kidnapping-for-profit case relating to the dismantling and theft of a warehouse. Shortly thereafter, Judge Artiaga reduced the warehouse-related charges against the defendants to a misdemeanor; she subsequently resigned (see chap. 6).[21]

· At 7:10 A.M. on May 11, 1988, Judge Jorge Alberto Serrano Panameño, forty-five, was shot dead by gunmen who pulled alongside his car and sprayed him with bullets. Serrano, a civilian, had served three years as first military judge of first instance and was responsible for two politically controversial cases at the time of his death. He was killed just days before he was expected to rule on an amnesty petition filed by the attorneys for three military officers jailed since April 1986 in the kidnapping-for-profit case. He was responsible for the portion of the case relating to the more serious charges—arms possession, kidnapping, extortion, and so forth. In a statement televised the day before his murder, Judge Serrano indicated that he would not grant amnesty in connection with the kidnapping charges against the three. It was widely reported that he was under considerable pressure to grant amnesty and that he had turned down a number of bribes. In another case before him, the Zona Rosa murders, he had ruled that amnesty must be granted to the three men charged—all guerrillas. His ruling, although affirmed later by a military appeals court, was overturned by President Duarte.[22]

- FMLN members killed José Apolinario Martínez, justice of the peace of Carolina, San Miguel, on June 14, 1988, according to Tutela Legal. On May 2, 1987, Martínez had received a letter warning him to resign "or he would pay the consequences."[23]
- In late 1988 and early 1989 the FMLN, in what it considered an effort to combat the army's counterinsurgency strategy, launched attacks and threats against civilian officials in conflictive areas, including mayors and judges. According to accounts in the Salvadoran press, at least seven justices of the peace resigned in early 1989 under FMLN pressure, those in Tapalhuaca, La Paz; San Ildefonso, San Vicente; Ereguayquin and Nueva Granada, Usulután; Metapán, Santa Ana; Villa Dolores, Cabañas; and Oratorio de Concepción, Cuscatlán.[24]
- On April 19, 1989, guerrilla commandos killed Attorney General José Roberto García Alvarado (see chap. 4).
- On November 16, 1989, the National Guard arrested Salvador Antonio Ibarra, attorney for the Lutheran legal aid and human rights agency, Socorro Jurídico Luterano, when he appeared at guard headquarters as an attorney representing detained foreign Lutheran workers. Ibarra was held for nine days, interrogated, kicked, and threatened. Immediately upon his release, he agreed to represent Jennifer Jean Casolo, a U.S. church worker arrested, charged with possession of arms of war, and eventually released for lack of evidence. On December 12, in the course of representing her, Ibarra made statements to the press suggesting that Casolo would be released. That same day, he told reporters, there was an attempt to kill him. Ibarra's sister and two others were arrested at his house on December 14, when police apparently came looking for him. They were released the next day.[25]
- On November 28, 1989, Francisco José ("Chachi") Guerrero, former president of the Supreme Court, presidential candidate, and foreign minister, was shot dead by the FMLN (see chap. 4).
- On April 13, 1990, unknown men fatally wounded Roberto Huezo Nativi, second justice of the peace in Santa Rosa de Lima, La Unión. He died in a health center shortly afterward.[26]
- On June 4, 1990, about 1:00 P.M., gunmen killed José Armando Peña Argueta, an appellate judge in San Salvador. Peña had driven home and was waiting in his car for his garage door to open when a red vehicle approached and discharged several unknown armed men, who

shot him dead. Peña had previously served as president of the Bar Association of El Salvador.

He had been attacked before, by the security forces. On August 28, 1987, plainclothes soldiers kidnapped Peña, freeing him in exchange for a large sum of cash. Even though his captors vowed to kill him if he spoke publicly about the crime, Peña brought civil suit against National Police agent Julio César Amaya Flores and Treasury Police agent Ricardo Antonio Flores, in the Sixth Criminal Court in San Salvador. In the course of the proceedings, Peña complained that a lawyer and family members of one of the defendants came to his house to arrange a deal. The two accused men were ultimately convicted of extortion and sentenced to seven years in prison, which was affirmed on appeal.

In November 1989, Peña initiated eviction proceedings against the mother of a member of a military investigative commission. The woman threatened to avenge the eviction. In December 1989 the house where Peña was living was machine-gunned by unknown persons, prompting him to leave the country until January 1990.[27]

About 1:00 P.M. on July 23, 1990, two unknown men dressed in civilian clothing shot and killed José Heriberto Rubio, another justice of the peace in Santa Rosa de Lima, on a bus. After firing several shots, the two men ran from the bus and escaped. Rubio had assumed the post of justice of the peace fifteen days earlier. According to family members, Rubio had received threats from guerrillas five years earlier for failing to pay FMLN war taxes.[28]

U.S. POLICY: THE JUDICIAL SYSTEM DODGE

Successive U.S. administrations have laid much of the blame for the failure to end human rights violations in El Salvador on the weak and ineffective judicial system. Thus, in January 1982 officials in the Reagan administration said, "Along with the general disintegration of institutions in El Salvador after the October 1979 coup, the judicial system had nearly collapsed by January 1981." The State Department, report issued two years later, on January 16, 1984, lamented the "effective collapse of the administration of criminal justice in cases with political overtones." And at the end of the decade the Bush administration found that the "judicial process continued to be hindered by archaic procedures, inadequate facilities, intimidation of judges, and corruption."[29]

These criticisms of the judicial system are justified, if misplaced. The system barely functions at all, as evidenced by the failure, in more than ten years of war, to convict a single military officer of a human rights violation. Its shortcomings are, however, no excuse for the failure to end political murders, which continue mainly because the high command of the armed forces lacks the will to end them. Focusing on the judicial system—with its attendant problems of fear, corruption, and inefficiency—diverts attention from the true source of the problem: the intransigent opposition of the military to the rule of law. No matter how technically competent and materially equipped, civilian judges cannot compel a hostile army to submit to its dictates. The armed forces has the responsibility and the power to bring about change.

In August 1984 newly elected President Duarte pledged to make human rights a central focus of his administration and appointed a special commission to investigate five highly publicized political killings, including the 1980 murder of Archbishop Romero, the 1983 Las Hojas massacre, the 1981 murder of forty-one people in Armenia, the 1981 killing of two U.S. land reform advisers and their Salvadoran colleague, and the 1980 disappearance and killing of the U.S. freelance journalist John Sullivan. The commission, known as the Cestoni Commission after its chair, Dr. Benjamín Cestoni (later head of the governmental Human Rights Commission), conducted only one inquiry during the year it existed, and failed to make headway in any of those cases.[30]

In late 1984 the U.S. government initiated a grant program to assist the Salvadoran judicial system. The agreement, ratified by the Legislative Assembly in 1984 and amended in 1985, had four components: the Commission on Investigations, the Revisory Commission on Salvadoran Legislation (CORELESAL), the Judicial Protection Unit, and the Judicial Administration and Training Program. From 1984 through 1990 the U.S. Agency for International Development (AID) has provided $13.7 million to the Judicial Reform Program.[31]

With $5.5. million in funding from 1985 through 1988, the Commission on Investigations is the most important component of the program. The commission includes both a Special Investigative Unit (SIU) to conduct investigations and a Forensic Laboratory. The SIU has thirty-nine detectives, all members of the security forces, who continue to draw military salary and are subject to military discipline and dependent on the military for career advancement and retirement benefits.[32] This conflict of interest—military officers are required to investigate allegations that their colleagues are implicated in abuses—has prevented the SIU from fulfilling its role as an impartial investigative unit.

Another problem plaguing the SIU has been that the Salvadoran code of criminal procedure permits only expressly specified "auxiliary organs" of the judicial system to present evidence in judicial proceedings: the SIU has never been a designated auxiliary organ. Hence, an appellate court reversed the decision of the trial court to try one of two remaining defendants in the case of the September 1988 army massacre of ten peasants in San Francisco, largely on the grounds that the evidence against him had been produced by the SIU, which had no formal judicial status (see chaps. 3 and 6).

The SIU has failed to investigate certain cases of obvious human rights significance or has inexplicably delayed its investigations. It did not investigate the 1988 Puerta del Diablo killings, and it did not begin work on the San Francisco massacre until nearly four months after it took place.[33] Furthermore, even great activity on its part has not led to effective prosecutions of culpable parties. Thus, although the SIU played a major role in the investigation into the assassination of Archbishop Romero, that case is effectively dead (see chap. 6); and although it has, according to U.S. Embassy officials and court records, undertaken an investigation into the October 1989 bombing of the FENASTRAS headquarters, it has denied two requests by the presiding judge in the case to turn over the results of its inquiry.[34]

The Forensic Laboratory is located on the premises of the Armed Forces General Staff, inside a building owned by the Ministry of Defense. To enter, people must identify themselves at the same guard post used by all visitors, a substantial deterrent to witnesses to crimes in which the military is implicated.

The other components of the Judicial Reform Program have had no greater effect on human rights developments than the SIU. The Revisory Commission on Salvadoran Legislation has proposed numerous legal reforms, many of which have yet to be adopted, but it has not addressed two areas that merit substantial legal change: the absence of a military selective service law and the antiquated labor code, which denies the rights to organize and strike to all agricultural workers. Although CORELESAL did draft a reform of the draconian Decree 50, the government shelved the proposal and instead submitted Decree 618, virtually identical to Decree 50, for passage by the Legislative Assembly in March 1987. The Judicial Protection Unit, which was, according to one State Department official, "ill conceived from the beginning," has yet to find a function.[35] The Judicial Administration and Training Program has succeeded in remedying some of the most egregious material and technical deficiencies of the judicial system. Yet new filing cabinets and training in U.S. law have understandably failed to address the questions of political will and military resistance that have plagued the judicial system throughout the decade.

THE POLICE FORCES

Though technically separate from AID's Administration of Justice Program, programs to train and assist the Salvadoran police forces have also been justified in the name of democratization and institution building. According to U.S. government officials, equipping the police forces and giving them professional training would lower the incidence of torture and other abuses of authority, for police would have fewer incentives to violate investigative norms.[36] There is little evidence, however, that this is the case. In spite of five years of training in U.S. police methods, the Salvadoran security forces continue to torture prisoners, using beating, simulated drowning, rape, electric shock, stabbing, whipping, and near asphyxiation, as well as other cruel and degrading treatment, such as deprivation of sleep, food, and water, death threats, prolonged standing or exercise, and confinement in tiny or very cold rooms. Members of the security forces enjoy the same immunity from prosecution as their military counterparts do, a fact that no doubt accounts for the persistence of gross human rights abuses among their ranks.

Police-training programs in El Salvador have had a checkered past. Between 1957 and 1974, AID's Office of Public Safety spent over $2.1 million to train 448 members of the security forces and to provide them with weapons, vehicles, riot control gear, and communications equipment. A U.S. public safety adviser worked with the intelligence units of the National Police, National Guard, and Immigration Service, some of the same units later identified by the Reagan administration as the nerve centers of death squad activity.[37] A U.S. official also provided equipment to an intelligence unit headed by Col. (later Gen.) José Alberto ("Chele") Medrano, organizer of the rural paramilitary network called ORDEN, which the Inter-American Commission on Human Rights of the Organization of American States later blamed for "torture and physical and psychological mistreatment."[38]

Recipients of U.S. training under the Office of Public Safety were more distinguished by their brutality than by their respect for human rights. These included rightist leader Roberto D'Aubuisson, widely linked to the death squads and to the assassination of Archbishop Romero, and Col. Roberto Mauricio Staben, implicated in a kidnapping-for-profit ring in 1986 (see chap. 6).[39]

The U.S. Congress cut off police assistance in 1974, after persistent reports associated recipients of U.S. training worldwide to serious human rights abuses, including torture and murder. The prohibition, known as Section 660 of the Foreign Assistance Act, banned U.S. support for "police, prisons, or other law enforcement forces" abroad. Beginning in the early 1980s, however, the Reagan administration renewed police training under a variety of guises. This occurred both with and without congressional knowledge and support. Between 1982 and 1986, for example, the Defense Department trained almost 2,800 members of the Salvadoran security forces to serve in eight police infantry battalions; the administration argued that the units performed primarily military rather than police duties and therefore that the training did not fall under the police aid ban.[40]

Similarly, in 1984 the U.S. military began training and equipping a Salvadoran Special Antiterrorist Command (CEAT), drawn from members of the Treasury Police, the most notorious of the security forces for their brutality and death squad connections. The Defense Department maintained that because CEAT was under the command of an army officer, training did not violate prohibitions on police assistance.[41] The Congress was not informed of the training until well after it began. The CEAT was used in 1985 to break up a hospital strike in which five people died, including four plainclothes policemen accidentally shot by their colleagues.[42]

The Congress formally waived the ban on police aid to El Salvador in August 1985, following the guerrilla attack in which four off-duty U.S. Marines died. The new law permitted the administration to grant police aid under reprogramming procedures and required it to certify progress by the Salvadoran government in eliminating abuses of prisoners. Before the amendment expired in late 1987, the administration committed seventeen million dollars to El Salvador for training and equipment. The bulk of the funds—almost fourteen million dollars—went for equipment, including shotguns, pistols, riot control gear, patrol vehicles, and radios. U.S. military advisers provided the training, which conflicted with the professed goal of the United States—separating the police from the army, navy, and air force and placing law enforcement personnel under civilian control.[43]

The Reagan administration made no new requests for police aid in 1988, partly because slow procurement procedures meant that deliveries of equipment continued well beyond 1987 and partly because it wished to avoid an acrimonious conflict with the Congress over the status of human rights in El Salvador. In the summer and fall of 1989, however, both the House and the Senate overturned the recommendations of their respective foreign affairs committees and adopted floor amendments renewing police aid to El Salvador. Bowing to human rights concerns, the Congress stipulated that the aid could not include firearms.[44]

In addition to aid provided through the waiver on Section 660, there are several other channels for police assistance to El Salvador.

Anti-Terrorism Assistance (ATA). In response to concerns about incidents of international terrorism, the Congress partially relaxed the worldwide ban on police aid in late 1983.[45] Under the ATA program, the United States provided $1.47 million to El Salvador and trained 254 police between 1986 and 1989. The courses were aimed exclusively at combating leftist, not rightist, terrorism, and included such topics as "anti-terrorist patrol techniques," "hostage negotiations," and "vital installation security."[46] Although the U.S. Embassy screened the participants, several members of the Congress alleged in

1986 that three of them had death squad connections. The State Department denied the allegations, but the Phoenix (Arizona) Police Department and Northwestern University withdrew their participation from the ATA program.[47]

International Criminal Investigative Training Assistance Program (ICITAP). A part of AID's Administration of Justice Program, ICITAP assists judges, prosecutors, and police in developing investigative and administrative skills; the aim is that prosecutions be based on physical evidence rather than on forced confessions. ICITAP also supports scholarships to enable foreign police to study at the Federal Bureau of Investigation (FBI) or in regional police schools.[48] Top Salvadoran police officials have participated in ICITAP-sponsored regional planning conferences, even though the Salvadorans do not meet the congressional requirement that only police under "judicial or prosecutorial control" be involved in the program.[49] By late 1990 approximately 425 Salvadorans had received training in such areas as interviewing suspects, victims, and witnesses and protecting the scene of a crime. Col. Nelson Iván López y López, the former director of El Salvador's Special Investigative Unit, attended the FBI Academy under ICITAP auspices. López y López may have been part of an attempt by the Salvadoran Armed Forces to deflect attention from army involvement in the 1989 murder of six Jesuit priests.[50]

Narcotics Control Training. The State Department's Bureau of International Narcotics Matters (INM) provides funding for other U.S. agencies to carry out training in enforcing antidrug laws in foreign countries. In El Salvador a small program of the Drug Enforcement Agency (DEA), under the Justice Department, has trained sixty-five police officers since 1986. The trainees frequently train other police.[51] In 1988 the *Washington Post* reported that Héctor Antonio Regalado, the founder of a death squad, had been hired by the DEA in early 1987 to teach marksmanship. When the embassy, which bears responsibility for all U.S. government activities in El Salvador, discovered its mistake, it reportedly pressed unsuccessfully for Regalado's arrest.[52]

6

IMPUNITY

Even though government forces in El Salvador have been responsible for tens of thousands of political killings, cases of torture, and forced disappearances since the outbreak of civil conflict in 1979, no military officer has ever been convicted of a politically motivated human rights offense. None has yet been tried, although seven officers are under indictment at the time of this writing. In spite of ten years of U.S. coaching and aid—U.S. military training with a purported human rights content and extensive aid to the judiciary and police for criminal investigations—the Salvadoran military remains utterly beyond the reach of the law. The very forces charged with protecting citizens not only remain the most deadly threat to their security but continue to act with complete impunity. [1]

The impunity of the armed forces and the death squads flows from the weakness and corruption of the judiciary and the overwhelming strength of the military and paramilitary groups, whose abuses the courts are—in theory—supposed to prosecute. Judges are protected by no one, and several have suffered violent reprisals (see chap. 5). Militants of the ARENA party, which has been closely identified with the death squads, have dominated the Supreme Court throughout the decade; and at every opportunity the Supreme Court has acted to thwart prosecutions of political killers. Although the United States has poured millions of dollars into the court system, the system remains impervious to reform. Disbursements of this aid were reportedly suspended in August 1990 as a result of U.S. frustration with the courts' handling of human rights cases. [2]

The treatment of human rights cases by Salvadoran authorities bears a direct relation to the level and persistence of international—and particularly U.S.—attention. Salvadoran authorities generally promise to investigate cases that have prompted an immediate protest from abroad. If the pressure is sustained for many years and is accompanied by threatened or actual curtailment of military aid, as for the murders of U.S. churchwomen and labor advisers discussed below, a measure of justice may be wrung out of the system. Yet violations that escape world attention do not elicit even hollow promises, as when the army massacred six neighborhood soccer players and a bread vendor in a poor San Salvador suburb on November 18, 1989 (see chap. 3).[3] The judge, noting the absence of international attention, commented frankly in February 1990 that "the case will be under investigation until it is forgotten."[4]

Alternatively, if international interest is expressed at the outset but subsequently wanes, the impetus for prosecution or compensation quickly evaporates. When the air force fired rockets at a house in northern Chalatenango province, killing five and wounding sixteen of the civilians hiding there (see chap. 2), the *New York Times* brought the case to international attention. The air force at first blamed the guerrillas but finally admitted responsibility and promised to indemnify the victims' families. Yet six months later, in the presence of Americas Watch, the head of the air force, Gen. Rafael Antonio Villamariona, told the human rights office of the army that the air force had not compensated anyone and had no plans to do so.[5]

Probably the most sweeping promise to provide justice in human rights cases was made by President Duarte, shortly after his inauguration in June 1984. In August he announced the establishment of a special commission to investigate political killings, its foremost task being to solve the murder of Archbishop Romero, the murder of two U.S. labor advisers and a Salvadoran colleague at the Sheraton Hotel, the disappearance of a U.S. reporter, and the massacres at Armenia and Las Hojas, Sonsonate. Duarte's term of office has since come and gone, yet with the exception of the Sheraton murders, these cases remain unsolved. Although two members of the National Guard were convicted in the Sheraton case, the intellectual authors of the crime escaped punishment despite considerable evidence implicating them, and the guardsmen were released under an amnesty law enacted in 1987.

AMNESTIES

Although the ineffectiveness of the judicial system and the omnipotence of the military have traditionally shielded those in uniform from criminal punishment for human rights abuses, an amnesty approved by the Salvadoran legislature on October 27, 1987, went so far as to legally close the door on prosecutions—and even investigations—of abuses committed up to October 22. By reinforcing the sense of military impunity, the amnesty contributed to an increase in political killings by government forces and death squads in the months that followed.[6]

The "full and absolute" amnesty passed by the assembly covered broadly defined political and related common crimes. Common crimes carried out by at least twenty individuals were also covered by the amnesty, to guarantee that the military would remain untouched for combat-related abuses. Offenses such as kidnapping, extortion, and drug trafficking were specifically barred, as was the murder of Archbishop Romero, excluded by a last-minute amendment made at the request of the Catholic Church.

Although the amnesty purported to contribute to national reconciliation in keeping with the Central American peace plan of August 1987, the treatment of guerrilla and government crimes was grossly unequal. Guerrillas were allowed fifteen days to apply for the amnesty, but all others—including the armed forces and right-wing criminals—could invoke the amnesty as a defense at any time. In practical terms, however, the amnesty freed many more prisoners accused of ties with the guerrillas—462—than members of the armed forces, for few men in uniform have ever been jailed for politically related crimes.[7]

The amnesty brought about the release of the National Guardsmen jailed for the 1981 Sheraton murders; it was applied to benefit military men implicated in the 1983 massacre at Las Hojas, although no soldiers had formally been charged; and it protected from prosecution members of the Arce Battalion who murdered five peasants in May 1987. In the last case, proceedings in the court in Ciudad Barrios, San Miguel, were dropped, although no individual suspects in the battalion had been identified and the army had denied responsibility.[8]

A group of imprisoned soldiers and former soldiers presented a proposal for a new amnesty to the Pardon and Amnesty Committee of the Legislative Assembly on December 8, 1989. The proposal asked that present and former members of the military who were being tried for crimes, as well as those who had already been convicted, be granted amnesty. As a parallel measure, some popular organizations demanded that leftist prisoners jailed since 1987 also receive amnesty. If the proposal had been adopted, military men accused in important human rights cases could have been freed, once again legalizing the de facto impunity with which agents of the state violate human rights in El Salvador.

The themes of impunity and amnesty have become major points of debate in the ongoing negotiations between the government and the FMLN under the auspices of the United Nations. Human rights groups and the Catholic Church are pressing for any agreement that emerges from the talks to include provisions for accountability for past abuses. The FMLN has proposed a massive purge of officers implicated in human rights violations and the dissolution of the Treasury Police, the National Guard, and the Atlacatl Battalion because of their history of human rights violations. For its part, the government has proposed a general amnesty for government forces, guerrillas, and prisoners held on politically related offenses.[9] The vast gulf between the positions of the two sides is a measure of the tremendous polarization of a nation in its eleventh year of civil war, a nation that has yet to resolve any of the underlying causes of the conflict.

FAILED OR INCOMPLETE PROSECUTIONS

The overwhelming majority of atrocities committed by government forces in El Salvador have never been investigated, let alone brought to trial. In the rare cases in which investigations or prosecutions were launched, the victims have generally been either U.S. citizens or extremely prominent individuals. A few cases involve massacres. Pathetic as the outcomes are, they show the system at its best, not its worst. The failure of efforts to prosecute even these select cases has provided a clear message of reassurance to the killers within and outside the Salvadoran Armed Forces: no matter how prominent the victim or how audacious the crime, you can always get away with murder.

Archbishop Romero, March 24, 1980

The assassination of Archbishop Oscar Arnulfo Romero as he performed mass is perhaps the most dramatic example of the impunity with which the military and the death squads in El Salvador carry out their crimes. Although the murder deprived the Salvadoran people of a venerated leader and attracted unprecedented international attention and outrage and although the government promised repeatedly that the killers would be discovered and punished, no arrests were ever made and no investigation completed. Even more significantly, evidence of official involvement in the murder and cover-up has yet to be probed seriously. Ten years after the assassination, there is little prospect that the killers will ever be identified, prosecuted, or punished. This case merits a detailed treatment here because it so perfectly demonstrates denial of justice and the failure to establish the truth about a repugnant crime.

From the start it was clear that any serious efforts to investigate the crime would be blocked, nor would the police, prosecutors, and judges do much more than go through the motions of investigating. The judge who was originally assigned the case, Atilio Ramírez Amaya, was prevented from carrying out a probing investigation by death threats and an assassination attempt, which prompted him to flee the country shortly after the archbishop's murder. Others with information on the crime also suffered persecution. On July 5, 1980, security forces raided the office of Socorro Jurídico, the human rights office of the Archdiocese of San Salvador, and seized documents with evidence of military involvement in the crime. In April 1981 a witness, Napoleón Martínez, was abducted, never to reappear.[10] Within months of the killing, accumulated evidence based on documents and accounts by military insiders began to link military officers, right-wing civilians, and Maj. Roberto D'Aubuisson, army officer and head of the ARENA party, to the crime. Yet these leads were virtually ignored; and although President Duarte had promised that the special investigative commission formed in 1984 would assign top priority to the murder, little effort was expended until 1986–87, when the Christian Democratic administration faced a serious electoral threat from ARENA. The scope of this tardy effort was circumscribed by its political objectives: rather than concentrate on leads indicating broad military and security force involvement, the Christian Democrats appeared determined only to prove the case against the ARENA leader.[11] Even this limited attempt ground to a halt in December 1988, when the ARENA-dominated Supreme Court blocked extradition proceedings against a D'Aubuisson associate, Alvaro Saravia, an alleged participant in the crime residing in Miami. Since then, all efforts to prosecute the crime have ceased.[12]

For six weeks following the murder, the National Police carried out a half-hearted investigation, which established little beyond the fact that the fatal shot had been fired from the front door of the chapel and that a vehicle may have been used. For the next six years the case was opened and closed several times but was never pursued with enthusiasm. The U.S. Central Intelligence Agency carried out its own investigation of the matter but did not release the results, even to congressional intelligence committees.[13]

In testimony before the Senate Foreign Relations Committee in April 1981, Robert E. White, the U.S. ambassador to El Salvador at the time of the killing, disclosed the existence of a diary that had been seized from D'Aubuisson's bodyguard, Capt. Alvaro Saravia, when D'Aubuisson, Saravia, and other officers were caught plotting a coup at a farmhouse outside San Salvador in May 1980. White said the diary provided "compelling, if not 100 percent conclusive" evidence "that D'Aubuisson and his group" were responsible for Romero's death.[14] The diary, which covered January through July 1980, contained entries showing deliveries of arms and ammunition as well as payments to army officers and others linked to death squads. Also noted in the diary was an Operation Pineapple, which required a special night-vision scope, a .257-caliber weapon, four automatic pistols, grenades, one driver, four security men, and a sharpshooter. The code name is believed to refer to the archbishop's assassination, though D'Aubuisson has said it does not.[15]

Several years later, in hearings held in February 1984, White said that in November 1980 a U.S. diplomat had received information from a Salvadoran military officer who participated in the planning of the murder. The officer was present at a March 22, 1980, meeting convened by D'Aubuisson in a San Salvador safe house. White said the twelve or so men present drew lots for what they deemed the honor of assassinating the archbishop. The witness, disappointed that he did not win the lottery, provided the bullets used in the murder so that he might participate vicariously. Lt. Francisco Amaya Rosa won the lottery, and he chose Walter Antonio Alvarez, a sharpshooter, to pull the trigger.

Months after the crime, according to White's account, D'Aubuisson had Alvarez, by then a man who knew too much, murdered.[16]

Col. Roberto Santiváñez, director of the former Salvadoran National Security Agency (ANSESAL), offered interpretations of several of the D'Aubuisson diary entries in press interviews in March 1985, after he was fired as the Salvadoran consul in New Orleans for having secretly met with members of the U.S. Congress. Based on his reading of the diary and his contacts in the Salvadoran military, Santiváñez asserted that the Romero assassination was carried out by two Salvadoran National Guardsmen and two former Nicaraguan National Guardsmen under orders from D'Aubuisson. Santiváñez believed the murder had broad support from the National Guard; he said the guardsmen cheered when the killers returned to the barracks upon completing their mission.[17] (Nearly a decade later, a group of army officers expressed similar delight at the news that six Jesuit priests had been slain.)[18]

Santiváñez alleged that Ricardo Lau, formerly a colonel in the Nicaraguan National Guard and later chief of intelligence for the U.S.-backed Nicaraguan contras, trained the unit that carried out the assassination, and received a payment of $120,000 in connection with the assassination three days after it was done.[19] On the page for March 27, 1980, the diary includes a telephone number for a "Coronel Ricardo La o [sic]" and two references to payments for Nicaraguan assistance, one for forty thousand dollars and another for eighty thousand dollars. Santiváñez asserted that wealthy Salvadorans made these payments to Lau for arranging the Romero assassination. He said Lau "was working directly for D'Aubuisson" at the time.[20] Santiváñez's version of what transpired differs from the version offered subsequently by the self-professed getaway driver, who claimed to have driven a lone, unidentified assassin to and from the killing (see below).

Apparently in response to White's accusations of February 1984 and in anticipation of the March elections, D'Aubuisson went on national television to present a videotaped confession by a self-proclaimed FMLN defector who called himself Pedro Lobo (Peter Wolf). Lobo claimed that he was involved in planning the assassination of Archbishop Romero, which was carried out by leftist guerrillas. The videotaped confession was later shown to be false.[21]

In the middle of 1985 an ex-convict named Adalberto Salazar Collier turned himself in to the National Guard for protection from unidentified men who had sought him out at his place of work. Salazar Collier said that while he was incarcerated in a Honduran penitentiary, Salvadoran and Honduran officials had bribed him to act the part of Pedro Lobo. Although he implicated several Salvadoran military officers in what amounted to a cover-up of the crime, there was apparently no attempt to bring charges against those involved. Prosecutors were able to ascertain that Salazar Collier was in prison in El Salvador at the time of the Romero assassination; he was therefore unlikely to have participated.[22]

In November 1987, in the heat of campaigning for the March 1988 general elections and on the eve of the return from exile of FDR leader Guillermo Manuel Ungo, President Duarte held a press conference to announce that his government had solved the Romero case. The announcement was based on the testimony of Antonio Amado Garay, who claimed that he drove a single assassin to and from the scene of the archbishop's murder on orders from Saravia. Garay also said that he overheard Saravia report to D'Aubuisson that the murder had been carried out, to which D'Aubuisson responded that Saravia had acted too soon; Saravia then insisted that he had done what D'Aubuisson had ordered.[23]

With this witness in hand, the Salvadoran authorities charged Saravia with participation in the murder plot, the first and only indictment since the murder. (Charges were not filed against D'Aubuisson; to do so would require that the ARENA-controlled Legislative Assembly lift the immunity granted to legislators.) The Foreign Ministry issued a request for Saravia's extradition from the United States, where he was living illegally, which a U.S. magistrate granted.[24]

Yet in December 1988, while the magistrate's opinion was on appeal, the Salvadoran Supreme Court ruled the extradition request invalid. Its legal arguments were notably unconvincing: the court argued that Garay's testimony contradicted that of another witness concerning the position in which the assassin stood when he fired the fatal shot.[25] However, a significantly lower burden of evidence is required for an extradition request and detention order than for a conviction; the minor discrepancy in the testimony ought not to have ruled out Saravia's arrest and extradition. The court also ruled that Garay's testimony, coming more than seven years after the crime was committed, was too old to be admissible.[26] By this standard, the case must effectively be closed, for evidence of a crime committed in 1980 is highly unlikely to be much less than eleven years old. Finally, the court held that the Foreign Ministry lacked the authority to issue extradition requests, a ruling one journalist described as "a delightfully brazen double-cross": the president of the Supreme Court, Francisco José ("Chachi") Guerrero, is said to have privately advised the Salvadoran attorney general and the U.S. ambassador to make the request through the Foreign Ministry, a procedure which the court then ruled invalid.[27]

Frustrated in its attempt to extradite Saravia, the Duarte government preempted television programming on all stations on February 5 and 7, 1989, to broadcast two videotapes laying out its case against D'Aubuisson and Saravia.[28] The government also released the name of the purported assassin, another D'Aubuisson associate, Dr. Héctor Antonio Regalado. (A dentist nicknamed Dr. Death, Regalado reportedly organized a death squad disguised as a Boy Scout troop in the late 1970s, only to execute its members in December

1980 out of fear they might talk.)[29] According to the government videotapes, Garay identified Regalado as the murderer in the Romero case based on police sketches of three men. Nonetheless, the identity of the gunman has been a subject of some dispute. As noted above, the Salvadoran source providing information to the U.S. Embassy during Ambassador White's tenure claimed that an individual named Walter Antonio Alvarez, who was handpicked by Lieutenant Amaya Rosa, fired the shot. Meanwhile, a former death squad agent providing information to the *Washington Post* in 1988 said that a National Police detective, Edgar Sigfredo Pérez Linares, shot Romero. "Jorge," the *Post*'s informant, claimed that on three occasions he heard Pérez Linares and other members of a death squad organized by D'Aubuisson brag about murdering Romero. "You should have seen how much blood came out of him—that's because I got him right in the heart," said Pérez Linares. Two Salvadoran officials cited by the *Post* called Jorge's account credible, asserting that a police drawing of the gunman based on Garay's description closely resembled Pérez Linares and no other suspect. Pérez Linares, also a suspect in the kidnapping-for-profit ring uncovered in April 1986, was killed under mysterious circumstances in May 1986.[30]

A Salvadoran army captain, Eduardo Ernesto Alfonso Avila, was also supposedly involved in the murder. The *Albuquerque Journal,* which conducted an in-depth investigation of death squad activity in El Salvador in 1983, presented the bizarre tale of Avila's alleged confession to an American acquaintance. According to a May 1982 cable from the U.S. Embassy in Panama to the U.S. Embassy in San Salvador, Avila told a U.S. acquaintance of participating in the January 1981 murder of two U.S. labor advisers and their Salvadoran colleague and planning to kill Archbishop Romero. Distraught by a belated sense of remorse, he took an overdose of Valium and went to the acquaintance for aid. The cable quotes Avila as admitting that "he personally planned and had two others assist him in the killing of Archbishop Romero. He indicated that he had used a dark car on this occasion and that he had spent three months planning the execution." According to the *Albuquerque Journal,* U.S. sources had previously been told that Avila had confessed to his involvement in Romero's murder to another person.[31]

The autopsy performed shortly after the archbishop's assassination failed to determine the precise caliber of the weapon used; the extensive fragmentation of the bullet suggested that an explosive projectile had been used, but the small size of the fragments prevented their precise identification.[32] One intriguing piece of evidence about the weapon was apparently ignored. In September 1987, Attorney General Roberto Girón Flores made public the 1986 declaration of Gloria Kahan Guzmán, a friend of Col. Roberto Mauricio Staben's; Staben is a powerful tandona member repeatedly linked to atrocities. Kahan said that she was friends with Staben when he was second in command at the cavalry barracks in La Libertad. One evening, while she was visiting Staben and an army lieutenant, Rodolfo Isidro López Sibrián, Staben showed her a telescopic rifle that he claimed was used to kill Archbishop Romero. Kahan had originally made her statement to the military judge investigating a military kidnapping ring in which Staben was implicated, yet that judge did nothing about the allegation, saying that it was beyond his jurisdiction. U.S. Embassy cable traffic shows that polygraph examinations supported the truth of Kahan's statements, yet Colonel Staben was never questioned in connection with the archbishop's death.[33]

The Romero case is a stark measure of the denial of both truth and justice to the victims of politically motivated human rights violations in El Salvador. The fact that ten years after the murder of such a prominent and revered leader there is little possibility that anyone connected with the killing will be punished speaks volumes about what the countless anonymous victims of military and paramilitary terror in El Salvador can expect from the courts. Equally sad, the more modest goal of establishing with certainty the truth about responsibility for this crime seems nearly as remote.

U.S. Churchwomen, December 2, 1980

The murder of four U.S. churchwomen has been one of a handful of politically motivated crimes by government forces for which at least some of the perpetrators have been criminally punished. Indeed, the court convicted members of the regular Salvadoran security forces of a politically motivated murder for the first time when it ruled on this case.[34] Five National Guardsmen remain in prison today, serving thirty years each. Nonetheless, serious questions as to whether the killers acted on higher orders remain uninvestigated, and there has been no effort to prosecute the officers who participated in an elaborate cover-up of the crime.

National Guard troops and their commander, Subsgt. Luis Antonio Colindres Alemán, picked up, raped, and killed the Maryknoll sisters Ita Ford and Maura Clarke, the Ursuline nun Dorothy Kazel, and the lay church worker Jean Donovan on December 2, 1980. Donovan and Kazel had been to the airport earlier that afternoon to pick up two colleagues, at which time they had attracted the attention of a National Guardsman. He later stated that he found them "suspicious" because of the size of their handbags. When the women left the airport and when they returned later that day to pick up Sisters Ford and Clarke, the guardsman, Margarito Pérez Nieto, telephoned his detachment commander, Subsgt. Colindres Alemán, to report his suspicions. Upon returning to National Guard headquarters about 7:00 P.M., Pérez Nieto reported on the women for the third time. Colindres Alemán then ordered five guardsmen to change into civilian clothes and, armed with G-3 rifles, to accompany him on an unspecified mission.[35]

Having instructed Pérez Nieto to stop all traffic leaving the airport at a checkpoint for ten minutes, except the nuns' vehicle, Colindres Alemán and his subordinates themselves stopped the sisters' white Toyota van on the airport access road, interrogated the women, and searched the van. Some guardsmen then drove the nuns in their van while the others followed in a National Guard jeep, which broke down and was abandoned near the town of Rosario de la Paz. One guardsman stayed behind with the jeep. The five others crowded into the van, which they drove to an isolated spot fifteen miles from the airport. There they ordered the women out of the van, raped them, and, on Colindres Alemán's orders, shot each in the head. They later burned the women's van and some of their belongings, apparently to avoid detection. Early the next morning, villagers from nearby Santiago Nonualco found the women's bodies sprawled along the roadside.[36]

Efforts by the guardsmen's superiors to cover up the crime began immediately. Senior National Guard officers knew the identity of the killers within days of the crime and took immediate steps to protect them. The murderers were transferred from the airport post and their rifles switched to frustrate the outcome of ballistics tests performed by the FBI. Official Salvadoran investigations begun in the aftermath of the crimes absolved the security forces of all involvement, even though the investigators knew this to be false. According to an analysis prepared for the State Department by a U.S. judge, Harold R. Tyler, Jr., the Salvadoran cover-up may have extended as high as Col. Carlos Eugenio Vides Casanova, then commander of the National Guard and subsequently minister of defense (now retired). It was only after the FBI and an officer at the U.S. Embassy developed their own evidence implicating the guardsmen that Colonel Vides Casanova ordered the arrest of the five guardsmen on April 29, 1981.[37] Even though covering up a crime is itself a crime under Salvadoran law, no effort was made to prosecute Colindres Aléman or anyone higher up who might be responsible.

On May 25, 1984, a jury found the five National Guardsmen guilty of the murder of the churchwomen. Several weeks later, Judge Bernardo Rauda Murcia sentenced them to thirty years' imprisonment, the maximum sentence authorized under Salvadoran law.[38] Lawyers for the defendants failed to secure their release under the October 1987 amnesty for political criminals and those involved in similar common crimes, for the judge decided that the murders were common crimes not connected to the civil war.[39]

One outstanding question is whether Colindres Alemán detained and murdered the churchwomen at his own initiative or under higher orders; he apparently told two participants in the crime that he acted under orders, and several others, including the former Salvadoran intelligence chief Roberto Santiváñez, have insisted that he did so.[40] The most exhaustive study of the issue, Judge Tyler's report of December 1983, tended to discount the possibility that higher officers had ordered the killings. Nonetheless, the report qualified this finding, noting that Salvadoran authorities had "done little" to address the issue.[41]

Further evidence supporting the theory of higher involvement emerged one and a half years after the publication of the Tyler report, when the defense attorney for one of the killers said that he had been forced to take part in a conspiracy to protect higher officers in the case. The lawyer, Salvador Antonio Ibarra, was appointed counsel for the guardsman Carlos Joaquín Contreras Palacios in December 1982. He was quickly joined in the defense by two attorneys with close ties to the National Guard and the military leadership. At a meeting shortly after the appointments were announced, the two attorneys reportedly ordered Ibarra to "keep [his] hands off" the case and insisted that he not contradict a statement that the possibility of a cover-up had been thoroughly investigated and rejected. Ibarra told the *New York Times* that he never met with his client, partly as a result of this pressure. Yet he refused to join with the two attorneys in public statements absolving military officers of a cover-up. A few months later, he was visited by a woman who identified herself as his client's common-law wife. She said that all five guardsmen had told her that they were merely carrying out orders "from San Salvador."[42] Ibarra refused to join an appeal that the charges against the guardsmen be dismissed.

On October 30, 1983, after it became clear that Ibarra would not cooperate, he was detained and tortured by men he believed to be members of the National Guard. He was released after the U.S. Embassy and the ICRC interceded, and was granted asylum in the United States.[43]

U.S. Labor Advisers and Colleague, January 3, 1981

The murder of two U.S. labor advisers and their Salvadoran colleague as they sipped coffee in the San Salvador Sheraton Hotel is, like the churchwomen's case, one in which very strong pressure from Washington brought about a highly unusual measure of justice: the conviction in February 1986 of the two National Guardsmen who fired the shots. Although Cpls. Santiago Gómez Gónzalez and José Dimas Valle Acevedo were each sentenced to the maximum term of thirty years, in December 1987 they were granted amnesty when a judge ruled that the murders fell under the definition of a politically motivated crime. An appeal by the attorney general, backed by the U.S. Embassy, failed, and the men were released. Meanwhile, the officers and wealthy civilians who ordered the killings have escaped justice entirely, despite strong pressure from the United States that they also be prosecuted.

José Rodolfo Viera, the head of El Salvador's land reform agency, is believed to have been targeted because he and his colleague Leonel Gómez had publicized evidence of corruption at the agency under its previous management by an army colonel. Viera's companions on the night of January 3, Mark David Pearlman and Michael Hammer of the AFL-CIO's American Institute for Free Labor Development, were most likely killed because they were dining with Viera.[44]

The convicted killers served as bodyguards to Lt. Rodolfo Isidro López Sibrián and to Capt. Eduardo Ernesto Alfonso Avila, implicated in the Romero case, both of whom were dining that night at the Sheraton with the wealthy Salvadoran businessmen Ricardo Sol Meza and Hans Christ, co-owners of the hotel, and Maj. Mario Denis Morán. According to the defendants' pretrial testimony, López Sibrián and Avila ordered them to kill the victims and gave them the weapons, and Christ led them to the dining-room door and pointed out the victims' table.[45]

A main roadblock in convicting those who ordered this and other crimes has been the inadmissibility under Salvadoran law of codefendant testimony, in this case the murderers' statements that they acted under higher orders. In addition, López Sibrián was allowed to dye his red hair black, shave his mustache, and put on glasses and makeup before appearing in a police lineup for identification by the defendants. They were naturally unable to identify him as one of the officers who told them to kill the labor advisers. Avila's uncle was a member of the Supreme Court that allowed this farce.[46]

Yet these obstacles could have been overcome, had there been the will to prosecute López Sibrián and Avila, both close associates of ARENA leader D'Aubuisson. In June 1985 two new witnesses provided direct evidence of their guilt. Patsy Walker, wife of the former U.S. military attaché to El Salvador, testified in court that Avila had told her of his involvement in the killings and had threatened to kill her children if she passed on the information. She added that he had also told her that a man named Fosforito, or Little Match, was aware of everything that happened at the Sheraton. López Sibrián is known as Fosforito because of his red hair.[47] A Costa Rican citizen named Carlos Francisco Aguilar also testified that Avila had confessed his role in the Sheraton and other killings and had stated that López Sibrián was part of what he called "operations." The new evidence was introduced too late to convict López Sibrián, who had already been granted a "definite stay of proceedings" by the Supreme Court, and the trial court deemed it insufficient to warrant Avila's arrest.[48]

Although Ricardo Sol Meza was briefly arrested and the extradition of Hans Christ was requested—he had moved to Miami—the Salvadoran courts quickly absolved both of involvement in the crime.[49] Maj. Denis Morán's role was never probed. (Morán was reportedly one of the officers whose removal then Vice President George Bush urged in his December 1983 visit to El Salvador. He has been promoted to colonel and is currently the Salvadoran military attaché in Guatemala.)

Las Hojas Cooperative, February 22, 1983

The massacre of more than seventy peasants of the Las Hojas cooperative in western Sonsonate province (see chap. 3) received wide press attention abroad and a prompt promise by the defense minister, Gen. José Guillermo García, for a full investigation and justice. García's pledge was one of the first in a series of similar promises from Salvadoran authorities, President Duarte included, that would not be carried out in this case.

Four years later, Attorney General Roberto Girón Flores took the unprecedented step of obtaining from the court an arrest warrant for Col. Elmer González Araujo, the commander of the Sonsonate garrison at the time of the massacre. Prior to this arrest order, no disciplinary action had been taken against any of the soldiers who took part.[50] (Years later, in November 1989, Col. Oscar Alberto León Linares, one of the officers implicated in the massacre, commanded the powerful Atlacatl Battalion, which murdered six Jesuit priests, their housekeeper, and her daughter.)[51] Indeed, while the perpetrators of the Las Hojas massacre enjoyed complete liberty, Salvadoran authorities arrested Fermín García Guardado, the father of one of victims, after he complained about the case to Salvadoran and U.S. authorities.

Due to the powerful opposition of González Araujo's military colleagues, the 1987 arrest order was never carried out. However, the order seriously strained the governing alliance between civilian and military authorities and was to some degree responsible, it was said, for the eventual removal of Col. Carlos Reynaldo López Nuila, vice minister of defense for public security, who was believed by the armed forces to support the order. Indeed, the 1987 amnesty law was crafted in part to let the military off the hook in the Las Hojas case and several other pending cases in which soldiers on patrol were involved in massacres.

After two lower courts ruled that the amnesty did apply to the Las Hojas massacre because it named fewer than twenty defendants, the attorney general appealed to the Supreme Court. The Supreme Court ruled, however, that more than twenty soldiers took part in the operation, even if not all were charged.[52] The commanders who ordered the massacre and the troops who carried it out will thus never be held accountable for their crime.

Kidnapping for Profit, 1982–1985

Senior U.S. diplomatic officials touted the case of the kidnapping-for-profit ring as a test case for the Salvadoran justice system. Because the victims were members of the conservative Salvadoran elite, it was widely believed that justice would prevail. Instead, the case has illustrated the worst Salvador has to offer—with suspects and judges offered bribes, intimidated, and killed while judicial proceedings have gone nowhere.[53]

An investigation by the SIU, aided by the Venezuelan police, uncovered a multimillion-dollar right-wing kidnapping ring whose operatives, often posing as leftist guerrillas, seized and held for ransom at least five wealthy Salvadoran businessmen between 1982 and 1985. The accused were apparently motivated by profit, not politics, although many of them have been linked to politically motivated death squad activities over the years.[54]

Three suspects were arrested in April 1986: Rodolfo Isidro López Sibrián, the former National Guard intelligence officer who eluded justice for his role in the Sheraton murders; his father-in-law, Orlando Llovera Ballete, a member of ARENA and a D'Aubuisson crony; and Maj. José Alfredo Jiménez. The most important military officer implicated was Col. Staben, head of the U.S.-trained Arce Rapid Reaction Battalion and, until May 1990, commander of the Seventh Military Detachment in Ahuachapán.[55] According to a statement by López Sibrián, reportedly seconded by two other witnesses, Staben was the "intellectual chief" of the ring, responsible with other officers for pinpointing the victims and dividing up the ransom. Yet Staben went free without even appearing for questioning, thanks to the personal intervention of President Duarte, who reinstated him to his command on May 7, 1986.[56]

Shortly before his scheduled arrest, another officer, Lt. Col. Joaquín Zacapa Astasio, was reportedly granted a fifteen-day vacation and advised to leave the country, which he did. Two other suspects, Cornejo Arango and Carlos Zacapa, also fled the country. Not long after the case was broken, three former National Police detectives implicated in the ring—Ramón Erasmo Oporto, Moisés López Arriola, and Edgar Sigfredo Pérez Linares (also implicated in the Romero case)—died under suspicious circumstances, two of them reportedly in police custody.

In early April 1987, Judge Miriam Artiaga Alvarez, presiding over a separate but related case (the dismantling and theft of a warehouse) against López Sibrián, Llovera, and Jiménez, reduced the charges against them after her house was machine-gunned twice. She subsequently resigned. On May 11, 1988, unidentified armed men shot and killed the military judge presiding over the main case against the defendants, Judge Jorge Alberto Serrano Panameño, who had recently told the press he would not grant amnesty for the kidnapping charges. He was killed days before he was to rule on an amnesty petition filed by the defense. Serrano told Americas Watch and others months before his death that he had turned down bribes from individuals connected to the kidnappers.

In late 1988 the judge who replaced Serrano amnestied the defendants in connection with the charge of illegal possession of firearms—the charge that had brought the case under the jurisdiction of the military court—and referred the case to Juan Héctor Larios Larios, the third criminal judge of San Salvador. On March 31, 1989, Judge Larios dismissed all charges against the eight defendants in the kidnapping case and ordered that the three defendants in custody—López Sibrián, Llovera, and Jiménez—be released immediately. Twenty minutes after this dramatic step, Judge Larios stepped down from the criminal court as part of a scheduled rotation.[57]

The decision created a major scandal and threatened to seriously damage the reputation of President-elect Alfredo Cristiani, with whose ARENA party many of the defendants (as well as many of the victims) were affiliated. Within days a new judge had reexamined the evidence and reversed the earlier ruling. The reversal did not, however, prevent the escape of Llovera, the only defendant actually freed after Judge Larios's ruling. On April 23, 1990, charges were dropped against two military men and three civilians who had never been captured and against Major Jiménez, who had been detained since 1986. The court also ruled that the cases against López Sibrián and Llovera (still at large) proceed to trial on the kidnapping charges but that the charges of robbery against them be dismissed. On April 26, 1990, President Cristiani instructed the attorney general to appeal the dismissal of the robbery charges, and attorneys for the two remaining defendants appealed the upholding of the kidnapping charges.[58]

San Francisco Peasants, September 21, 1988

The Bush administration has made prosecution of this massacre of ten peasants by the army (see chap. 3) a major priority in its dealings with El Salvador. Vice President Dan Quayle warned that U.S. aid would be affected if the killers were not brought to justice, and U.S. Ambassador William Walker held a "photo opportunity" with the judge to show U.S. interest. The *Miami Herald* reported on August 16, 1990, that setbacks in the prosecution of this and the kidnapping-for-profit case had prompted the Bush administration to suspend two million dollars in U.S. aid to the judiciary. State Department and embassy officials consulted by Americas Watch would not confirm or deny the cut in aid but reiterated their frustration with the handling of the two cases.

Immediately following the massacre, the soldiers of the Jiboa Battalion, commanded by the head of military intelligence of the Fifth Brigade, Maj. Mauricio Beltrán Granados, engaged in an elaborate cover-up to make the murders look like combat deaths. They smeared blood on the uniform of one of the soldiers, as though he had been wounded, and planted guerrilla arms and propaganda at the scene of the massacre. When questioned by army, police, and court investigators, the men of the battalion all provided rehearsed, false testimony. After an autopsy showed that the firefight story was untrue, the head of the Fifth Brigade, Col. José Emilio Chávez Cáceres, put forward another claim, that the FMLN had returned at night and shot the corpses to make it look as if they had been executed by the army.

On February 3, 1989, Vice President Quayle visited El Salvador and made an unusually tough pitch for the punishment of those who committed the massacre. His suggestion that military aid might be threatened by the failure to curb or prosecute military atrocities, reminiscent of the remarks made by then Vice President George Bush when he visited El Salvador in December 1983, was one rarely aired by either the Reagan or the Bush administration. It prompted a serious and rapid investigation by the Armed Forces General Staff: on February 20 the military authorities gave the green light for the prosecutions, directing the SIU to question soldiers from the Jiboa Battalion.

On March 12, 1989, five months after the massacre and five weeks after Quayle's visit, the general staff publicly announced it had discovered that a massacre had been deceitfully covered up by the head of military intelligence of the Fifth Brigade, and was consigning the case to the courts. It cleared Colonel Chávez Cáceres, a member of the tandona, of any wrongdoing but accused two officers, including Major Beltrán (who was not a member of a Military School class), three noncommissioned officers, and four soldiers. All the accused were detained by the security forces, although they continued to receive their salaries. On March 15, 1989, Judge Edis Alcides Guandique Carballo of San Sebastián formally ordered the judicial detention of the nine defendants. An additional three soldiers were subsequently detained in connection with the massacre.

On February 7, 1990, Judge Guandique dismissed charges against all but two defendants, to Major Beltrán and Subsgt. Rafael González Villalobos.[59] Defense lawyers appealed their indictment, and the attorney general appealed the dismissal of the case against the other soldiers, whom Judge Guandique had found either to have not been at the murder site at the time of the massacre or to have not participated in the killing.

On May 2, 1990, the appeals court in San Vicente affirmed Judge Guandique's ruling that the case against Major Beltrán should proceed to trial, as well as the dismissal of charges against the remaining defendants, but reversed the decision to try Subsergeant González Villalobos. The court reasoned that the principal evidence against the subsergeant—his confession and the testimony of another soldier, both taken by the SIU—was not admissible because the SIU was not an officially established auxiliary organ of the judiciary. Only the case against Major Beltrán is set to proceed to jury selection and trial.

Members of the Press, March 1989

Mauricio Pineda Deleón. A soldier shot and killed Mauricio Pineda, a television soundman for Salvadoran Channel 12, as he rode in the back of a clearly marked press vehicle in San Miguel on the day of the 1989 presidential elections. Although the soldiers manning a checkpoint tried to justify the shooting by asserting that someone in the car had fired in their direction, a videotape taken by two of the journalists after the shooting shows that the television crew was unarmed and that the car was clearly identified as a press vehicle. In addition, although military spokespersons later contended that the soldier intended only to stop the car, the journalists said that they were not signaled to halt.[60]

Cpl. José Antonio Orellana Guevara, twenty-four, of the Arce Battalion was arrested shortly after the shooting. After an eight-hour trial on June 6, 1990, a jury in the Second Criminal Court in San Miguel rendered a verdict of not guilty.[61] During the trial about thirty soldiers of the Arce Battalion in mufti, including two officers, entered the courtroom and watched the proceedings. Marcos Antonio Guevara, who covered the trial for Channel 12, described the impact of the soldiers' presence: "They were telling the jury in so many words that if they delivered a guilty verdict, they would have to contend with the Arce Battalion. The jury members live there. They leave the court alone and have their skins to think about."[62] The decision may be appealed.

Roberto Navas Alvarez and Luis Galdámez. On March 18, 1989, the night before the presidential elections, air force soldiers on the Boulevard del Ejército, which runs between San Salvador and Ilopango, killed Roberto Navas and wounded Luis Galdámez as the two were on a motorbike heading for San Bartolo, where Galdámez lives. Navas, who was driving, was killed instantly by two bullets. Galdámez was badly injured by one bullet, which shattered his left arm and entered his lung. Both men were photographers for Reuters.[63]

The air force maintains that the soldiers fired only after the journalists openly defied clear signals to stop at three successive checkpoints and only in order to stop a speeding vehicle. (Ironically, the guerrillas had declared a national traffic stoppage during the elections.) Yet physical evidence and Galdámez's testimony disprove those contentions. The placement of Navas's body and the position of the motorcycle suggest that the bike was either stopped or almost stopped when the shots were fired. Neither Galdámez, Navas, nor the bike exhibited scratches or dirt, casting further doubt on the notion that the bike was moving rapidly at the time. Air force soldiers on the scene did not quickly secure medical attention for Galdámez, despite his grave condition. Officials at the hospital told Reuters that Galdámez was not brought there until 11:30 or 11:45 that evening, at least two and a half hours after the shooting. The hospital would have been a fifteen-minute ride away.

Three air force soldiers, Benjamín Caballero Pleitez, Nicolás Rodríquez Huezo, and Lt. Nelson Saúl Solano Reyes were charged on May 9, 1989, and have since been confined to a military base. For several months, however, the investigation has been stalled. When interviewed by Americas Watch in late July 1990, José Angel Vanegas Guzmán, the judge of first instance for Soyapango, described the case as "in the investigative stage," although he admitted that he had not read the case and thus had not been doing much investigating. In mid-September 1990, Galdámez had not yet been questioned or given an opportunity to testify regarding what happened on the night of March 18.

The Jesuits, Their Housekeeper, and Her Daughter, November 16, 1989

On November 11, 1989, the FMLN launched an urban offensive that, by many accounts, led the Salvadoran Armed Forces high command to doubt its ability to maintain military control of San Salvador. On November 13, members of an elite Special Commando Unit of the U.S.-trained Atlacatl Battalion searched the Jesuit residence at the Central American University in San Salvador. At approximately 2:30 A.M. on November 16, members of that same unit summarily executed six priests, their housekeeper, and her daughter. Nine members of the armed forces (including Col. Alfredo Benavides Moreno, then head of the Salvadoran Military School) have been charged with participation in the murders, and another member with destruction of evidence. Three more have been charged with perjury.[64] The judge added new charges of terrorism and conspiracy to commit terrorism against the defendants in November 1990. Yet the process by which the accused were identified remains unclear, and significant questions remain as to higher-up responsibility for ordering the attack.[65]

Such evidence as exists in the case has been produced by the SIU, which has conducted at best a superficial investigation. A conflict of interest—in that SIU agents are all security force members—has prevented a complete accounting of armed forces involvement. Particularly troubling have been the difficulties Judge Ricardo Zamora of the Fourth Criminal Court has confronted in exploring the likely possibility that senior officers ordered Colonel Benavides Morales to carry out the murders. Among the obstacles Judge Zamora has had to overcome are the destruction and fabrication of evidence, false testimony by Salvadoran military officers, and the reticence on the part of the United States to provide relevant information (see chap. 8).

Furthermore, the provision of Salvadoran law that prohibits one codefendant from testifying against another presents a serious obstacle to the prosecution. Plea bargaining and immunity from prosecution in exchange for testimony may be common in the United States, but no such practices are customary in El Salvador. A precedent for allowing codefendant testimony has nonetheless been commonly overlooked: in the 1986 kidnapping-for-profit case (see above), the Salvadoran legislature approved a law that allows codefendant testimony in cases involving drug trafficking, kidnappings, or extortion. It could be broadened to include cases of murder. Whether such a law could be applied retroactively to an investigation in process without violating the principal of nonretroactivity in penal law has been widely debated, but it is the opinion of respected attorneys that such legislation would be of a procedural and not a penal nature and thus applicable to cases in progress.

Concerned lest the U.S.-supported armed forces continue to enjoy immunity from prosecution for the massacre, the Speaker of the U.S. House of Representatives constituted a Special Task Force on El Salvador to report on the progress of the case. On April 30, 1990, the Moakley report—named for the chair of the task force, Rep. John Joseph Moakley—concluded that none of the soldiers currently detained would likely have been arrested or charged if not for the testimony of a U.S. major, who said that knowledge of Benavides Morales's participation in the crime had been communicated to and then concealed by the head of the SIU, Lt. Col. Manuel Antonio Rivas. (Although the Moakley report did not name the major, he has since been identified in the press and elsewhere as Maj. Eric Buckland.) The report charged that the investigation of the case and preparations to prosecute those detained and charged had been completely stalled to date.[66]

Four months after the publication of the report, Moakley issued a dramatic press statement accusing the Salvadoran high command of engaging in "a conspiracy to obstruct justice in the Jesuits' case." He cited the following elements of a cover-up:

- · Logbooks from the Military School showing, among other things, the comings and goings of vehicles on the night of the murders were burned, apparently on the orders of a senior military officer.
- · When Judge Zamora requested the presence in court of the four cadets on duty at the Military School on the night of the murders, the

wrong four cadets were produced; when the right ones showed up, they claimed to have seen nothing.

· The Military Honor Commission that allegedly chose the nine defendants from among members of the armed forces falsely denied that it had written "even the skimpy report it did prepare in the case," nor has it otherwise indicated how it chose the defendants.

· Capt. Carlos Fernando Herrera Carranza, who worked for the National Intelligence Directorate (DNI), lied to investigators by asserting that he had reported the murders at a meeting of fellow intelligence officers on November 16 after he heard of the killings on the radio. Yet his announcement came before any stations had begun broadcasting the news.

· Col. Carlos Armando Avilés, who reportedly was instrumental in breaking the case by telling Major Buckland of the military responsibility, testified in court that he had not told him any such thing and barely knew him regardless. In fact, the two worked "side by side" for months, according to the Moakley statement, and Colonel Avilés specifically requested Major Buckland's assignment to El Salvador.

· The armed forces provided the judge with an apparently fabricated logbook from the Military School.

· An assistant to the employee of the Military School in charge of checking weapons in and out on the night of the murders has twice ignored a subpoena to testify before Judge Zamora.[67]

Later Moakley revealed that Major Buckland had told the FBI that he and Salvadoran Defense Minister René Ponce had advance knowledge of an army plot against the Jesuits. The U.S. Embassy and the State Department withheld this bit of information from Salvadoran investigators, including Judge Zamora, for ten months, until Moakley made it public (see chap. 8).[68] President Cristiani himself withheld the seven-page report of the Honor Commission from the court until someone informed the judge of its existence. Moreover, it was not until July 12, 1990, that Cristiani also publicly revealed that he had personally authorized the November 13 search of the Jesuit residence, now thought to be a reconnaissance mission in preparation for the murders. (It was later learned that Cristiani endorsed the mission after it had already taken place.)

The defense slowed the process by submitting a series of petitions for a change of venue to the court in Santa Tecla; the appeals court refused to hear the third such petition, submitted on July 20, 1990. In early December, Judge Zamora formally ordered the case to go to trial.[69] A trial date has not yet been set, and the defense has attempted to drag out proceedings further by filing appeals and habeas corpus petitions. In his August 15, 1990, press release Rep.

Moakley said he did not believe that military officers would have withheld, destroyed, and falsified evidence or repeatedly committed perjury "without at least the tacit consent of the High Command. Even more important, I believe that the High Command's goal, from the beginning, has been to control the investigation and to limit the number and rank of the officers who will be held responsible for the crimes. As a result, some individuals who may have direct knowledge of the murders have been shielded from serious investigation."

Moakley's analysis is on the mark. Although Judge Zamora is not above criticism for leaving persons or issues uninvestigated, most observers have praised his courage and initiative. The real obstacles in this case have been created by the armed forces.

7

REFUGEES AND THE DISPLACED

Of those directly victimized by the war in El Salvador, the largest number are people who have had to flee their homes, either to take refuge outside the country or to seek some haven within it. Since 1979 at least one fourth of the entire population of the country has had to abandon possessions, homes, and communities; many have had to endure separation from family members and friends. These separations have often become permanent.

The refugees and the displaced, those who have left the country and those who have left their communities but not the country, are widely viewed as incidental victims. To a degree, this is accurate. Yet as in some other conflicts in the post–World War II era, many people have also been forced to leave their homes as a consequence of deliberate efforts to depopulate zones of the country for strategic purposes. In the case of El Salvador, virtually all the forcible depopulation is attributable to the armed forces. That is not to absolve the guerrillas from blame. Some civilians left home because the guerrillas insisted that they incorporate themselves into the guerrilla struggle, because the guerrillas' use of land mines made it too dangerous for them to pursue their agricultural livelihoods or because the guerrillas suspected them of being informers for the armed forces and threatened them. Yet it has not been in the interests of the guerrillas to depopulate the territories in which their forces operate, for they depend on local peasants for the food their combatants require; they depend on local residents for information; and at times they depend on their own ability to blend into the civilian population to obtain or impart information or escape capture. Many peasants where guerrillas have been active are members of the families of the guerrillas, a further reason not to harm the local people.

The armed forces do not depend on the local population for supplies; on the contrary, it has been in their interest to depopulate parts of the country in order to deny supplies, information, and the opportunity to blend into the civilian population to the guerrillas. Whatever the background of individual members of the armed forces, their family and place of origin have not discernibly affected strategic decisions that contribute to depopulation. Much of the conduct of the armed forces, at least through the mid-1980s, reflected their view that depopulation was militarily useful.

The refugees and the displaced have scattered. Some have entered the United States, initially as illegal aliens; a typical estimate of the number of immigrants from El Salvador is more than a half million since 1980. Others, probably more than 200,000, have settled in Mexico and elsewhere in Central America. The U.S. Bureau of the Census, which has attempted to monitor the flow of refugees from Central America, has found that

> Salvadorans began fleeing their country en masse in April 1980 as the conflict between government troops and opposition forces escalated after the assassination of Catholic Archbishop Oscar Romero. By the beginning of 1981, some 90,000 Salvadoran refugees were scattered throughout Middle America, the majority in Mexico and Honduras. . . . The outflow accelerated in the first half of 1981, when an additional 150,000 people fled the country (or, as migrant workers, remained in Guatemala), and subsided during the latter half of the year, when the net outflow was around 40,000. The amount of external displacement of Salvadorans in the region appears to have peaked at the beginning of 1982 when over 280,000 Salvadorans sought asylum in Mexico, Guatemala, Honduras, Nicaragua, Costa Rica, and Panama.

According to the Bureau of the Census, the number of refugees in Central America fell somewhat thereafter, apparently because some of the Salvadorans migrated onward. Probably the majority went to the United States.[1]

Several thousand Salvadorans have been resettled in an orderly fashion in countries with active programs to provide refuge to Salvadorans fleeing political persecution, first and foremost Canada and secondarily Australia. The most visible refugees were twenty thousand who had settled by mid-decade in three camps on the Honduran side of the border with El Salvador. In recent years most of the refugees in those camps have repatriated to El Salvador voluntarily, though relatively few of the Salvadorans residing with the general population in the United States, Mexico, or elsewhere in Central America have gone back of their own accord. From 1980 to 1986 the United States sent back 48,209 Salvadorans, but many of them probably left El Salvador to again take refuge outside the country.[2]

By the beginning of 1984 about 500,000 Salvadorans had been internally displaced; half of those were registered with their own government as displaced persons. Salvadoran government figures on the registered displaced put the number at 2,000 in January 1980; 34,503 in November 1980; 165,503 in May 1981; 197,199 in November 1981; 248,743 in September 1982; and 289,758, the high point, in July 1983.[3] The number of displaced persons who did not register with the government probably grew during this period in roughly similar proportions, though precise figures are not available.

Within El Salvador the displaced fall into three categories: those who flocked to San Salvador and a few other cities and towns, creating shantytowns on their outskirts or, in some cases, crowding into the homes of relatives already living there; those who became seminomads in zones controlled by the guerrillas, periodically moving to escape ground sweeps and aerial attacks by the armed forces; and those who settled in a number of camps for the displaced operated by the government, the Catholic Archdiocese of San Salvador, other churches, and some other charitable organizations. Just as the refugees in the camps in Honduras were the most visible part of the population that had fled the country, so the residents of the camps within the country were the most visible part of the displaced population. By October 1983, when the Salvadoran government took a census of displaced persons, there were 35,510 registered displaced persons living in approximately 117 camps.[4] Many of those living in church-administered camps were not registered.

In January 1984 an Americas Watch delegation visited the town of San Francisco Gotera to investigate the circumstances in which the displaced people lived. The situation there indicated what might be found elsewhere in the country, too.

Much of Morazán Department was guerrilla controlled, but San Francisco Gotera itself, the site of a large army base, was controlled by the armed forces. Periodically the army went into areas that were controlled by the guerrillas—who generally retreated or scattered rather than engage in pitched battles and then resumed control when the army went back to its base in San Francisco Gotera. At times the armed forces engaged in more sustained efforts to drive out the guerrillas, and on a number of occasions, peasants were caught up in military sweeps, and many of them were killed. In December 1981, Morazán was the site of the massacres at El Mozote, in which seven hundred to one thousand peasants were killed, the bloodiest massacres of the entire conflict (see chap. 3).

Although thousands of people continued to try to eke out an existence in the rural areas of Morazán, many peasants left. Among them were some who fled to the departmental capital, San Francisco Gotera, figuring that they would be safe from army ground sweeps near an army base. Before the war the town had a population of five thousand, but by the time of Americas Watch's visit in January 1984, the number had swollen to include twelve thousand displaced people, many of them living in an enormous camp. Living conditions in this camp were miserable: it was crowded; the housing was terrible; sanitation was poor; and the food was barely adequate. Yet it provided a measure of safety.[5]

In the course of the January 1984 investigation, Americas Watch examined the demographic composition of several camps housing the unregistered displaced, including those in San Franciso Gotera. At the time, 71.5 percent of the camp residents were children under fifteen years of age; in comparison, children under fifteen accounted for 45.6 percent of the general population and 51.4 percent of the registered displaced in and out of camps.[6] As was evident to visitors, most of the other camp residents were adult women and elderly or disabled men. Healthy, able adult men were nowhere to be seen.

Several related factors contributed to this disparity between the demographic composition of the camps and the general population. Most important, for men who seemed capable of combat to reside there would have been extremely dangerous. The armed forces viewed the camps as shelters for the wives and children of the guerrillas. No doubt their suspicion was well founded in some cases, though the number of guerrilla combatants never exceeded ten thousand or twelve thousand, in the estimation of the Salvadoran Armed Forces and the U.S. Embassy, so the great majority of the camp residents clearly did not fit into this category. Yet the armed forces frequently raided the camps in an apparent effort to find guerrillas. Any young healthy adult male found in such a raid was at great peril. Some young men were actually guerrillas; some had died in the repression of the early 1980s, which took its heaviest toll among young males; other men, unencumbered by wives and children, settled outside the country, many entering the United States as illegal aliens. Figures are not available, but it seems likely that this last category has been the largest.

The absence of males suitable for combat did not prevent the armed forces from conducting frequent raids on the camps in the early years of the war. Americas Watch chronicled some of the raids. A few episodes are typical.

· At 7:00 A.M. on January 11, 1981, a tank, two trucks, and hundreds of soldiers invaded the archdiocesan camp for the displaced in the parish of Soyapango in San Salvador. The army occupied the parish and the camp for fifteen days. The refugees were evacuated and transferred elsewhere.[7]
· In March 1981 the army entered La Bermuda, a camp eighteen miles northeast of San Salvador. Up to a hundred people were forcibly removed. A foreign news photographer who was at the scene subsequently related his experience to Americas Watch: "The Army personnel told me I couldn't take photos, but I did anyway. I followed some Army personnel out to the road with some of their detainees, including this girl in the photo. She was about sixteen and was weeping. The Army personnel took her and several others into some bushes, and then I heard shooting, a lot, and the atmosphere became very tense. . . . My sixth sense told me to get out, so I did.

The Green Cross later confirmed that bodies had been found there, a group of civilians."[8]

· Army and National Guard units evicted more than two thousand displaced persons from the La Bermuda camp on July 14, 1981. Some were relocated to a former penitentiary then used as a camp for the displaced.[9] From there some people eventually went to Bethania Camp, operated by a French humanitarian organization, Medecins du Monde,where they suffered more raids. An American pediatrician, Dr. Arthur Warner, who began working at Bethania Camp as a volunteer in June 1983, described his first visit: "[It] was interrupted by a tension-filled two-hour intrusion and search by a 20-man, fully armed platoon. They arrived at 8:30 A.M. in two brand-new 4 × 4 Ford troop carriers and directed menacing warnings at me and the refugee population at large." The camp was also raided the day before an Americas Watch visit in January 1984.[10]

· The Domus Mariae Camp of the Archdiocese of San Salvador in the Mejicanos section of the capital was the target of frequent raids, including one on December 31, 1980, in which an eighteen-year-old boy was taken away. His tortured body was found on January 9, 1981, along with the bodies of two other people. Other raids occurred on August 20, 1980; October 10, 1980; January 11, 1981; February 16, 1981; February 17, 1981, at 6:00 A.M. and at 1:00 P.M.; and on March 17, 1981.[11]

The list of such episodes in 1980–84 could be greatly extended and would include many raids punctuated by violent abuses. Until the middle of the decade the displaced were a mostly invisible portion of the Salvadoran population, and little attention was paid to their victimization. Thereafter, with human rights groups and others paying increased attention to abuses against them, the number of raids declined sharply in both frequency and ferocity.

When the camps were the targets of military raids, relief workers employed by the Archdiocese of San Salvador and other agencies that ministered to the displaced were themselves frequent victims of harassment and worse. One case investigated closely by Americas Watch represents the dangers of conducting such relief efforts.

Marco Antonio Coto Vega, a twenty-seven-year-old law student, and his wife, Dinora Rodríguez de Coto, a twenty-eight-year-old medical student, were both employed in the relief program for the displaced run by the Archdiocese of San Salvador.[12] On July 27, 1983, Marco Antonio was picked up on his way to get food supplies for the San Roque camp. Four armed men pulled him into a microbus with tinted windows and handcuffed and blindfolded him.

In the microbus his abductors interrogated him about the relief operation and the destination of the food. When he failed to answer, they administered electric shocks to his temples. Later his head was pressed against a window, his blindfold was removed, and he was asked to identify passers-by. Then he was taken to the National Police headquarters. Over a number of days he was interrogated further about the relief effort and tortured to elicit answers. His interrogators accused him of taking food to the guerrillas and said the San Roque camp was used to train guerrillas.

Two days after Marco Antonio was picked up, he learned that his wife had also been taken. She had been alarmed when he failed to return home and went to search for him, without success, at the archdiocese offices and at the San Roque camp. The next evening, July 28, while she was waiting for him at home, armed men came to the house and seized her. She gave medical consultations twice a week at the archdiocese-run La Basilica camp, and they told her they had seen her at the camps. An official who arrived decided that the whole family should be detained: Dinora, her mother, her twin two-year-old daughters, and her cousin were all taken away. As they were put into a vehicle, Dinora saw that the street was filled with soldiers, about fifty of them. The family was taken to the National Police headquarters, the adults blindfolded.

Dinora's questioning lasted several days and went along the same lines as the interrogation of her husband. She was blindfolded at all times; at one point, an interrogator took her slip off and began molesting her.

The disappearance of the Cotos soon became known outside El Salvador; it became an issue when a U.S. delegation visited the country, in September, a week or so after they were detained. The delegation included Rep. James Shannon of Massachusetts and Holly Burkhalter, a member of the Americas Watch staff both of whom knew of the case. Shannon raised the matter repeatedly during visits with Salvadoran officials, including President Magaña. After promising to look into it, Magaña phoned Shannon to tell him that he had "found" the Cotos. Dinora's mother, daughters, and cousin were released unharmed; Marco Antonio was sent to a prison after sixteen days of detention, and Dinora was sent to prison after fifteen days of detention. The Cotos were visited in their respective prisons by representatives of Americas Watch in January 1984.[13] When they were released in March and allowed to leave El Salvador, the government of Austria provided asylum to the family. No charges were ever filed against them.

Their story is hardly unique. Many relief workers have been subjected to human rights abuses, apparently because the Salvadoran Armed Forces considered that furnishing food and other supplies to the displaced constituted a form of assistance to the guerrillas. A few more examples follow.[14]

- Roxana Guadelupe Funes, supervisor of sewing at the archdiocesan camp of San Roque, was arrested on July 29, 1983, tortured, sexually abused, held in prison without charges for eight months, then released, whereupon she went into exile.
- Gustavo Adolfo Zelada, a teacher at San Roque, was detained with Funes. Tortured and held in prison without charges for seven months, he went into exile when he was released.
- Dr. Angel Ibarra, director of medical services in the camps for displaced persons operated by the Lutheran Synod of El Salvador, was abducted by the National Police on April 26, 1983, along with the Rev. Medardo Gómez, the head of the Lutheran Church in El Salvador. Ibarra was tortured in the National Police headquarters; his feet and eardrums were given electric shocks, his shoulder was dislocated, and he received internal injuries. The Rev. Gómez was released on April 29, but Dr. Ibarra remained in Mariona prison until October 26, 1983, when he left the country.
- Ramón Grande García, accountant for the camps operated by the Lutheran Church, was arrested on November 8, 1983, then tortured and imprisoned. His sister, secretary to the head of the Lutheran Church, her two-year-old son, Ramón and his sister's father, their brother, their nephew, and a friend were also detained for several days.
- Wilfredo Amaya, regional director of Caritas, a Catholic Church–run relief agency, was abducted by several armed men on May 6, 1983, and tortured by the National Police. He was released five days later.
- Pedro Posada, who had undertaken a three-month assignment for the Archdiocese of San Salvador to work on matters concerning displaced persons, disappeared on December 9, 1982.

The armed forces also attacked the displaced and those who ministered to them more randomly. In early 1984, Americas Watch learned that on several occasions the Salvadoran air force had bombed groups of displaced persons who had gathered to obtain medical assistance from mobile health units of the International Committee of the Red Cross. The agreement that permitted the ICRC to provide assistance to displaced Salvadorans required it to tell the armed forces in advance of the movements of its vehicles, presumably to make certain that its humanitarian missions did not get caught up in combat. The ICRC suspended medical services to the displaced after the agreement was signed because planes came in to attack several times as its vehicles were leaving places where displaced people had assembled to get Red Cross services. Americas Watch complained of the bombing of the displaced to U.S. Ambassador Thomas Pickering, who promised to investigate. He said that if he found that Red Cross workers has been attacked while they were assisting displaced people, he would put an end to the attacks. Thereafter the attacks ended.[15]

After 1984 the number of attacks on camps for the displaced and those who ministered to the displaced declined markedly, though they did not cease entirely. One target was the Catholic Church–run center for the displaced at San José Calle Real, not far from San Salvador, which opened in August 1985. It housed more than five hundred people and also served as a medical clinic for Salvadorans from nearby rural areas and, from January 1987 through April 1988, as a temporary refuge for wounded FMLN combatants evacuated from war zones by the ICRC under an agreement with the government. The injured guerrillas stayed at the center until they could be evacuated for medical treatment abroad. In late 1987 and early 1988 armed uniformed soldiers entered San José Calle Real four times. On January 17, 1988, troops fired on the center for over two and a half hours, injuring one ex-guerrilla and terrorizing the displaced persons living there. On January 24, 1988, six armed men in civilian clothes ordered a center employee to get out of a church vehicle he was driving and beat him with their rifle butts. Other employees at the center also suffered harassment, and in August 1987 the day care center at the Fe y Esperanza camp for the displaced, also run by the church, was bombed.[16]

Another way in which the Salvadoran Armed Forces demonstrated their antagonism toward the displaced was by attempting to cut off the delivery of food and medicine to civilians living a seminomadic existence in conflict zones or in zones controlled by the guerrillas. The ICRC has provided such aid throughout the decade, authorized to do so by the Salvadoran Armed Forces. Unofficially, certain military commanders frequently denied passage to ICRC vehicles seeking to cross military lines to provide humanitarian services to the displaced. Col. Sigifredo Ochoa Pérez, army commander in Chalatenango Department during the mid-1980s, was particularly obstructive. He publicly insisted that all those residing in the area were guerrillas; accordingly, he thought that blocking the delivery of food and medicine to them was legitimate. Yet several thousand civilians were trying to eke out an existence in the area even though many had been displaced from their original homes. Denying access to the ICRC caused considerable hardship.

In recent years military hostility toward the displaced has been central to another issue: the resettlement of communities that were abandoned in the early years of the war. The armed forces oppose resettlement: not only do they consider displaced persons potential sources of food and other logistical support for the guerrillas but they also apparently think displaced persons are family members of the guerrillas or guerrillas themselves.

On August 7, 1987, when the Salvadoran government was one of five Central American nations that convened in Guatemala City to adopt a peace plan for the region, it committed itself to "give urgent attention to groups of refugees and displaced persons brought about by the regional crisis, through protection and assistance, particularly in areas of education, health, work and security, and wherever voluntary and individually expressed, to facilitate in the repatriation, resettlement and relocation [of these persons]." With this obligation in mind, the Salvadoran government and its armed forces permitted several large repatriations of refugees from Honduras. Additional refugees returned individually or in small groups. In 1990 three Salvadoran refugee camps in Honduras—Colomoncagua, San Antonio, and Buenos Aires—were closed down as a result of these repatriations.[17] Only the Mesa Grande camp remained open at the end of 1990, with two thousand refugees. During the second half of the decade, starting with the resettlement of Tenancingo at the beginning of 1986—the town that had been abandoned after it was bombed by the Salvadoran air force in 1983 (see chap. 3)—several thousand internally displaced people returned to their former communities in conflict zones.

The armed forces periodically hampered resettlement efforts, even making violent attacks on those returning to their communities. On April 8, 1986, during the course of a one-day military operation in Arcatao, the community in Chalatenango that had been home to many of those killed in the Sumpul River massacre in May 1980, townspeople were rounded up and accused of being guerrillas; some were picked out by the troops for special abuse—several men were tortured, and four resettlers were murdered. Arcatao continued to be a special target for raids by the armed forces; in March 1988, for example, two residents were killed when the air force fired rockets at the town.[18]

Some refugees and displaced persons returning to their communities were victimized by the guerrillas. In organizing the resettlement of Tenancingo, the Archdiocese of San Salvador had negotiated agreements with both the armed forces and the FMLN that their combatants would stay out of the town. These agreements were crucial because either side could use the presence of the other as a pretext to make the town a battle zone. Yet both sides violated their agreements with the church, and those who had resettled the town suffered the consequences. In Arcatao, subsequent to the April 1986 incident in which the armed forces executed four men, the guerrillas reportedly executed the three men who had fingered the victims.[19]

With the resettlement of refugees and the displaced the harassment of relief workers was renewed. A number of incidents took place in 1988: in Panchimilama, La Paz, Lutheran church workers were detained and threatened on several occasions; in Guarjila, Chalatenango, at a repatriation site for refugees returning from Honduras, two North American relief workers were arrested (earlier in the year, a delegation of U.S. citizens was expelled); and in April, Medecins du Monde, which had worked extensively with the displaced in El Salvador since the beginning of the decade, announced the closing of its mission in the country because of the harassment—including threats and detentions—suffered by its doctors and other personnel. Nor has the military abandoned its practice of periodically blocking the delivery of food and relief supplies, further hampering the process of resettlement and causing further hardship for the returning civilians.[20]

After a decade in which at least a fourth of El Salvador's citizens were forced to flee from their homes and their communities, the process of displacement appears to have largely halted and to a small extent reversed. Although several thousand displaced persons and refugees have returned to their communities, they represent only a small fraction of the more than one million Salvadorans who left the country or moved to safer places in other cities and departments. The "urgent attention" to refugees and the displaced and their repatriation and resettlement that was required more than three years ago by the Central American peace plan is nowhere to be seen. At best, what has transpired since then is a grudging acceptance of efforts by a handful of Salvadorans to return home, a process made arduous and perilous by the actions of the armed forces. This is certainly far from the facilitation that the government was committed to. The armed forces continue to regard the returning civilians with great suspicion, seeing their potential for providing a revitalized popular base for the guerrillas. Under the circumstances, it is hardly surprising that so few who fled should have made the attempt to go back: their victimization persists.

8

THE ROLE OF THE UNITED STATES

For most of the twentieth century El Salvador was in a backwater of U.S. foreign policy. That the military stole two elections from civilian politicians, in 1972 and 1977, hardly raised eyebrows in Washington. In the mid-1970s a congressional subcommittee held hearings about human rights abuses and electoral fraud there, but concern about the internal political situation never spread beyond a small circle of liberal Democrats and church and human rights activists. According to a State Department official in 1977, the United States had "no strategic interests" in El Salvador.[1]

A more intense U.S. preoccupation with the country began in 1979, when Sandinista guerrillas overthrew the Somoza dictatorship in Nicaragua. The specter of other Central American states falling, like a row of dominoes, to leftist revolutionaries—most of the countries were ruled by repressive military governments—led to a flurry of regional diplomatic activity by the Carter administration. But U.S. involvement in El Salvador only began in earnest when officers of the Salvadoran army, themselves fearful of sharing Somoza's fate, overthrew the government in October 1979 and installed a civilian-military junta that promised social reform and an end to human rights abuses.

The Carter administration was concerned that the junta consolidate its rule, in order to serve as a buffer against growing political polarization. But a series of juntas were dissolved and re-formed through mid-1980 as civilian representatives decried their inability to curb the power of the military and stop indiscriminate terror by the army and security forces.

The Carter administration supported socioeconomic reform in El Salvador, and the U.S. Embassy pressed the army to curb its human rights violations. But as the threat of leftist violence grew, so did U.S. anxiety, and with it a willingness to support the armed forces. The Carter administration slowly expanded a program of security assistance, the rationale for it being, then as throughout the Reagan years, that assistance would provide a lever for the United States to press for human rights improvements. At first the aid was "nonlethal": trucks, jeeps, night-vision devices, tear gas. Prominent Salvadorans denounced even this much aid. In February 1980, following reports that the Carter administration intended to increase nonlethal aid and send additional military advisers, Archbishop Oscar Romero wrote to President Carter. Previous aid, he said, had allowed the security forces to "repress the people even more violently, using lethal weapons.[2]

Days after Romero was assassinated on March 24, 1980, a subcommittee of the Congress approved the administration's request for almost $6 million in nonlethal aid to El Salvador. But the violence, contrary to administration predictions, accelerated throughout 1980. Repression in the cities swelled the ranks of a small rural guerrilla movement, active since the early 1970s. At year's end, in a move that assured El Salvador's place on the front pages of U.S. newspapers, Salvadoran security forces murdered three U.S. nuns and a Catholic lay worker. No incident, until the 1989 murders of six Jesuit priests, their housekeeper, and her daughter captured the attention of U.S. policymakers or the public.

If 1980 closed with a reminder of the brutality of the Salvadoran military, 1981 opened with the darkening clouds of civil war. Hoping to catch the incoming Reagan administration off guard, the Salvadoran guerrillas launched what they called a final offensive in an attempt to take power. Cuba and Nicaragua, apparently believing the guerrillas' inflated estimates of their strength, provided arms and ammunition. The Carter administration denounced the foreign interference and provided weapons to the Salvadoran army for almost the first time in five years.[3]

But the Reagan administration seized the opportunity to convert the failed offensive into a global crusade against communist intervention in the Western Hemisphere. In late February 1981, Secretary of State Alexander Haig vowed to "draw the line" in El Salvador, thus positing the Salvadoran conflict to be part of a global struggle between East and West in which major security issues were at stake. He set the stage for Reagan foreign policy over the next several years, declaring that "international terrorism," emanating from the Soviet Union and its allies, would take the place of human rights as an organizing principle of U.S. foreign policy.[4] Over the ten years that the United States has been intensely involved in the politics of El Salvador, one major policy goal has predominated: to prevent Salvadoran guerrillas from seizing power through violence. Because the U.S. public has overwhelmingly opposed committing U.S. troops to fight in El Salvador, the central task of defending the regime has fallen to the Salvadoran Armed Forces. The United States has been in the unenviable position of having to justify its support of the Salvadoran army even while the army was murdering thousands of civilians.

As much as Reagan administration officials may have wished to distance the United States from human rights concerns, these concerns remained central to U.S. policy. The Congress insisted on linking El Salvador's human rights performance to U.S. approval of economic and military aid. But both the administration and the Congress viewed human rights as a means to an end: unless human rights abuses were stopped, the army would continue to alienate the Salvadoran population and ensure a steady stream of recruits for the guerrillas, and the civilian government would never gain credibility through elections. It is precisely because the U.S. policy on human rights in El Salvador has derived from the larger goal of prosecuting the war against communism that it has lacked both consistency and credibility.

In tracing the evolution of U.S. policy over the decade with particular emphasis on the U.S. human rights policy, or rather, its failure,we do not wish to convey the impression that the United States had the power to work its will unimpeded in El Salvador. Instead, we believe that providing almost four billion dollars in economic and military aid over a ten-year period (see app. A) gave the United States substantial leverage to effect change in Salvadoran behavior. Because the Salvadoran army saw time and time again, however, that U.S. aid would flow regardless of military conduct, U.S. influence has been squandered. During the Reagan years in particular, not only did the United States fail to press for improvements (with a notable exception, discussed below), but in an effort to maintain backing for U.S. policy, it misrepresented the record of the Salvadoran government and smeared critics who challenged that record. In so doing, the administration needlessly polarized the debate in the United States and did a grave injustice to the thousands of civilian victims of government terror in El Salvador.

THE REAGAN YEARS

During the first months of 1981, El Salvador figured prominently in the foreign policy of the Reagan administration. The State Department produced a massive "white paper" on El Salvador, based on captured documents allegedly proving the role of communist countries in promoting the insurgency. High-level emissaries circulated the report in European and Latin American capitals but found only limited support for U.S. policy. With equal fanfare, the administration nearly tripled military aid in March and sent new teams of U.S. military advisers to train Salvadoran troops in counterinsurgency. The administration was remarkably silent on human rights abuses, apparently because it viewed such reports as guerrilla disinformation, according to a former U.S. ambassador.[5] To the extent that Reagan officials discussed political violence at all, they blamed it on the left. This was in a year when the legal aid office affiliated with the Catholic archdiocese in San Salvador tabulated 2,644 murders of noncombatant civilians by government and allied paramilitary forces in one month, a level that the administration would retroactively accept when it sought to show "progress" in the human rights situation in subsequent years.[6]

The administration committed other blunders in its initial policy offensive. Secretary Haig angered members of the Congress when he suggested— contrary to the evidence—that the U.S. churchwomen had been killed in an "exchange of fire" and that their vehicle might have "run a roadblock" set up by the Salvadoran Armed Forces, thus echoing earlier charges by the U.N. representative Jeane Kirkpatrick that the nuns were "political activists on behalf of the [opposition] Frente [Democratic Revolutionary Front]."[7] In addition, members of the Congress feared that increasing the amount of military aid and the number of advisers meant that the United States was seeking a military solution in El Salvador, when what was needed was social reform and an end to human rights abuses. The aid and the advisers raised a further concern: that the United States might land troops in El Salvador, an eventuality opposed by a large majority in the Congress, as well as the public at large.

To register its concern over the direction of U.S. policy, the Congress adopted a certification requirement in the foreign aid bill in late 1981. To qualify the Salvadoran government for military aid, the administration had to report every six months that the Salvadoran government was "making a concerted and significant effort to comply with internationally recognized human rights" and "achieving substantial control over all elements of its armed forces" in order to end human rights abuses. The certification provided a needed corrective to the emphasis in administration policy, even if it demonstrated congressional unwillingness to cut aid in response to Salvadoran government atrocities.

Until President Reagan vetoed the certification in late 1983, the six-month requirement structured the debate over U.S. policy in El Salvador. To maintain a flow of assistance to the Salvadoran Armed Forces, the administration made the necessary certification four times, even though the human rights situation in El Salvador remained appalling. Over the two-year period in which the certification requirement remained in effect, the administration gradually moderated its denial that any abuses emanated from the Salvadoran army and the security forces. But the movement toward modernization was timid and was overshadowed by the effort to exculpate the military for any complicity in atrocities against civilians. The following examples highlight the administration's approach.

In issuing its reports to the Congress, the State Department and U.S. Embassy in San Salvador relied primarily on the Salvadoran press for information about abuses, despite the conservative bias of the two major dailies and despite the admission of an embassy official that the Salvadoran press is "inherently biased, not accurate, and not competent by U.S. standards."[8] (Two papers critical of the government were forced to close in 1980 and 1981, when their editors were murdered or their presses bombed.) The U.S. Embassy admitted the limitations of press reports, noting in a January 1982 cable that the newspapers "only report deaths in areas where they momentarily have correspondents or in areas into which correspondents do not fear to enter. . . . This is certainly an underreporting of events."[9] Embassy and State Department officials acknowledged repeatedly that their reporting was deficient but claimed that it at least had the virtue of consistency.[10]

In other instances, the State Department simply reported as fact information provided to the embassy by the Salvadoran Armed Forces. That was the main source of information about the number of soldiers disciplined for human rights abuses. To support the claim that the Salvadoran government was achieving control over wayward elements of the military, the State Department asserted in July 1982 that 109 members of the armed forces had been disciplined for human rights abuses. This statistic was averred despite the admonition by the embassy that the figure could not be confirmed independently and should therefore be used "with proper caveats."[11]

Even while relying on questionable methodology in gathering its human rights information, the administration disparaged human rights monitors in San Salvador who gathered information from survivors or eyewitnesses. To start with, its criticism focused on Socorro Jurídico, the legal aid office affiliated with the Archdiocese of San Salvador; State Department officials accused it of a leftist bias because it only reported on human rights violations by the government—the practice of most human rights organizations worldwide. The administration's attacks probably contributed to the decision by the archdiocese to form a new office in 1982, Tutela Legal, which reported on both sides to the conflict.

Even this was not enough, however. In December 1982, U.S. Ambassador Deane Hinton said that human rights groups were "courageous" but "have an evident political bias" in favor of the left. In 1983 the State Department claimed that Tutela Legal's sources included "announcements by guerrilla groups" and that the civilians whose deaths it reported were "mostly guerrilla supporters." The first statement was false. The second was irrelevant, except to suggest that civilians who died deserved their fate. After a temporary improvement in relations between the embassy and Tutela Legal in mid-1983, the embassy renewed its aspersions in early 1984, asserting that 80 percent of the civilian deaths reported by Tutela Legal were those of "guerrilla 'masas'" and by implication, therefore, not human rights abuses.[12]

In January 1982 the *New York Times* and the *Washington Post* carried lengthy stories about the massacres of hundreds of civilians that was committed by the U.S.-trained Atlacatl Battalion in El Mozote. In testimony before the Congress, the assistant secretary of state for inter-American affairs, Thomas O. Enders, denied that government troops had "systematically massacred civilians" and claimed that the embassy had "sent two Embassy officers to investigate." In fact, according to the report of a House Intelligence Subcommittee later that year, the embassy officers "never reached the towns where the alleged events occurred," though they flew over El Mozote in a helicopter. Enders's claim that the civilians might have died in a military confrontation, rather than massacres, came from a "man from a town several miles away from El Mozote [who] 'intimated' that he knew of violent fighting," according to the congressional report (emphasis in the original).[13]

In several of the certifications, promises by the Salvadoran military were substituted for actual improvements, and those promises look even more ludicrous in hindsight. In substantiating its claim that the Salvadoran government was achieving control over elements of the military, for example, it is reported in the second certification that the "Minister of Defense has ordered that all violations of citizens' rights be stopped immediately and [has] directed punishment of military offenders."[14] In 1990, eight years later, no Salvadoran officer had yet been prosecuted for a human rights abuse, despite the tens of thousands of civilian murders committed by troops under their command.

In March 1983, Secretary of State George Shultz told the Congress that "if they [Salvadoran Armed Forces] don't clean up their act, the support is going to dry up, and they've been told that and they know that and that will happen."[15] In fact, however, the Reagan administration opposed every attempt by the Congress to reduce or eliminate aid and, in the years following Shultz's remark, expanded it dramatically, despite ongoing human rights abuses. The same hyperbole was evident in early 1984, when the State Department heralded as a "major development" the arrest of Capt. Eduardo Alfonso Avila in connection with the January 1981 murder of two AIFLD labor advisers and the head of the Salvadoran land reform agency.[16] In fact, Avila was held briefly for a minor military infraction, and in July 1985 a Salvadoran judge ruled that there was insufficient evidence to indict him. Avila's uncle served on the Salvadoran Supreme Court.

In attempting to exculpate the Salvadoran armed and security forces for responsibility for abuses, both the Reagan and the Carter administrations portrayed human rights violations as emanating from extremists or shadowy death squads operating with no connection to the security forces. The Carter administration drew this picture first when, for example, the deputy assistant secretary of state for inter-American affairs, John Bushnell, testified that "much of this violence is the result of attacks from the extreme right and the extreme left. . . . Some members of the military, individual officers, have been involved. . . . But it is not government-directed violence."[17] In December 1981, U.N. Ambassador Jeane Kirkpatrick also used polarities when she told the United Nations that "in El Salvador, murderous traditionalists confront murderous revolutionaries—with only the government working to moderate and attempting to pacify adversaries."[18]

By the time of the fourth and last certification, the administration admitted that some of the "armed rightist terrorists" responsible for human rights abuses included "some members of the security forces," but it still generally implied that these were rogue elements engaging in practices uncharacteristic of the armed forces. A year later, however, a Senate Intelligence Committee inquiry into the death squads, which relied on the same cable traffic that the administration used in preparing its reports to the Congress, concluded that "significant political violence—including death squad activities—has been associated with elements of the Salvadoran security establishment, especially the security services. The U.S. government has information which corroborates public claims that death squad activities, as well as other abuses provoked by extreme right-wing officers or their associates, have originated in the Salvadoran security services, including the National Police, National Guard and Treasury Police."[19]

At times the pattern of denial and obfuscation was broken. But even when high-ranking U.S. officials spoke out against the abuses, the content of their message was quickly diluted by contradictory statements from others in the administration. In October 1982, for example, Ambassador Hinton told the American Chamber of Commerce in San Salvador that "since 1979 perhaps as many as 30,000 Salvadorans have been MURDERED, not killed in battle, MURDERED" (emphasis in the original). Within days of the speech, however, an "anonymous" White House official publicly disavowed Hinton's remarks, expressing "surprise" and "concern" that "the decibel level had risen higher than our policy has allowed in the past."[20] The criticism undercut whatever impact Hinton's speech might have had in El Salvador. When the State Department subsequently circulated Hinton's speech, it toned down his remarks, saying that the Salvadorans had been "killed illegally, that is, not in battle."[21] In late 1983 an upsurge in death squad killings, increased guerrilla effectiveness in the countryside, and fears that the Congress would not approve requested levels of military aid focused renewed high-level attention on the problem of government-sponsored violence. In early November, for example, the tortured bodies of nine people, including three members of a peasant cooperative and two pregnant women, were found stuffed in grain sacks in the town of Zaragoza. The newly arrived U.S. ambassador, Thomas Pickering, condemned the incident, in November 1983 asking members of the American Chamber of

Commerce who among them could "excuse" or "justify" atrocities against civilians.[22]

The Salvadoran presidential elections scheduled for mid-1984 provided an additional context for a U.S. preoccupation with political violence. U.S. officials viewed the holding of credible elections as central to gaining the loyalty of Salvadoran citizens toward the government, and to convincing the attentive U.S. public that a legitimate democratic process was underway in El Salvador. Rampant murder undercut both objectives.

In late November, the U.S. Embassy in San Salvador began leaking to journalists the names of officers implicated in death squad murders. In December, at Pickering's request, Vice-President Bush visited El Salvador and publicly condemned "death squad terrorists." Privately, Bush demanded the removal of a number of active duty Army and security force officers and one civilian connected with the violence, and reportedly threatened that Congress would not sustain aid if the murders continued.[23]

In the months following Bush's visit, the number of death squad victims fell sharply. The decline illustrated that military officers directed and controlled death squad killings, a charge the administration had long denied, and that U.S. pressure could be effective when applied.[24] At the same time, focusing on death squad murders once again deflected attention from the Salvadoran army and the security forces, which were principally responsible for the deaths of Salvadoran civilians. Just weeks after Bush's visit, the embassy tacitly admitted government responsibility for civilian deaths, charging that guerrilla masas, or supporters, constituted the bulk of civilians killed during military operations. The allegation that civilians living in conflict zones were "something other than innocent civilian bystanders," however, implied that they deserved their fate at the hands of the armed forces.[25]

Bush's visit might have marked a turning point in U.S. policy on human rights except that his message was contradicted by other senior officials. In early November, Under Secretary of Defense Fred Ikle said that death squads were "in fact enjoying the protection of the Communist guerrillas." Later that month President Reagan pocket-vetoed the certification linking U.S. aid to human rights improvements. He subsequently told a group of high school students that guerrillas were carrying out death squad murders to smear El Salvador's reputation, because "the right wing will be blamed for it."[26] Throughout the first half of 1984 the administration defended the Salvadoran Armed Forces against charges that they engaged in indiscriminate bombing in the countryside. In fact, by the middle of the year, the forced displacement of Salvadoran civilians in conflict zones because of aerial bombardment had become the dominant human rights issue in El Salvador.[27]

The Advent of Democracy in El Salvador

The denial of human rights abuses in El Salvador had both practical and ideological roots. The Congress had tied military aid to human rights improvements, thus compelling the administration to deny the existence of abuses in order to maintain a flow of U.S. assistance. At a deeper level, however, administration officials believed that communist regimes were by definition violators of human rights; the administration could rationalize anticommunist crusades, such as the one to defeat the Salvadoran rebels, in the name of human rights. As Secretary of State George Shultz put it, "We know well that the protection of human rights and liberties over the long term can only be insured by a democratic form of government." Or as the assistant secretary of state for human rights, Elliott Abrams, claimed: "Generally speaking, democratic governments are far less likely to engage in torture than non-democratic governments. This is because such institutions as freedom of speech, freedom of the press, freedom of assembly and association, and free elections have built respect for human rights into the very foundations of democratic government."[28]

The administration thus had strong ideological reasons to promote democracy in El Salvador. There were more instrumental purposes as well. The Congress, insisting that the war against communism was more than a military enterprise, proposed a negotiated, political solution to the Salvadoran conflict. Some policymakers in the Reagan administration also recognized that efforts at political reform were necessary, given El Salvador's history of fraudulent elections, if the Salvadoran government was to gain legitimacy. Even so, the administration equated democracy with its procedural aspect—elections—subordinating, except for rhetorical purposes, such crucial issues as civilian control of the military and the rule of law.[29]

El Salvador first held elections for a Constituent Assembly in March 1982. Large numbers of people turned out to vote, providing the Reagan administration with a distinct public relations victory. In spite of the massive turnout, U.S. officials had to become deeply involved in postelectoral political jockeying in order to prevent the reputed death squad leader Roberto D'Aubuisson from being named provisional president. In the end the assembly appointed Alvaro Magaña, a more neutral figure. After March 1982 the administration regularly cited the elections as evidence of an improved human rights climate, as if the holding of an election implied the advent of the rule of law.

In fact, continued lawlessness in the months leading up to the March 1984 presidential elections was one of the reasons Vice President Bush traveled to El Salvador in December 1983. The resurgence of death squad activity—this time aimed at government officials and members of the Christian Democratic Party—threatened the very political center the administration was attempting to foster. In a further attempt to undermine the right, the Reagan administration channeled covert funds to bolster the candidacy of José Napoleón Duarte against his ARENA party opponent, Roberto D'Aubuisson. Duarte beat D'Aubuisson in a May 1984 runoff, a victory widely hailed as a triumph for democracy and U.S. policy. In the wake of Duarte's election, the Congress approved record amounts of military aid to El Salvador. The defeated D'Aubuisson, meanwhile, reportedly stood at the center of a plot to assassinate Ambassador Pickering, whom D'Aubuisson apparently blamed for the routing of ARENA at the polls.[30] For the next several years a bipartisan consensus over support for the Duarte government removed El Salvador from the central place it had held in the raging foreign policy debates of the early 1980s.

Duarte's election had several contradictory effects on the human rights situation in El Salvador. On the one hand, the subsequent expansion of military aid intensified the air war against Salvadoran insurgents, who by late 1983 were moving about the countryside in company-size units, each about a hundred strong. The helicopter fleet of the Salvadoran Armed Forces more than doubled in size during 1984 and came to include C-47 gunships, provided by the United States, whose fifty-caliber machine guns could fire fifteen hundred rounds per minute. The air war forced the guerrillas to break back down into smaller units. But in 1984, as previously, the principal victims of aerial attacks were Salvadoran citizens living in conflict zones. President Duarte issued rules of engagement in September 1984 in an effort to reduce their impact on the civilian population. Yet the attacks continued, as did the forced displacement they caused, both facilitated by the augmented U.S. assistance program.[31]

On the other hand, certain forms of political violence, notably death squad killings and disappearances, temporarily declined through the end of 1987, only to rise again in 1988. Reports of extreme forms of torture by the security forces also sharply decreased during this period. Nonetheless, detainees held for politically motivated offenses continued to suffer ill-treatment at the hands of the security forces, including prolonged standing or exercises; sleep, food, or water deprivation; death threats; and confinement in very cold or very small rooms. Between August 1984 and September 1988 there were no mass killings by the army in the countryside.

These developments in mid-decade notwithstanding, it was difficult to call the overall human rights situation improved, as the Reagan administration did. The army and the security forces were responsible for a considerable number of ongoing abuses. In 1985, for example, there were nineteen hundred political killings and disappearances, 90 percent of which were attributed to government forces. Such numbers appear small only by comparison to the carnage earlier in the decade.[32] Moreover, as long as no officers were punished for human rights offenses, the structure that permitted such abuses to continue remained intact.

The impunity enjoyed by members of the armed forces meant that abuses would ebb and flow but never be eliminated.

Even though a state of siege still severely restricted civil and political rights during Duarte's first two years in office, organized groups that had supported Duarte's candidacy did express more and more political dissent. These protests took on an increasingly antigovernment tone as the Duarte administration failed to deliver on campaign promises to end the war or to reverse the national economic decline and as it was forced to adopt austerity measures that were unpopular with the labor-peasant coalition that had helped elect Duarte to office. Ironically, the Christian Democratic victory in the assembly elections of March 1985 may have contributed to the popular discontent by conveying the impression that the government was finally in a position to move forward on its program of social and economic reforms. In addition, several media reports indicated that the guerrillas were attempting to rebuild their base of support in the cities in order to destabilize the government and that they had improved ties to the trade union movement in particular.[33]

The U.S. response to these developments in mid-decade hurt the cause of human rights in El Salvador. In its zeal to support Duarte and to protect the U.S. aid program, the Reagan administration sought to portray the FMLN as the main source of human rights violations. The U.S. Embassy in San Salvador, under the stewardship of Ambassador Edwin G. Corr, regularly smeared human rights groups that said otherwise, a counterproductive policy of shooting the messenger rather than taking stock of the ample bad news emanating from Duarte's administration.

Reporting on Political Violence

The administration interpreted reductions in some forms of human rights abuses in 1984–85 as a license to deny any culpability on the part of the Salvadoran government in ongoing violations. In establishing categories of political violence for reporting purposes in 1985, for example, the embassy omitted the armed forces as a possible source of political violence.[34] In addition, the embassy capitalized on an increase of abuses by the guerrillas to claim that the FMLN was chiefly responsible for the violence against civilians. The use of land mines, the kidnapping and assassination of mayors and other political figures, the killing of four U.S. Marines and nine others in a sidewalk café in San Salvador, and the kidnapping of President Duarte's daughter provided sufficient grounds for condemnation (see chap. 4).

But the focus on guerrilla abuses to the exclusion of others at best scored points in a propaganda war, at worst distorted the record and made it impossible for the United States to press for an end to government-sponsored violence. As

Archbishop Arturo Rivera Damas of San Salvador noted in condemning the café murders, it was hypocritical to speak out against left-wing terrorism while remaining silent about the bombings, ground sweeps, and forced relocations carried out by the government in the countryside.[35]

Seizing on the emotions aroused by the café massacre, administration supporters in the Congress moved to restore aid to the security forces in El Salvador, a move long sought by the Reagan administration.[36] The administration argued that police training was especially urgent to meet an increased guerrilla threat in urban areas and that training by the United States would serve to improve the human rights practices of Salvadoran security forces—the same argument it had made in the case of military aid provided to the army. Critics countered that police aid only implicated the United States in ongoing abuses by the security forces and should not be provided in the absence of a system of accountability for human rights violations. There was, moreover, little evidence that units trained by the United States through its military assistance program had an improved human rights record, a problem illustrated by the repeated involvement of the U.S.-trained Atlacatl Battalion in brutal massacres.[37]

Washington debated police aid but otherwise paid little attention to the war in El Salvador after Duarte's election, though it did express concerns over the air war. But even after the Congress approved the police aid program, it continued to be mired in controversy. In the summer of 1986 members of Congress alleged that three Salvadoran officers brought to the United States for antiterrorism training had participated in death squad activities. According to subsequent news reports, another officer in the U.S. training program was linked to the torture of a prisoner.[38] Following the revelations, the Phoenix (Arizona) City Council voted to terminate the training of members of Salvadoran security forces by its police force. Between 1985 and 1989 the United States provided close to twenty million dollars to the Salvadoran security forces through a variety of programs (see chap. 5).

The Reagan administration's practice of discrediting human rights monitors and victims had its origins in its human rights reporting early in the decade. But the practice of claiming that information about abuses came from guerrilla sources or that the victims were themselves guerrillas picked up in 1986 and continued through the end of Reagan's term in office.[39] Such claims may have been useful in an expanded psychological operations war against the guerrillas, but they needlessly endangered the lives of many innocent civilians, including U.S. citizens and human rights monitors whom the United States should have endeavored to protect.

In 1986, for example, the U.S. Embassy circulated an "analysis" of a 1985 Americas Watch report on El Salvador to the Congress and to the press. The embassy charged that the report was "based primarily on pro-FMLN sources, and relie[d] heavily on testimony from FMLN supporters from the guerrilla stronghold of Guazapa." Although the embassy had no way of knowing the political sympathies of the victims, and indeed regularly labeled all people from zones of conflict as guerrilla supporters, its accusation seemed primarily a way of justifying the army's attack against civilians in the Guazapa area. In any case, the military and security forces ordinarily chose victims precisely because they were thought to have some links with the left, a consideration that does not obviate a citizen's right to fair treatment or necessarily nullify the credibility of his or her testimony.[40]

The embassy practice of accepting declarations by the armed forces at face value meanwhile gave a false picture of the human rights situation. For example, embassy officials dismissed an account of a January 1987 bombardment of the northern town of San Diego as rebel propaganda. When reporters who traveled to the area documented the attack, embassy spokespersons were forced to admit that they had based their denial on reports by the Salvadoran air force.[41]

The dismissal of human rights victims and their testimony as FMLN-inspired was particularly characteristic of the Reagan administration's handling of labor rights violations. The Salvadoran government cracked down harshly on labor unions in 1985–87, applying such labels as "subversive" or "guerrilla-linked" to justify the repression of active unionists in the industrial, agricultural, and service sectors. Although many of the victims were affiliated with antigovernment unions, members of progovernment unions, including the AFL-CIO-supported UCS, a peasant association, were also punished when they attempted to exercise their constitutionally guaranteed rights to bargain collectively, organize, or strike.[42]

Because U.S. trade law provides that respect for labor rights be considered in granting U.S. trade preferences, Americas Watch filed several petitions with the U.S. Trade Representative that documented cases of violations of workers' rights in El Salvador. In response to these petitions, the administration first denied there were such cases and then justified attacks on trade unionists on the grounds that the victims were supporters of the guerrillas. The administration also denounced those who reported on labor abuses as politically motivated.[43] It thus displayed a paradoxical attitude toward democratic freedoms in El Salvador, policymakers simultaneously praising the opening of political space in El Salvador under President Duarte and condemning its use by groups critical of the government. Labeling dissidents FMLN supporters justified the persecution of individuals on the basis of their alleged political leanings, even though their activities were protected by the Salvadoran Constitution and international human rights laws.[44]

Of all the attempts to discredit critics of the government, perhaps none was so pernicious as the embassy's denunciation of human rights monitors. In a country where thousands have been murdered or have disappeared for far less offense than speaking out against government abuses, the embassy's campaign to protect the Salvadoran government by defaming its critics was unconscionable. This is especially true given the number of Salvadorans who have lost their lives carrying out human rights or humanitarian work.

An episode in mid-1986 demonstrates the embassy's attitude. In late May a woman named Luz Janeth Alfaro Peña held a press conference at the Treasury Police headquarters. Alfaro claimed to have been an FMLN member who worked on and off for several years with the nongovernmental Human Rights Commission. She announced that several well-known human rights and humanitarian organizations, including the nongovernmental Human Rights Commission and the Social Secretariat of the Archdiocese of San Salvador, were front groups for the FMLN. Perhaps her most sensational claim was that 95 percent of the food and other assistance that church-sponsored relief groups collected abroad went to the FMLN with the approval of Archbishop Rivera Damas. She said that the Lutheran, Baptist, and Episcopal churches were also helping the guerrillas. Alfaro's allegations led to the arrest of ten leaders of various human rights organizations, many of whom were abused or tortured in detention and all of whom were forced to sign statements that they later repudiated. Eight people associated with the Social Secretariat received death threats and were told to leave the country.[45]

The U.S. Embassy colluded in the trial-by-press-conference atmosphere by using Alfaro's denunciations to further its own campaign against FMLN "front groups." Later on the same day as Alfaro made her announcement, the embassy issued a statement affirming that "the Salvadoran security forces are in the process of rolling up a group of FMLN members who have been running front organizations devoted to disinformation on human rights issues." Referring to Alfaro's allegations, the embassy stated: "This latest information makes it clear that [the Committee of Mothers and Families of the Detained, Disappeared, and Assassinated of El Salvador and the nongovernmental Human Rights Commission] have been thoroughly penetrated by the FMLN and subject to manipulation by these admitted Marxist-Leninist groups for a number of years."[46]

The embassy's statement showed utter disregard for the requirements of due process and appeared to justify the Salvadoran government's tarring of all humanitarian workers as subversive. In response to protests by U.S. churches and human rights groups, the embassy issued a clarification of its initial denunciation several weeks later: "The blanket charges by Janeth Luz Alfaro are unjustly tainting some Church and human rights organizations working in El Salvador. . . . Many church groups have played a major role in providing humanitarian support and sustenance to the truly needy . . . and . . . are vital to the well being of the country."[47]

In spite of the retraction, the embassy continued its criticism; it pounded away at Tutela Legal in particular, the principal source of reliable information about human rights in El Salvador. In 1986 the embassy circulated a cable attacking the group, "whose methodology is questionable and whose statistics we have shown to be badly flawed and biased." In fact, on only one occasion did the embassy demonstrate weakness or error in Tutela Legal's methodology, which involved the numbers it gave for victims of indiscriminate attacks by the military in the mid-1980s. The analysis in the embassy cable did not note Tutela Legal's improved methodology in that area, an oversight that appeared deliberate.[48]

In 1987 the embassy continued to openly criticize the human rights office of the archdiocese as "biased" and "inaccurate."[49] In 1988 it distributed a press packet labeling Americas Watch materials and articles by a respected journalist "leftist propaganda." Circulating the packet to diplomats and the press corps in San Salvador was a particularly poor use of embassy resources, conveying once again that the problem with human rights in El Salvador was not with those who committed violations but rather with those who documented them.[50]

It is no small indication of the legacy of the Reagan administration that death squad killings and army massacres were on the rise in 1988, prompting even the governmental Human Rights Commission to observe that "the violence of the past is resurgent in the nation, threatening to drown us in a bloodbath of uncontrollable and disastrous consequences."[51] In July, Secretary Shultz traveled to El Salvador and reportedly pressed top military officials to curb human rights abuses; and before leaving El Salvador in August 1988, Ambassador Corr reportedly met with leaders of the ARENA party to express concern about the rise in death squad activity.[52] But after years of covering up or denying such abuses, the United States was in an awkward position to protest their resurgence.

In perhaps final testimony to the failure of eight years of Reagan policy in El Salvador, soldiers of the army's Fifth Brigade summarily executed ten captured peasants in the town of San Francisco, San Sebastián, in September. Soldiers under the command of an army major blindfolded and bound seven men and three women from the town and led them to a secluded spot. Then the soldiers detonated captured guerrilla mines, which they placed around the area, hoping to hide their own hand in the murders. When the mines failed to kill the captives, the major ordered the soldiers to shoot them at point-blank range. The soldiers then planted guerrilla arms and propaganda at the scene, concocting an elaborate cover-up, which held that the peasants were killed during a guerrilla ambush.[53] Scarcely a month after the San Francisco massacre, the State Department praised the "dramatic decline in human rights abuses by government forces and the radical right" in El Salvador.[54]

THE BUSH ADMINISTRATION

In its first months in office, the Bush administration took steps that distinguished it from its predecessor. The U.S. Congress, too, began peering at the policy of unquestioned support for the Salvadoran government. With the contra war over in Nicaragua, with rightists controlling the Salvadoran Legislative Assembly and expected to win the March 1989 presidential elections and with U.S. budget constraints forcing hard choices to be made over competing spending priorities, El Salvador was once again bubbling to the surface of foreign policy concerns. Vice President Quayle visited San Salvador in early February 1989, in a trip that many compared with Bush's visit in December 1983. In statements to the press, Quayle described his purpose as conveying "a very emphatic, strong message" that military leaders must "work for the elimination of human rights abuses."[55] In private, he warned that aid might be cut off if conditions did not improve. As a test, Quayle insisted that those responsible for the San Francisco massacre of September 1988 be brought to justice.[56] Within days of Quayle's visit, the Army Fifth Brigade remitted three of four soldiers sought by a local judge for their involvement in the murders. By mid-March nine soldiers, including a major in the army, were detained by court order.[57] (Over a year later, only the major remained in custody, and charges had been dismissed against eight of the defendants; see chap. 6.)

Quayle again traveled to El Salvador after the inauguration of ARENA President Alfredo Cristiani, this time reportedly out of concern that rightist sectors of ARENA were pressing for a return to their bloody practices of the past.[58] In the spirit of expanding contacts with the extreme right in order to influence them, Quayle met with Roberto D'Aubuisson, shunned by U.S. officials since 1984, when he was allegedly involved in a plot to assassinate Ambassador Pickering. The need to court the right—now holding formal power—diluted whatever human rights message Quayle might have sought to convey on this second trip. In July 1989, U.S. Ambassador William Walker invited D'Aubuisson to the embassy's Fourth of July celebration, thus furthering the ex-major's restitution in U.S. eyes.

Although the Bush administration took several highly visible steps regarding human rights in 1989, the Cold War reflexes of the Reagan years characterized administration responses to the November 1989 guerrilla offensive and the murder of six Jesuit priests, their housekeeper, and her daughter. Its reluctance to criticize the Salvadoran army for abuses committed during the course of the fighting (even as it roundly criticized the FMLN) had the unfortunate effect of condoning abuses by government forces. In addition, in the immediate aftermath of the murder of the Jesuits, U.S. officials sought to minimize the possibility that the army was responsible, even though strong circumstantial evidence implicated the armed forces. While condemning the murders, Ambassador Walker speculated that they were the work of the FMLN; the assistant secretary of state for inter-American affairs, Bernard Aronson, ventured that the killings were the work of the "violent right."[59] After President Cristiani named nine soldiers, including a colonel, as responsible for the killings in January 1990, U.S. officials seemed particularly eager to contain the investigation and avoid implicating the armed forces high command. Such efforts made it appear that the United States was less interested in a full airing of the truth than in minimizing the political damage of the Jesuit killings to the Salvadoran army and to U.S. policy. Some examples follow.

· Officials of the Bush administration failed to acknowledge any army violations of the rules of war during the FMLN urban offensive, instead shifting the blame for any harm to civilians solely to the rebels. Although the guerrillas were responsible for numerous violations, the administration's silence on the subject of army abuses sent the message that "anything goes" when the army faced hard combat. The administration made no remarks on instances of indiscriminate fire in heavily populated neighborhoods, the torture of detainees, and targeted killings by the armed forces; by contrast, officials scored FMLN behavior.[60]
· The State Department defended President Cristiani's decision to refuse a call by the International Committee of the Red Cross for a temporary cease-fire to evacuate wounded civilians from areas of fighting. The administration acceded to such a call, however, to evacuate U.S. military trainers trapped in the Sheraton Hotel.[61]
· Ambassador Walker initially defended the Salvadoran Armed Forces' raids of church and relief organizations, comparing the arrest of humanitarian workers to the U.S. internment of the Japanese during World War II. (The United States has since admitted its wrongdoing and paid reparations to these U.S. citizens of Japanese descent.) When a U.S. citizen, Jennifer Jean Casolo, was arrested by the security forces, allegedly for harboring weapons for the guerrillas, U.S.

officials made numerous statements indicating a strong presumption of her guilt. After weeks of protest by U.S.-based religious and human rights groups over the treatment of religious workers, Secretary of State James Baker III wrote to Cristiani to express his "deep concern."[62]

· The administration sought aggressively to discredit the testimony of an important witness in the Jesuit murder case, Lucia Barrera de Cerna. After being accompanied to the United States by a U.S. Embassy official, Cerna and her husband were held virtually incommunicado for several days and, without their own attorney or another trusted person present, were interrogated by the FBI and a Salvadoran military investigator. Cerna was given lie detector tests and was treated more as a suspect than as the sole witness to come forward with information about the killings. The administration supported assertions by the Salvadoran government that Cerna's testimony was not credible because she failed the lie detector tests, neglecting to note that she failed after she changed her story to say that she had seen nothing on the night of November 16. Cerna's claim to have seen uniformed soldiers carry out the murders was borne out by the subsequent arrest orders for nine army soldiers.[63]

Similarly, the U.S. Embassy informed on an important Salvadoran military source, Col. Carlos Armando Avilés, who had received information that the head of the Salvadoran Military School had confessed his involvement in the crime to a senior Salvadoran officer investigating the Jesuit murders. After Avilés shared his discovery with a U.S. military adviser, embassy officials provided members of the Salvadoran high command with the name of their source. Avilés subsequently changed his story.[64] Both the Cerna and Avilés episodes sent a powerful message to anyone with information about the Jesuit murders: they could not trust the U.S. Embassy.

· In spite of the administration's public insistence that a resolution of the Jesuit case was important to the United States, U.S. policy was inconsistent. The administration concealed from congressional and Salvadoran investigators key information that, if true, would implicate the Salvadoran high command in at least a cover-up of the murders. The embassy and the State Department withheld information provided by a U.S. major concerning advance knowledge of a plot against the Jesuits. According to an addendum to an affidavit provided by Maj. Eric Buckland to the FBI on January 11, 1990, and recanted seven days later, Salvadoran Army Chief of Staff René Emilio

Ponce knew of Col. Alfredo Benavides Moreno's plans to kill the priests and sent Col. Avilés to the Military School approximately ten days before the murder to try to talk him out of it.[65] The information contained in Buckland's affidavit was shared with the congressional task force headed by Rep. Joe Moakley ten months after it was known by the Bush administration and then only when someone leaked it. It took months for U.S. officials even to ask Col. Ponce or other senior Salvadoran officers what they might know about the murders.[66]

Moakley has accused the high command of being "engaged in a conspiracy to obstruct justice."[67]

· U.S. agencies, including the State Department, have refused to release documents requested by the Jesuits and others pertaining to the Jesuit murders on the grounds that to do so would imperil U.S. national security. What the administration may be protecting, however, is politically damaging information indicating that the United States knew far more about the murders than officials have let on. One of the first people to see the bodies of the murdered priests, for example, was apparently a CIA official working at the National Intelligence Directorate of the Salvadoran Armed Forces. He reportedly told a Salvadoran counterpart that the military was responsible. In addition, U.S. advisers slept at the high command headquarters during the November guerrilla offensive.[68] Given this and a decade of close relationships between U.S. and Salvadoran military and intelligence officials, it is inconceivable that U.S. officials did not have extensive knowledge of who was involved in the murders.

In the months following the November 1989 guerrilla offensive, there were some positive changes in the policy of the Bush administration. Both Secretary Baker and Assistant Secretary Aronson went on record in favor of a negotiated settlement to the Salvadoran conflict; and Aronson, stating that the guerrillas had legitimate concerns for their safety should they lay down their weapons after a cease-fire, implied that the administration recognized the need for military reform. The shift in emphasis away from a futile search for a military solution toward negotiation is welcome. It remains to be seen, however, what position the United States will adopt on the thorny issue of reform of the armed forces and punishment of those guilty of human rights abuses and how much leverage the United States will apply in pursuit of those goals. The administration did slow the delivery of military aid in August 1990 to protest the military's lack of cooperation in the Jesuit case, but it opposed congressional efforts that summer to reduce military aid by half in order to forward the Jesuit investigation and create an incentive for both sides in the conflict to negotiate.

A DECADE OF FAILURE

Before leaving El Salvador in July 1988, Ambassador Corr listed five areas in which the United States supported El Salvador's attempt "to establish a viable constitutional democracy": the creation of institutions and attitudes necessary for a constitutional democracy; the quest for peace, through the effective conduct of the war and the search for national conciliation; economic improvement and a fairer distribution of the nation's wealth; the reduction of human rights abuses and the improvement of the judicial system; and the search for peace and democracy in all of Central America. "Salvadoran failure in any one of these areas," Corr said, "would mean eventual failure in all of them, and, consequently, failure to attain a constitutional democracy."[69] If judged by Ambassador Corr's own criteria, Salvadoran democracy and U.S. attempts to promote it must be considered a failure.

Ten years and close to four billion dollars after Secretary of State Alexander Haig vowed to "draw the line" in El Salvador, one line has clearly been drawn: the guerrillas have not seized power. But military stalemate does not translate into military victory, and El Salvador's civil society has paid an exorbitant price for what the United States deems vital to its own security.

Five elections were held in El Salvador between 1982 and 1990, but the casting of ballots did not establish the rule of law, the supremacy of civilian authority over the authority of the armed forces, or the guarantee of fundamental human rights for the Salvadoran people. The Jesuit murders and the languishing investigation thereof serve as only the most prominent reminder that the armed forces remain a law unto themselves, beyond civilian control and answerable to virtually no one. It is of no small symbolic importance that leftists are not the only ones to suffer in the new "democracy." Col. Adolfo Arnoldo Majano, who served on the first civilian-military junta, which took power in 1979, and who was once hailed by U.S. officials as proof that the Salvadoran army had broken with the past and launched a new era of reform, fled the country for fear of his life.

Ten years ago, when the United States deepened its involvement in El Salvador's civil war, policymakers claimed that vital U.S. security interests were at stake. In 1990, with the Soviet Union mired in internal difficulties and its empire crumbled, it is hard to see what, beyond inertia, sustains the U.S. effort. Some may argue that there are legitimate internal reasons for striving to keep the FMLN from power. But the terror of the last decade and the U.S. defense of those who carried it out belie any claim that the interests of the Salvadoran people reside at the heart of U.S. policy.

The central problem is that the United States has treated human rights and the rule of law as secondary objectives, in service of its own strategic goals. U.S. policy must reverse those priorities; the United States must stand prepared to withdraw its support if humanitarian goals show little hope of being accomplished.

9

CONCLUSION: HUMAN RIGHTS
AND DEMOCRACY

Although the number of political murders and disappearances in El Salvador has declined markedly over the last decade, the human rights situation has not fundamentally changed. Opposition politicians like Rubén Zamora once again live, work, and even campaign in El Salvador, but violence still severely limits their ability to organize. The press offers considerably more diversity than it did several years ago; but reporters are still shot by soldiers, and the liberal daily *Diario Latino* was burned to the ground in February 1991. The Jesuit-run Central American University is recovering from the massacre of its leadership in November 1989, but the killers, and those who ordered the crime, have still not been brought to justice. Most significantly, political killings, though less frequent than in the early 1980s, remain routine and continue to go unpunished.

During this same decade six national elections have been held, largely as a result of U.S. policy—one for a constituent assembly to draft a new constitution and then two for president and three for Legislative Assembly. By 1989, when the first peaceful transfer of presidential power from one party to another was accomplished in the eye of a storm of sustained army and guerrilla violence, one could reasonably ask, Why has the U.S. success in promoting elections in El Salvador not brought about more substantial human rights improvements? The reason lies in the limited nature of the political opening that elections have created and their failure to bring about the rule of law.

The two major sources of human rights violations in the last decade have been the military–death squad apparatus and, to a lesser extent, the guerrillas. Elections have left the power of each virtually untouched. Elected officials cannot easily exert authority over an insurgent army; however, their failure to exercise more than marginal influence over the Armed Forces of El Salvador, which supposedly operate at their command, lies at the heart of the country's still-tragic human rights situation.

The military has flouted the authority of the civilian president time and time again, from its refusal to honor a ten-day holiday truce negotiated between

President Duarte and the FMLN in December 1985, to its preventing Duarte from firing his air force commander in 1986, to the murder of the Jesuits and their household staff in November 1989.[1] The most glaring symbol of the weakness of the civilian government is its failure to convict a single military officer of a human rights violation despite a decade of military atrocities. The right to vote loses much of its luster when no matter who is elected, the army, air force, and security forces continue to kill, certain that they will never have to answer for their crimes. Democracy without the rule of law is not worthy of the name.

The failure to prosecute and convict military human rights violators on a regular basis—to make punishment the predictable result of politically motivated crime—allows the perpetrators of violence to terrorize the population at places and times of their choosing. And the continuance of terror—less selective in some years, more selective in others, but always determined by the will of military leaders rather than the rules of civilian justice—discourages the popular participation needed to establish genuine democracy.

Elected officials, powerless as they have been to end military murder and intimidation, have demonstrated no greater ability to undercut the guerrillas by addressing the grossly unequal economic and political relations that are the root causes of the war. The decade began with an ambitious land reform program, which was curtailed long before its initial aims had been realized. In the mid-1980s, Duarte's expansive promises to his populist base went unfulfilled. By the dawn of the 1990s, President Cristiani's ARENA government had succeeded in uniting both the moderate and militant wings of a popular movement against its antireformist policies.

From the outset the principal goal of U.S. policy has been to vanquish the guerrillas. Elections have been a component of that policy, incorporated primarily to marshal U.S. public and congressional support behind the war effort, as well as to offer the Salvadoran people an electoral alternative to the armed struggle. For a time, at least until the Jesuits and their staff were murdered, the Congress appeared satisfied that democracy was flowering in El Salvador. The massacre of the six priests, their housekeeper, and her daughter produced the most serious congressional questioning of U.S. policy toward El Salvador in a decade. Yet the failure of elections to produce democracy in El Salvador had been evident all along in the persistence of armed conflict and the inability of left-of-center politicians to participate in elections freely without fear of reprisals.

It may well be, now that the end of the Cold War has removed El Salvador from the prism of superpower rivalry, that the parties to the conflict can develop the shared tolerance of difference that is essential if genuine democracy is to take root and human rights are to be respected. Room for hope lies in the pursuit, more than a year later, of the peace talks initiated in January 1990 between the government and the guerrillas, with skilled mediation by the United Nations. Also encouraging is the acknowledgment by both the government and the guerrillas that reform of the armed forces is essential to establishing peace. Yet the extent to which the military will accept far-reaching reforms, including the purging and prosecution of human rights abusers from its ranks, remains open to serious question. The reform of the armed forces—and accountability for human rights abuses—is both the challenge and the hope of the future in El Salvador.

APPENDIX A

U.S. AID TO EL SALVADOR, 1980–1992
(millions of dollars)

Fiscal Year	Economic	Military	Total
1980	58.2	6.0	64.2
1981	113.6	35.5	149.4
1982	182.2	82.0	264.2
1983	245.5	81.3	326.8
1984	215.9	196.6	412.5
1985	434.0	136.2	570.2
1986	322.6	121.8	444.4
1987	462.9	111.5	574.4
1988	314.1	81.5	395.6
1989	307.0	81.4	388.4
1990	245.2	81.0	326.2
1991[a]	223.0	85.0	308.0
1992[b]	207.8	86.4	294.2
Total	3,332.3	1,186.2	4,518.5

Source: Congressional Research Service, Library of Congress, based on figures from U.S. Department of State, AID.

Note: Economic assistance includes Development Assistance; Economic Support Funds; food assistance (P.L. 480, Titles I and II); and disaster assistance.

  Military assistance includes Military Assistance Program funds, military training grants, and Foreign Military Sales financing.

[a]The figures are estimates. The Congress withheld half the military aid pending progress in the Jesuit murder investigation and in peace talks between the Salvadoran government and the FMLN. The administration released the withheld aid on January 15, 1991, but did not immediately provide it to the Salvadoran government.

[b]The figures represent the request from the administration to Congress.

APPENDIX B

PARTIAL CHRONOLOGY OF HUMAN RIGHTS
EVENTS IN EL SALVADOR, 1979–1991

1979

October 15: A group of young military officers overthrows the government of Gen. Carlos Humberto Romero and forms a ruling junta with prominent civilian politicians. The junta declares its intention to restore the rule of law, bring peace, and respect the 1962 Constitution.

October 16: The junta issues Decree 3, granting amnesty to all political prisoners and Salvadorans in exile.

October 26: The junta issues Decree 9, establishing the Special Committee to Investigate Missing Political Prisoners to discover the fate of the "disappeared" under the Romero and Molina regimes.

November 6: The junta formally dissolves ORDEN, the right-wing paramilitary organization responsible for many human rights abuses. However, no effective measures are taken to disband the death squads, which continue to operate.

November 23: The special commission recommends the prosecution of former Presidents Molina and Romero, as well as several high-ranking officials in their administrations, for human rights violations. Formal charges are never brought against these individuals. The commission fails to find still alive any of the people who had disappeared, although it did find the remains of some of the disappeared, as well as clandestine jails and torture centers. Although there are almost no political disappearances while the committee operates, they begin again after its final report in January 1980.

1980

January 3: Two of the three civilian members of the junta, Guillermo Manuel Ungo and Román Mayorga, resign along with all the civilian cabinet members after the military rejects civilian control over the armed forces.

January 22: The largest demonstration in the country's history takes place in San Salvador in commemoration of the 1932 rebellion and subsequent massacre. Sharpshooters and guards fire into the crowd from atop the National Palace, killing between twenty and fifty-two demonstrators.

February 8: The junta issues Decree 114, stating it will only recognize the validity of the 1962 Constitution insofar as it is compatible with its own objectives.

March 3: Christian Democrat Héctor Dada, who joined the junta following the resignations of Ungo and Mayorga, resigns to protest repression by the military. He is replaced by José Napoleón Duarte.

March 6: The junta declares a nationwide state of emergency. Pursuant to the Constitution, being in a state of emergency means the suspension of the freedoms of movement and residence, assembly, and expression and suspension of the inviolability of correspondence. Military tribunals are vested with jurisdiction over civilians charged with offenses against the peace and security of the state.

The junta promulgates an agrarian reform law. Many peasants are subsequently killed when they attempt to claim land under the reform, which is never fully implemented.

March 24: Archbishop Oscar Arnulfo Romero, a strong advocate of human rights and social reforms, is assassinated while saying mass in San Salvador. The judge initially responsible for investigating the archbishop's death later flees El Salvador after several death threats and an attempt on his life.

March 30: Security forces fire on people gathered for Archbishop Romero's funeral.

April: The FDR is established and begins to operate as the political arm of the revolutionary opposition.

May 7: Army Maj. Roberto D'Aubuisson and his supporters are arrested at a farm near Santa Tecla for plotting a coup. Also captured is a diary linking D'Aubuisson with the assassination of Archbishop Romero.

May 14: Thousands of Salvadorans fleeing into Honduras to escape army operations are attacked by Salvadoran troops on the ground and in helicopters, as well as by members of the paramilitary group ORDEN, as the victims cross the Sumpul River. At least six hundred are killed. The army turns increasingly to attacks on civilians living in guerrilla-controlled territory in order to deprive the guerrillas of a potential social base.

May 22: The junta issues two decrees modifying the Criminal Code and the Code of Criminal Procedure. Decree 264 expands the definition of terrorism and prohibits occupations of public buildings and places of employment and religious worship. Decree 265 bans the release on bond or parole of those accused or convicted of many politically motivated offenses.

June 24: Decree 296 is issued, prohibiting strikes by officials and employees of the state and its decentralized agencies and providing for immediate dismissal of those who organize strikes.

June 26: The Salvadoran military raids the National University, killing between twenty-two and forty students and beating and abusing many other students, faculty, and staff. The university closes. This incident is one of many attacks against educational institutions.

August 22: The junta issues Decree 366, empowering the executive to dissolve any professional association in a state agency or semiautonomous agency for participating in strikes or other interruptions of essential public services.

October 3: María Magdalena Henríquez, press secretary of the CDHES-NG, is abducted by uniformed police and is later found dead. Another human rights commission representative is found killed a few days later.

October: Five armed revolutionary groups form a coalition calling itself the Farabundo Martí National Liberation Front

November 1: Sixty-two people aged fourteen to twenty-two are abducted by security forces making a systematic search of two villages in Soyapango. Their bodies are later found, bearing marks of torture.

November 27: Six leaders of the FDR are kidnapped from San José High School in San Salvador, where they were preparing for a news conference. The badly mutilated corpses of the FDR leaders are later found east of the capital.

December 2: Four U.S. churchwomen (three nuns and a lay church worker) are picked up, sexually abused, and killed by National Guardsmen after leaving the principal airport. Several other religious workers are also killed in 1980 in circumstances implicating government forces. U.S. military and economic aid is suspended shortly after the churchwomen's bodies are discovered.

December 3: The junta issues Decree 507, modifying judicial procedures concerning crimes against the state. Military courts are given jurisdiction over so-called politically motivated crimes. The decree also allows for lengthy administrative detention, thus facilitating torture, and suspends traditional rules of evidence.

December 17: The Carter administration claims that the investigation into the killing of the churchwomen is progressing and restores U.S. economic aid.

1981

January 3: The president of the Salvadoran Institute for Agrarian Reform, José Rodolfo Viera, and two top U.S. officials of the AIFLD, Mark David Pearlman and Michael Hammer, are assassinated in the San Salvador Sheraton Hotel under orders from two National Guard officers Lt. Rodolfo Isidro López Sibrián and Capt. Eduardo Alfonso Avila. The officers are later absolved of the murders; their bodyguards, comvicted of the killings in 1986, are freed under the 1987 amnesty.

January 10: The FMLN launches a so-called final offensive nationwide but does not succeed in overthrowing the government.

The junta imposes a 7:00 P.M. to 5:00 A.M. curfew. Socorro Jurídico, the legal aid office of the San Salvador archdiocese, estimates that by February 18 the government has shot 168 people since the curfew was established.

January: *El Independiente,* the last independent newspaper in El Salvador, closes after eight of its employees are imprisoned and army tanks and trucks surround its office. It had been attacked on three other occasions, and its editor was the target of several assassination attempts.

January 14: Responding to the guerrilla offensive, the Carter administration restores military aid suspended after the U.S. churchwomen were killed.

January 17: President Jimmy Carter invokes special executive authority to send five million dollars in emergency military aid to El Salvador.

February 26: Decree 603 ratifies the closing of the National University.

March 17: As thousands of Salvadoran refugees attempt to flee across the Lempa River, the Salvadoran air force bombs them from helicopters while the army fires mortars and machine guns at them. Twenty to thirty are killed, and 189 are reported missing.

April 7: In the "massacre of Monte Carmelo," more than twenty people are taken forcibly from their homes in a suburb of San Salvador and shot, apparently by police and others collaborating with them.

May 29: The armed forces issue a list of 138 persons deemed responsible for the "chaos" in the country, including prominent civilian politicians.

October 15: Martial law and the curfew are formally lifted. However, abductions and killings by security forces still occur at night, leading many Salvadorans to continue observing the curfew.

October 20–29: A counterinsurgency operation by security forces on the southern bank of the Lempa River results in the murder or kidnapping of 147 noncombatants.

November: The CDHES-NG reports that at least four hundred bodies have been dumped at the El Playón lava bed over the past two years. The area, which is fifteen miles from San Salvador, is frequently patrolled by government troops. U.S. Embassy officials encounter six fresh bodies on a November 14 visit.

During an armed forces counterinsurgency operation in Cabañas, approximately one thousand fleeing civilians are trapped by helicopter and ground fire for thirteen days while Honduran troops block the border. Fifty to one hundred refugees are killed.

December 11: Massacres take place in the hamlet of El Mozote and nine other villages in Morazán in what comes to be known as the El Mozote massacres. Government troops murder up to one thousand peasants, including many children.

1982

January 28: U.S. President Reagan certifies that El Salvador has complied with the human rights conditions for receiving military assistance. He makes this certification every six months until late 1983, when he uses a pocket veto to kill a bill that would have extended the certification requirement.

January 30–31: Uniformed troops conduct operations in the San Antonio Abad neighborhood of San Salvador in which thirty-two civilians are killed and others are detained.

January 31: Army troops kill 150 civilians in Nueva Trinidad, a hamlet in Chalatenango.

March: At least eleven hamlets in San Vicente are attacked from the air during military "pacification programs," which include blanket bombings of inhabited villages. On March 10, five thousand peasants from the San Esteban Catarina jurisdiction of San Vicente fleeing from army troops and bombings are pursued by helicopter and mortar fire. Later they are caught in a surprise bombing in the area where they have taken refuge.

March 10: A death list of thirty-five Salvadoran and foreign journalists is issued by a group calling itself the Anticommunist Alliance of El Salvador.

March 17: Four Dutch journalists are killed in what may have been an army ambush. One of them was detained by Treasury Police on March 11.

March 28: Elections for the Constituent Assembly are held in an atmosphere of intimidation and violence. The electorate is presented with a limited choice because the parties of the left cannot participate freely and safely. The right wing receives the most votes, and the PCN and the ARENA party put together a governing coalition.

April 22: Roberto D'Aubuisson, the ARENA leader implicated in the murder of Archbishop Romero, is chosen as president of the Constituent Assembly.

April 27: The Constituent Assembly issues Decree 3, recognizing the Constitution of 1962 as the basic law of the republic and abrogating previous government statutes of exception to the Constitution, including parts of the land reform program. Decree 507, which denies many due process rights, remains in effect.

April 29: The presidency of El Salvador goes to Alvaro Magaña, a banker with close ties to the military. Three vice presidents are selected, representing the PCN, ARENA, and the Christian Democratic Party.

May 18: Decree 6 is issued, suspending key provisions of the land reform program. Massive evictions of peasants from the land ensue.

May 31: Socorro Jurídico, the legal aid office of the Archdiocese of San Salvador, is reorganized. Socorro Jurídico continues to operate but is no longer associated with the archdiocese, and a new office, Tutela Legal, is created. It is mandated to compile statistics on violence by the guerrillas as well as the government.

Late July: The leader of the Christian Democratic Party, José Napoleón Duarte, charges the extreme right with the murders of hundreds of Christian Democratic mayors and other activists.

July 27: The Reagan administration again certifies that the Salvadoran government is meeting the human rights requirements for receiving U.S. military aid.

August: During a military campaign in San Vicente, government troops massacre three hundred to four hundred civilians.

August 3: President Magaña and four of the five parties that participated in the March elections sign the Pact of Apaneca, establishing the basic platform of the government. Respect for human rights is among the stated objectives, and a governmental Human Rights Commission is established to "protect, watch over, and promote" human rights.

October 8–17: Seventeen leaders of labor unions and the FDR are kidnapped by heavily armed men. The army later discloses that eight are held in military jails.

1983

February 22: Uniformed army soldiers abduct people from the farming cooperative of Las Hojas and surrounding communities in the department of Sonsonate. Approximately seventy are killed. Some corpses are found with their hands tied behind their backs, shot in the back of the head. The CDH later submits a confidential report to President Magaña, but no significant disciplinary action is taken.

March 16: Marianela García Villas, president of the CDHES-NG, is killed in an army ambush of a group of displaced persons.

May 4: The Constituent Assembly issues Decree 210, declaring amnesty for certain politically motivated crimes committed by civilians, whether under prosecution or not. Five hundred thirty-three political prisoners are released by June 24. The law also applies to those who turn themselves in.

May 25: Guerrillas kill a U.S. military adviser, Lt. Comdr. Albert A. Schaufelberger III, while he waits in his car for his girlfriend at the Catholic University in San Salvador.

August 25: Treasury Police arrest Pedro Daniel Alvarado Rivera, who "confesses" to the May 25 FMLN execution of Lt. Comdr. Schaufelberger. On November 12 the U.S. Embassy states that Alvarado was not involved in the killing and that his confession was obtained under duress. Two and a half years later he is freed by the military judge.

September: Following a September 25 confrontation between the army and the guerrillas in the town of Tenancingo, twenty-five miles northeast of the capital, the armed forces undertake a bombing raid that kills about one hundred civilians.

October 7: Víctor Manuel Quintanilla Ramos, the highest-ranking FDR spokesperson still in El Salvador, is found strangled along with three other victims. A death squad takes credit for the slayings. His death demonstrates the impossibility of any FDR representative taking part in the electoral process in the upcoming 1984 presidential elections.

Mid-November: Troops of the U.S.-trained Atlacatl Battalion kill several score civilians in the towns of Copapayo, San Nicolás, and La Escopeta, about forty-five miles northeast of the capital. Twenty women and children are taken inside a house and shot; at least thirty people drown when soldiers firing automatic weapons drive them into Lake Suchitlán.

November 30: President Reagan pocket-vetoes the bill that would have continued to make U.S. military aid and arms sales to El Salvador conditional on certification that the government is "making a concerted and significant effort" to respect human rights and is achieving control over the armed forces. However, he allows legislation to take effect that withholds 30 percent of the military aid authorized for El Salvador until a verdict is reached in the case of the four U.S. churchwomen killed in 1980.

December 11: Vice President George Bush visits El Salvador and meets with top military leaders. He reportedly makes explicit threats that U.S. aid will end unless death squad activities and the disappearances of civilians are curbed, certain active-duty officers connected with the violence are removed, and the 1984 presidential elections are conducted without problems. The frequency of death squad killings diminishes significantly in coming months.

1984

February 24: The Legislative Assembly enacts Decree 50, the Law of Criminal Procedure Applicable during the Suspension of Constitutional Guarantees, formally replacing Decree 507 of the junta. Many provisions of the latter law are maintained. Incommunicado administrative detention is permitted for up to fifteen days. Appeal proceedings for convictions by military courts are instituted.

April and May: Fifteen hundred Salvadorans flee rural areas of northern Morazán when the FMLN attempts to forcibly recruit them.

May 6: The Christian Democrat leader José Napoleón Duarte is elected president of El Salvador, defeating Roberto D'Aubuisson of the ARENA party, whom Duarte in later years accuses of being the intellectual author of the murder of Archbishop Romero. Turnout is high, and the vote count appears fair.

May 25: Five former National Guardsmen are convicted of the 1980 murder of the four U.S. churchwomen. They are given the maximum sentence, thirty years' imprisonment. This is the first time that members of the regular Salvadoran security forces have been convicted of a politically motivated murder. Evidence of orders from higher up and a cover-up is not investigated.

July 17–22: Salvadoran army troops massacre sixty-eight civilians in the vicinity of Los Llanitos, Cabañas.

August: President Duarte announces the establishment of a commission to investigate five well-known political killings, including massacres in the villages of Armenia and Las Hojas, the assassination of Archbishop Romero, and the murders of several U.S. civilians.

August 28–30: Killings of civilians by the army occur in and around Las Vueltas, Chalatenango, culminating in a massacre on the banks of the Gualsinga River. At least fifty die, and others are missing. Elliott Abrams, U.S. assistant secretary of state, denies that this massacre or the massacre at Los Llanitos has occurred.

1985

March 1: Americas Watch opens a field office in San Salvador.

March 7: The Clara Elizabeta Ramírez Front of the FMLN assassinates Lt. Col. Ricardo Aristides Cienfuegos, head of COPREFA, at a San Salvador tennis club.

March 31: The Christian Democratic Party wins a majority of seats in the Legislative Assembly and a majority of municipal offices. The General Staff of the Armed Forces declines rightist demands to void the elections because of fraud.

May 16: The FMLN kills José Roberto Araujo, a military judge, in his car after he drops his daughter off at school.

June: The Legislative Assembly dismisses Attorney General José Francisco Guerrero, citing his failure to take convincing action in the assassinations of Archbishop Romero and Attorney General Mario Zamora Rivas.

The new minister of justice, Dr. Santiago Mendoza Aguilar, announces plans for a penal reform, including the establishment of a special commission to investigate conditions at Mariona prison, where male political prisoners are held. At the end of June, he announces the dismissal of twenty employees of the Ministry of Justice for their abuse of authority.

June 19: Members of the PRTC, part of the FMLN, attack off-duty U.S. Marines sitting in a café in the Zona Rosa neighborhood of San Salvador. Four marines and nine civilians are killed.

July: The Legislative Assembly ratifies the Judicial Reform Program agreement with AID. The $9.2 million U.S.-funded program provides for a Revisory Commission on Salvadoran Legislation; a Judicial Protection Unit to improve security for participants in criminal justice proceedings; a Commission on Investigations, consisting of a Special Investigative Unit and a Forensic Laboratory; and judicial administration and training programs.

September 10: The daughter of the president, Inés Guadalupe Duarte and a friend are kidnapped and held hostage by the FMLN. They and several mayors, kidnapped in prior months, are released on October 24 in exchange for political prisoners held by the government. The parties to the conflict agree not to target each other's family members.

October: The Central American University, José Simeón Cañas, run by the Jesuits, opens the Institute of Human Rights (IDHUCA).

November: José Vladimir Centeno and his brother Jaime Ernesto are subjected to a media trial for their alleged involvement in the October 26 FMLN kidnapping of Col. Omar Napoleón Avalos that illustrates the lack of effective due process. Their videotaped confession is broadcast on November 18, and they are subsequently made to appear at a news conference. Later they claim they were forced to rehearse their confession under torture. The telephone workers' union, to which their father belongs, calls a strike in support of their release. Three union officials are arrested on November 23.

November 22: President Duarte makes a major statement on labor policy at a time of renewed union activity. While granting some of the public employees' economic demands, he also announces measures to prevent strikes.

December: The Supreme Court holds that the dismissal of Attorney General Guerrero by the Legislative Assembly was unconstitutional. He is reinstated.

1986

January 10: The Salvadoran Armed Forces launch Operation Phoenix, an offensive to remove rebels from their traditional stronghold on Guazapa volcano. One of the stated objectives is to dislodge the masas—the civilian population that supports the guerrillas. Many civilians are captured and forcibly relocated by the army.

January 28: Fifty-six families begin resettling the town of Tenancingo, which was abandoned after air force bombardment in 1983. Under the sponsorship of the Archdiocese of San Salvador and Fundasal (a Salvadoran nonprofit organization), an effort is made to rebuild this town and secure guarantees by both sides in the conflict to stay away.

February: Three new death squads announce their existence with communiqués to the press.

Two National Guardsmen are convicted of the January 1981 murder of two U.S. labor advisers and a Salvadoran agrarian reform leader. Lieutenant López Sibrián and Captain Avila had been indicted for planning the assassinations, but charges against them were dismissed for insufficient evidence.

March 14: The Legislative Assembly extends the state of emergency, which has continued almost uninterrupted since 1980, for yet another thirty days but exempts freedom of expression from restrictions.

April: At the petition of the armed forces high command, the Legislative Assembly once again restricts freedom of expression when it again extends the state of emergency.

May 1: Two members of the coffee workers' union and their friend disappear in Santa Ana upon their return from a union march in San Salvador. Their mothers occupy the National Cathedral in protest, but the boys remain disappeared.

May–June: Ten leaders of COMADRES and the CDHES-NG are arrested and spend months in jail before being freed in a prisoner exchange, at which time they return to their work.

June: Peasants displaced by Operation Phoenix start to repopulate the area of El Barillo, Cuscatlán, in the company of foreign church workers. The foreigners are subsequently deported.

July: Displaced persons return to San José Las Flores, Chalatenango.

September 14: Msgr. Ricardo Urioste states in his homily at the National Cathedral that for the previous forty-five days the army has stopped food supplies from reaching six hundred civilians in San José Las Flores. This is one of many instances in which the armed forces restrict food deliveries to civilians.

1987

January: The state of emergency ends as twenty-seven right-wing deputies boycott voting in the Legislative Assembly, precluding the conduct of legislative business.

February 28: Decree 50, which had established special procedures for those detained for "security" reasons, lapses by its own terms. The expiration of the state of emergency prevents its renewal.

June 15: The Maximiliano Hernández Martínez Anticommunist Brigade, one of the most notorious paramilitary groups of the early 1980s, reappears with the publication of a death list threatening fourteen students and teachers at the National University.

July 28: The bodies of five young men are exhumed from a well in the village of Los Palitos, San Miguel, pursuant to a court order. They were killed on May 21, allegedly by members of the Arce Battalion.

August 7: President Duarte signs the Central American peace plan, obligating the government to negotiate with the FMLN, to take steps to increase political freedoms, to facilitate the return of refugees, to declare amnesty for politically motivated offenses, and to respect human rights.

October 10: A total of 4,300 Salvadoran refugees return from Mesa Grande, Honduras. Most move back to their original villages, many in eastern Chalatenango. Their resettlement is a concession by the Salvadoran military, which had long opposed the repopulation of conflict zones.

October 26: Herbert Ernesto Anaya Sanabría, head of the CDHES-NG, is murdered by unknown gunmen near his home in San Salvador.

October 27: The Christian Democrat–dominated Legislative Assembly grants amnesty to more than four hundred prisoners accused of politically motivated offenses. The law also effectively absolves all military and paramilitary groups for thousands of killings and other crimes attributed to them before October 22, 1987. The only politically motivated crime not forgiven under the amnesty is the 1980 assassination of Archbishop Romero.

November 8: Days before the two principal leaders of the FDR are to return from exile, the bodies of two young men are found on the road between La Libertad and San Salvador. The letters FDR are scrawled in red ink on the chests of both bodies.

November 21: Rubén Zamora, leader of the MPSC and vice president of the FDR, returns from exile.

November 22: President Duarte announces that the SIU has uncovered an important witness in the Romero assassination: the driver of the getaway car, whose testimony he summarizes on television.

November 23: Guillermo Manuel Ungo, president of the MNR and vice presidential candidate in 1972 when Duarte was presidential candidate, returns from exile to resume political activity inside El Salvador. In exile he was president of the FDR.

1988

January 5: The government claims in a television broadcast that the murder of Herbert Anaya has been solved, based on the confession of a nineteen-year-old boy, who said that he served as a lookout for FMLN assassins. His statement was made during twelve days of incommunicado detention, and on February 20 he recants the confession and denies any involvement. He is eventually freed for lack of evidence.

January 8: The head of intelligence for the army high command writes to the heads of the Catholic and Lutheran churches in El Salvador, asking them to "impede" the visits of foreign religious workers in areas of conflict. This is part of a campaign by the Salvadoran military to obstruct the activities of international relief and church workers in conflict zones.

February 17: Six civilians are killed when an FMLN mortar falling short of its target lands on their house just outside the Sixth Brigade barracks in Usulután.

May 11: Armed plainclothesmen kill Jorge Alberto Serrano Panameño, the military judge who was presiding over the trial of alleged death squad members engaged in a kidnapping-for-profit ring and in the 1985 murder of U.S. Marines and other civilians known as the Zona Rosa case. On July 28, Justice Minister Julio Alfredo Samayoa announces that he has proof that members of ARENA were involved in the killing. No arrests are made.

June 30: U.S. Secretary of State George Shultz visits El Salvador and reportedly presses top Salvadoran military officials to curb human rights abuses.

July 18: The Salvadoran Supreme Court approves the lower courts' grant of amnesty, under the October 1987 amnesty, to those charged with the 1983 massacre of peasants at the Las Hojas farming cooperative in Sonsonate.

September 21: Soldiers from the Jiboa Battalion of the Fifth Brigade massacre ten villagers from San Francisco, in San Vicente Department. The army first contends that the villagers were "subversives" killed by soldiers in "fierce combat," then claims that guerrillas killed the victims in the hope that the armed forces would be blamed.

1989

February 3: U.S. Vice President Dan Quayle visits El Salvador and delivers a sharp warning on human rights and the need to resolve the San Francisco case.

February 13: Soldiers of the Atlacatl Battalion attack an FMLN field hospital in El Chupadero, Chalatenango, killing ten people, including two women, a Mexican doctor and a Salvadoran nurse, both of whom were apparently raped.

February 16: In San Salvador, FMLN guerrillas kill Miguel Castellanos, an editor of the journal *Análisis* and ex-commander of the FPL, who collaborated extensively with the government after his capture in 1985.

March 12: The Armed Forces General Staff announces its discovery that a massacre had been carried out at San Francisco and subsequently covered up by the head of military intelligence at the Fifth Brigade. The case is consigned to a civilian court.

March 15: Dr. Francisco Peccorini, a professor of theology at the National University and a leading critic of the administration, is killed by the FMLN in San Salvador.

March 18–19: On the eve of the national elections, members of the Salvadoran Armed Forces kill two journalists, Roberto Navas and Mauricio Pineda Deleón; wound a third, Luis Galdámez; and fire on a vehicle carrying a fourth, Cornel Lagrouw, who is wounded in cross fire and dies en route to the hospital.

March 19: Alfredo Cristiani, of the ARENA party, is elected president.

April 14: The FMLN throws dynamite at the house of Vice President–elect José Francisco Merino López, slightly injuring a young girl and seriously damaging the house.

April 15: An Argentine doctor and a French nurse are killed at an FMLN field hospital after being captured, along with several Salvadoran FMLN personnel and a wounded combatant, by air force soldiers in San Ildefonso, San Vicente. An autopsy performed later in France shows that the nurse was tortured, mutilated, and probably raped.

April 19: Attorney General José Roberto García Alvarado is killed by the FMLN at an intersection in San Salvador by an explosive placed on top of his vehicle.

Treasury Police raid and search the offices of four organizations working with the displaced, the unemployed, and women; seventy-five are arrested, and several detainees are tortured.

May 22: Nine bus passengers are killed when an FMLN mine explodes under the bus at El León Pintado, Santa Ana.

June 1: President Cristiani is inaugurated.

June 9: Dr. José Alejandro Antonio Rodríguez Porth, newly appointed minister of the presidency, is killed along with his driver and orderly by shots fired by two unknown men in front of his San Salvador home. The FMLN denies involvement but remains the prime suspect.

June 21: Sister Mary Stanislaus Mackey, a U.S. citizen, is shot and wounded by armed men in a pickup truck who pull up alongside her vehicle.

June 30: Edgar Chacón, a well-known conservative theoretician, is shot dead in his car in San Salvador.

July: Soldiers from the First Brigade and the Atlacatl Battalion arrest seven young men from the Tres Ceibas and Camotepeque farming communities north of San Salvador and brutally beat them, resulting in the death of two. César Vielman Joya Martínez, one of two soldiers charged in the killings, flees the country; once abroad he alleges that he was a member of a death squad operating out of the First Brigade.

August 19: Two union members, Juan Francisco Massín and Sari Cristiani Chan-Chan, last seen in the custody of air force soldiers, disappear.

September 18: National Policemen and National Guardsmen arrest seventy-four people affiliated with the FENASTRAS labor federation and mistreat and rape some.

October 17: Ana Isabel Casanova, daughter of Col. Edgardo Casanova Vejar, commander of the Military School and cousin of former defense minister Gen. Carlos Eugenio Vides Casanova, is gunned down as she leaves her family home in Santa Tecla.

October 19: Explosions damage the homes of Rubén Zamora and Aronette Díaz, leaders of the UDN. Two of Zamora's bodyguards are injured.

October 30: Shells fired in an FMLN attack on the headquarters of the Armed Forces General Staff explode in nearby streets, killing a gas station attendant and wounding at least fifteen people.

October 31: Four persons are injured when a bomb explodes during predawn hours in the office of the COMADRES.

At 12:30 P.M. a powerful bomb destroys the headquarters of the FENASTRAS labor federation, killing ten people and injuring more than thirty.

November 2: The FMLN breaks off peace talks with the government.

November 11: FMLN guerrillas catapult six homemade mortars at the National Guard barracks in San Salvador, injuring three soldiers, killing two children, and wounding five other civilians. That evening the FMLN launches the most powerful military offensive of the war with coordinated attacks nationwide. Hundreds of civilians die over the next few weeks, as guerrillas and army soldiers wage pitched battles in major cities and air force firepower is deployed to dislodge guerrillas from densely populated neighborhoods.

November 12: Soldiers of the Second Brigade summarily execute several civilians and wounded or captured guerrillas in La Unión, Santa Ana.

November 16: In the predawn hours soldiers of the U.S.-trained Atlacatl Battalion, under orders from Col. Alfredo Guillermo Benavides Moreno, head of the Military School, enter the Central American University. They burn offices at the Monsignor Romero Pastoral Center and kill six Jesuit priests, including the rector and vice-rector of the university and the director of its Human Rights Institute, as well as their housekeeper and her daughter. The soldiers attempt to blame the FMLN for the crime by leaving a note supposedly signed by the FMLN.

November 18: Soldiers summarily execute seven unarmed young men in Colonia San Luis, Cuscatancingo, a northern suburb of San Salvador.

November 23: Lucía Barrera de Cerna, who testifies that she saw uniformed men firing at the Jesuit residence the night of the murders, is brought to the United States, where she is interrogated for four days by Salvadoran and U.S. officials, who subsequently assert that her testimony is of no value.

November 25: Jennifer Jean Casolo, a U.S. citizen and coordinator of delegations for Christian Education Seminars, is arrested after a large cache of weapons is found in her backyard.

November 29: Former Supreme Court president Francisco José ("Chachi") Guerrero is shot dead on a street in San Salvador by the FMLN.

The FMLN apparently kills five journalists after capturing them at the headquarters of the government news agency. The FMLN received fire from the building during its occupation of the rich San Salvador neighborhood of Escalón.

December 5: Mario Roberto Alvarez, secretary general of the Santa Ana local of the SICAFE coffee workers' union, is shot and severely injured by an unidentified man in plain clothes. He is the fourth SICAFE director to be shot—two died—in little more than a year.

Two members of the San Cayetano El Rosario cooperative in Ahuachapán are taken from their homes by uniformed soldiers and civil defense members. They remain disappeared until the announcement in February 1991 that they were in fact murdered.

December 13: Jennifer Jean Casolo is released on grounds of insufficient evidence and expelled from the country.

December 20: Col. Carlos Armando Avilés tells a U.S. Army major in El Salvador that the Salvadoran military and Col. Alfredo Benavides Morales are implicated in the murder of the Jesuits, according to subsequent testimony by the U.S. major. Avilés denies the truth of the major's testimony.

December 29: Four more members of the San Cayetano El Rosario cooperative are captured by armed men in civilian dress deployed with uniformed soldiers. The four men remain disappeared.

1990

January 2: Unbeknownst to U.S. Ambassador William Walker, the U.S. major informs his superiors in the U.S. Military Group at the embassy about the information from Colonel Avilés implicating the Salvadoran military in the massacre of the Jesuits. That same day Ambassador Walker tells a U.S. congressman that FMLN guerrillas might have committed the Jesuit killings dressed in army uniforms.

January 3: Without informing Ambassador Walker, the head of the U.S. Military Group in San Salvador confronts Col. René Emilio Ponce, chief of staff of the Salvadoran Armed Forces, with the U.S. major's information and names Colonel Avilés as the source. Avilés denies having made such statements but does not pass a lie detector test. He is confined to base, and his scheduled promotion to military attaché in Washington, D.C., is canceled.

January 7: President Cristiani announces that the Salvadoran military was involved in the murders of the Jesuits.

January 11: The government agrees to renew peace talks with the FMLN under the auspices of the United Nations. Several rounds of talks are held over the course of the year.

January 12: Héctor Oquelí Colindres, deputy secretary-general of the MNR, and Gilda Amparo Flores Arévalo, a Guatemalan attorney, are kidnapped by plainclothesmen in Guatemala City and found dead later that day.

January 13: President Cristiani identifies nine army soldiers, including Colonel Benavides Moreno, as those responsible for the murders of the Jesuits.

January 19: Fourth Criminal Court Judge Ricardo Zamora orders that the soldiers be provisionally detained for their role in the murders of the Jesuits. One of the nine implicated soldiers remains at large.

February 4: It is reported that senior armed forces officers met twice within hours of the Jesuit murders, suggesting that they may have known far more about the massacre far earlier than has been acknowledged to date.

February 8: The judge in the case of the San Francisco massacre by the army dismisses charges against nine of the defendants but orders Maj. Mauricio Beltrán Granados and Cpl. Rafael Rosales Villalobos to stand trial.

February 11: Two rockets fired from a Salvadoran air force helicopter hit a house in Corral de Piedra, Chalatenango, killing five civilians and wounding sixteen.

February 23: Former President Duarte dies of cancer.

April 11: The state of emergency lifted.

April 30: The U.S. House of Representatives Special Task Force on El Salvador, led by Rep. Joseph Moakley, releases a report on the progress of the Jesuit case that describes the investigation as completely stalled. The report concludes that none of the soldiers currently detained would likely have been arrested or charged if not for the testimony of the U.S. major (later identified as Maj. Eric Buckland).

May 2: An appeals court in San Vicente, ruling on the San Francisco army massacre, affirms the lower court ruling that Major Beltrán should be tried but reverses the decision to try Corporal Rosales.

May 21: The Arms Control and Foreign Policy Caucus of the U.S. Congress releases a report stating that fourteen of the fifteen highest-ranking army officers in El Salvador had commanded troops responsible for atrocities at some point during their careers.

June 6: Arce Battalion Cpl. José Antonio Orellana Guevara, who was arrested for the March 19, 1989, shooting death of the journalist Mauricio Pineda

Deleón, is acquitted after thirty nonuniformed soldiers enter the courtroom during the trial.

July 6: The Salvadoran military announces that it has detained Lt. Col. Camilo Hernández, who is accused of covering up the murder of the Jesuits and the two women by ordering the burning of the logbooks of the Military School.

July 26: Negotiators for the government and for the guerrillas reach a formal agreement on international verification of human rights conditions. Although the accord originally envisions U.N. verification following a cease-fire, the international body later agrees to begin monitoring compliance with the accord in 1991. Additional talks produce no new accords by the end of 1990.

August 15: Rep. Moakley issues a press statement accusing the Salvadoran high command of engaging in "a conspiracy to obstruct justice in the Jesuits' case." Noting that military officers have withheld, destroyed, and falsified evidence and repeatedly committed perjury in the case, he expresses doubt that this would occur "without at least the tacit consent of the High Command."

August 27: Army Sgt. Oscar Armando Solórzano Esquivel is arrested for perjury regarding the Jesuit murders.

September 5: Judge Zamora orders two soldiers, Héctor Antonio Guerrero Maravilla and Rufino Barrientos Ramos, detained on perjury charges in connection with the Jesuit murders.

September 27–28: The U.S. Trade Representative (USTR) holds hearings on labor rights violations in El Salvador. Representatives from Salvadoran trade unions—the UNOC and the FENASTRAS—and U.S. human rights and labor organizations, including Americas Watch and the AFL-CIO, submit petitions documenting labor rights violations. If the USTR decides that the Salvadoran government is not guaranteeing labor rights, trade benefits must by law be terminated; the decision is still pending at the end of 1990.

October 18: Rep. Moakley releases a statement announcing that in a signed affidavit, Major Buckland informed the FBI in January 1990 that he had learned that Colonel Benavides Morales had threatened the Jesuits at least ten days before the November 16 Jesuit murders. The affidavit stated that Defense Minister René Emilio Ponce (then head of the Joint Chiefs of Staff) had knowledge of those threats and had sent an intermediary to try to dissuade Colonel Benavides Morales from carrying them out. Major Buckland later retracts his story. Although the U.S. Embassy shares this information with President Cristiani, neither informs investigators or Judge Zamora until Moakley urgently requests that they do so.

November 5: The U.S. Congress cuts the $85 million in military aid to El Salvador by one half in 1991. The legislation limits military aid to $42.5 million unless President Bush determines that the FMLN is not negotiating in good faith in the U.N.-sponsored peace talks with the government, has launched an offensive that threatens the survival of the government, acquires lethal military aid from abroad, or engages in violence against noncombatants, in which case full aid will be restored. The law also calls for a complete cutoff of military assistance if President Bush determines that significant progress is not being made on the Jesuit case, if the government walks out of peace negotiations with the FMLN, or if it engages in violence against noncombatants.

November 20: Guerrillas launch a series of attacks against military and strategic targets throughout the country in order, they say, to "punish" the military and "accelerate" peace negotiations. Initial reports indicate the year-end offensive resulted in scores of dead or wounded combatants, as well as approximately two dozen civilian deaths and one hundred wounded.

December 6: Judge Zamora orders the defendants in the massacre of the Jesuits to stand trial.

1991

January 2: The FMLN shoots down a U.S. helicopter, which is transporting three U.S. Army servicemen, near the hamlet of San Francisco in Morazán Department. One of the U.S. officers is killed in the crash; the other two are allegedly executed by a guerrilla on the ground.

January 8: The two principal government prosecutors in the case of the murder of the Jesuits and their housekeeper and her daughter resign, charging the military with obstruction of justice and the Attorney General's Office with not "pursuing a clean investigation."

January 15: The Bush administration makes the determination allowing it to restore aid in full to the Salvadoran government unless the government and guerrillas reach a cease-fire in sixty days.

January 21: Armed men dressed in military uniforms massacre fifteen men, women, and children belonging to one family in the village of El Zapote Abajo near San Salvador. Two brothers—who had previously been members of the military—and a former civil defense member are captured by the authorities in connection with the crime. Two sisters are also detained and charged. The motive for the massacre and involvement by armed forces units remain unclear.

February 8: The National Police announces the arrest of four civil defense members for the murder of two members of the San Cayetano El Rosario cooperative in Ahuachapán who were captured on December 5, 1989. This marks the first official acknowledgment that any of six members of the co-op who disappeared in December 1989 were in fact dead. The fate of the other four co-op members remains unknown.

February 9: The offices of the daily *Diario Latino* are burned to the ground, forcing it to close down. A greatly reduced version of the paper begins publication several days later.

February 22: In a step hailed by the U.S. State Department as a "breakthrough," five members of the army high command ask the minister of justice to question ten middle-ranking officers who participated in a meeting at the Military School the evening before the massacre of the Jesuits and their staff. All but three of the officers had already testified, however, and new interviews failed to yield anything of substance. At the same time, the military officers insist that "institutional responsibility in the [Jesuit] case does not exist."

February 28: Guillermo Manuel Ungo dies of complications from surgery in Mexico City.

February 28: FMLN commanders, in a departure from previous policy, announce that the rebels will not enforce a nationwide boycott of voting in the upcoming elections for legislative and municipal posts.

March 10: Elections are held for Legislative Assembly and local positions. The governing ARENA party loses its absolute majority in the assembly and the left-of-center CD and UDN win seats in the legislature for the first time. The elections were preceded by a surge of violence against opposition candidates and campaign workers.

APPENDIX C

HUMAN RIGHTS AND HUMANITARIAN ORGANIZATIONS

Americas Watch, 485 Fifth Avenue, New York, N.Y. 10017, and 1522 K Street, N.W., Suite 910, Washington, D.C. 20005

Amnesty International, 99–119 Rosebery Avenue, London EC1R 4RE, U.K., and 322 8th Avenue, New York, N.Y. 10001

Central American Refugee Center, P. O. Box 53113, Washington, D.C. 20009

Committee in Solidarity with the People of El Salvador (CISPES), 19 West 21st Street, 2d floor, New York, N.Y. 10010

Committee to Protect Journalists, 485 Fifth Avenue, New York, N.Y. 10017

El Rescate Human Rights Department, 1813 West Pico Boulevard, Los Angeles, Calif. 90006

El Salvador Committee for Human Rights, 20 Compton Terrace, London N1 2UN, U.K.

El Salvador On Line, Washington Center for Central American Studies, P. O. Box 11095, Takoma Park, Md. 20912

Inter-American Commission on Human Rights, 1889 F Street, N.W., Washington, D.C. 20006

International Human Rights Law Group, 733 15th Street, N.W., Suite 1000, Washington, D.C. 20005

The Lawyers Committee for Human Rights, 330 Seventh Avenue, 10th floor, New York, N.Y. 10001

National Lawyers Guild, 853 Broadway, Room 1705, New York, N.Y. 10003

Socorro Jurídico Cristiano, Apartado Postal (06) 294, San Salvador,
El Salvador

Oficina de Tutela Legal del Arzobispado, Apartado 2253, San Salvador,
El Salvador

NOTES

CHAPTER 1: A BRIEF HISTORY

1. LeMoyne, "El Salvador's Forgotten War," pp. 106–7. Tutela Legal, the human rights office of the Archdiocese of San Salvador, and its predecessor, Socorro Jurídico, have compiled statistics on civilians killed on both sides of the armed conflict using documented cases and estimates when they were unable to conduct on-site investigations. These figures show more than forty thousand civilian casualties over the course of the decade.

2. Inter-American Development Bank, cited in Barry, *El Salvador*, p. 177.

3. The figures, from 1988 and 1989, were provided by the Inter-Hemispheric Education Resource Center, Albuquerque, N.Mex.

4. Barry, *El Salvador*, pp. 109–10, 177; *CEPAL Review* (Economic Commission for Latin America), April 1984.

5. Statistics from UNICEF, cited in El Rescate Human Rights Department, *El Salvador Chronology*, June 1990, p. 6.

6. Burke, "El sistema de plantación," pp. 473–86.

7. U.S. Department of State, AID, Office of Public Safety, *Report*, p. 23.

8. Ibid., p. 8.

9. Webre, *José Napoleón Duarte*, pp. 176–78.

10. *Report on the Situation of Human Rights in El Salvador*, pp. 153–58.

11. Arnson, *El Salvador*, pp. 34–35.

12. Ibid., pp. 43, 42.

13. "Central America 1980: Nicaragua, El Salvador, Guatemala," findings of an investigative mission sponsored by the Unitarian Universalist Service Committee, p. 18; *Amnesty International Annual Report, 1980*, p. 134.

14. Arnson, *El Salvador*, p. 49.

15. Dunkerley, *Power in the Isthmus*, p. 405.

16. Douglas Farah, "Death Squad Began as Scout Troop," *Washington Post*, August 29, 1988.

17. Bonner, *Weakness and Deceit*, pp. 311, 313.

18. Ibid., p. 138.

19. Robert J. McCartney, "U.S. Seen Assisting Duarte in Sunday's Salvadoran Vote," *Washington Post*, May 4, 1984; Philip Taubman, "CIA Said to Have Given Money to Two Salvadoran Parties," *New York Times*, May 12, 1984.

20. A disappearance occurs when government forces or their agents take a victim into custody but deny holding him or her. This practice has been used as a tool of repression in many countries. The victims are often tortured and killed and their bodies disposed of secretly. See Amnesty International, *Disappearances: A Workbook* (London: Amnesty International, 1981).

21. Dunkerley, *Power in the Isthmus,* p. 410.
22. Dillon, "Dateline El Salvador," p. 164.
23. Barry, *El Salvador,* p. 84.
24. Lane, "Pilot Shark of El Salvador," p. 28. This incident is also related in chap. 3. The Iran-contra scandal erupted when the U.S. Justice Department revealed in the fall of 1986 that profits from the secret sale of arms to Iran had been diverted to the Nicaraguan contras. The diversion took place when the Congress had banned military aid to the contra rebels.
25. Jefferson Morley, "Prisoner Duarte," *New York Review of Books,* December 4, 1986. This incident is related in chap. 6.
26. Lindsey Gruson, "Ten People Slain near Salvador Village," *New York Times,* September 24, 1988.
27. Morley, "Prisoner Duarte."
28. See Americas Watch, *Compliance, January 1988;* and Americas Watch, *Compliance, August 1979–August 1988.*
29. Americas Watch, *Human Rights,* pp. 7–8.
30. Gibb and Smyth, *El Salvador.*

CHAPTER 2: THE ASSAULT ON CIVIL SOCIETY

1. Targeted killings, also known as extrajudicial executions, are intentional murders of selected individuals, as distinct from indiscriminate attacks.
2. Americas Watch and American Civil Liberties Union (ACLU), *Report,* p. xxxiv; Americas Watch and ACLU, *Third Supplement ,* pp. 29–31; Americas Watch, *Civilian Toll,* pp. 17–18; Americas Watch, *Year of Reckoning,* p. 93.
3. Americas Watch, *Carnage Again,* pp. 40–41.
4. Americas Watch, *Year of Reckoning,* pp. 127–28, 146–47.
5. Frank Smyth, "The Truth Will Out," *Village Voice,* July 25, 1990.
6. James A. Goldston, "Down the Salvadoran Drain," *New York Times,* September 28, 1990.
7. Bennet, "Burying the Jesuits," p. 116.
8. Americas Watch and ACLU, *Report,* p. xxiv; U.S. Department of State, *Country Reports for 1989,* p. 569. The armed forces numbered fifteen thousand in mid-1981. Human rights violations by the FMLN are discussed in chap. 4.
9. Americas Watch and ACLU, *Supplement,* p. 269.
10. The Atlacatl Battalion's record includes the December 1981 massacres of up to a thousand at El Mozote, the November 1983 massacre at Lake Suchitlán, the July 1984 massacre at Los Llanitos, the August 1984 Gualsinga River massacre, the February 1989 murder of medical personnel and wounded combatants at an FMLN field hospital in Chalatenango, and the November 1989 massacre of six Jesuit priests and two witnesses, in addition to several individual cases of torture or murder. See U.S. Congress, Arms Control and Foreign Policy Caucus, "Abuses of Human Rights," which summarizes ten cases of atrocities by the Atlacatl Battalion based on reports by Americas Watch, the Lawyers Committee for Human Rights, and Tutela Legal. A visiting professor at the U.S. Army School of the Americas in Fort Benning, Georgia, described the Atlacatl soldiers as "particularly ferocious. . . . We've always had a hard time getting [them] to take prisoners instead of ears." Americas Watch, *Year of Reckoning,* pp. 157–59.

11. Letter from Michael Posner, executive director, Lawyers Committee for Human Rights, to Richard B. Cheney, U.S. secretary of defense, April 20, 1990.

12. U.S. Congress, Arms Control and Foreign Policy Caucus, "Barriers to Reform." Eleven of the fourteen linked to abuse received U.S. training. Martin McReynolds, "El Salvador Rights Record Challenged," *Miami Herald*, May 22, 1990.

13. U.S. Congress, Arms Control and Foreign Policy Caucus, "Barriers to Reform," p. 2; Bacevich et al., *American Military Policy*, p. 26.

14. Joel Millman, "El Salvador's Army: A Force unto Itself," *New York Times Magazine*, December 10, 1989, p. 95.

15. Amnesty International, *El Salvador: "Death Squads,"* p. 9.

16. Dickey, "Behind the Death Squads," p. 16.

17. Ibid., p. 17.

18. See, for example, U.S. Congress, Senate, Select Committee on Intelligence, *Recent Political Violence*, pp. 11, 15; U.S. Congress, House, Permanent Select Committee on Intelligence, *Report*, p. 17; Amnesty International, *El Salvador: "Death Squads"*; Dickey, "Behind the Death Squads," pp. 16–21; Craig Pyes, "A Dirty War in the Name of Freedom," *Albuquerque Journal*, December 18, 1983; Pyes, " 'The Doctor' Prescribes Torture for the Hesitant," *Albuquerque Journal*, December 20, 1983; Pyes, "The Businessmen Invest in the Murky Side of War," *Albuquerque Journal*, December 21, 1983; Pyes, "The New American Right Cooks Up a Hot Potato," *Albuquerque Journal*, December 22, 1983; Nairn, "Behind the Death Squads"; Farah, "Death Squad Began as Scout Troop," *Washington Post*, August 29, 1988.

19. Amnesty International, *El Salvador: "Death Squads,"* p. 8.

20. Americas Watch and ACLU, *As Bad as Ever*, p. 30.

21. Americas Watch and Lawyers Committee, *Free Fire*, p. 3.

22. Americas Watch, *Settling into Routine*, p. 41, quoting *El Mundo*, October 25, 1985, and *El Diario de Hoy*, October 27, 1985; ibid., p. 42, quoting *El Mundo*, December 10, 1985; ibid., quoting *El Mundo*, January 20, 1986.

23. As in the early 1980s, the brigade's communiqué was given to local newspapers and radio stations and used as a news item. The right-wing daily *El Diario de Hoy* published the list of threatened individuals. Americas Watch, *Civilian Toll*, pp. 210–11.

24. Americas Watch, *Year of Reckoning*, p. 59.

25. U.S. Department of State, *Country Reports for 1989*, pp. 570, 572.

26. Americas Watch and ACLU, *Second Supplement*, p. 62.

27. Americas Watch, *Year of Reckoning*, pp. 59–60.

28. Douglas Farah, "Salvadoran Death Squads Threaten Resurgence" and "Rightist Denies Past, Present Role in Squads," *Washington Post*, August 28, 1988; and Farah, "Death Squad Began as Scout Troop."

29. For example, a U.S. official in San Salvador told a reporter in 1983 that "every garrison of any size had death squads. It's that simple. . . . All of this comes out of a military intelligence function." Nairn, "Behind the Death Squads," p. 25. A Treasury Police defector gave detailed testimony about death squad killings to Amnesty International in June 1988, stating that these operations are based in the intelligence sections of each one of the security forces. Amnesty International, *El Salvador: "Death Squads,"* pp. 17–18.

30. Douglas Farah and Don Podesta, "Salvadoran Killings Cited," *Washington Post*, October 27, 1990.

31. The decision on his request for political asylum is pending and will not be

affected by the conviction. Robert F. Howe, "Death Squad Figure Guilty in Immigration Case," *Washington Post,* September 19, 1990.

32. See generally Americas Watch, *Labor Rights in El Salvador.*

33. In a response to an Americas Watch petition to review U.S. trade preferences for El Salvador because of violations of workers' rights, the Subcommittee on the Generalized System of Preferences of the U.S. Trade Representative stated that from June 1986 to May 1987 UNTS-affiliated unions and associations presented 73 percent of all contracts to the Ministry of Labor, and from June 1986 to February 1, 1988, they filed 64 percent of the collective-bargaining agreements. Americas Watch, "Petition before the U.S. Trade Representative," p. 16.

34. Americas Watch and ACLU, *Report,* pp. 53, 54.

35. Americas Watch and ACLU, *Supplement,* p. 56.

36. Americas Watch and ACLU, *Report,* p. xl.

37. Americas Watch and ACLU, *Second Supplement,* p. 22.

38. Americas Watch and ACLU, *As Bad as Ever,* pp. 10–11.

39. Americas Watch, *Civilian Toll,* p. 248.

40. Americas Watch, *Nightmare Revisited,* pp. 11–15.

41. Ibid., pp. 12–13.

42. Ibid., p. 19.

43. Americas Watch, *Year of Reckoning,* pp. 102–3.

44. Tutela Legal, *Weekly Report,* July 27–August 2, 1990, p. 5.

45. Americas Watch, *Year of Reckoning,* pp. 54–55. For details on the rest of the examples in this section see ibid., pp. 126, 123 (FENASTRAS); 61, 63 (SICAFE); 51–52 (San Cayetano cooperative).

46. Americas Watch, *Civilian Toll,* pp. 73–74.

47. Archbishop Romero, February 2, 1980, quoted in Swedish, *Like Grains of Wheat,* p. 23.

48. For a list of the victims and the circumstances surrounding their deaths or disappearances see Americas Watch, *Year of Reckoning,* pp. 171–78. For details on the Reyes, Abrego, and Serrano cases see ibid., pp. 175–77.

49. Americas Watch and ACLU, *Report,* p. 56.

50. "The Jesuit Vision," *Boston Globe,* November 17, 1989, excerpted from a letter written by Father Ellacuría three years earlier in response to a series of articles on Central America by Edward R. F. Sheehan.

51. U.S. District Court for the Central District of California, transcript, January 16, 1987, pp. 49–51.

52. Ana Arana, "Jesuit Massacre Came on Heels of Army Meeting," *Baltimore Sun,* February 4, 1990; and Douglas Farah, "U.S. Pressure in Jesuit Probe Said to Alienate Salvadoran Officers," *Washington Post,* February 6, 1990. The National Intelligence Directorate shares a building with the CIA.

53. Speaker's Task Force on El Salvador, "Interim Report," p. 10.

54. Lawyers Committee, *Jesuit Case a Year Later,* p. 30.

55. Americas Watch and ACLU, *Report,* pp. 56–57.

56. Americas Watch and ACLU, *As Bad as Ever,* p. 33.

57. Americas Watch, *Nightmare Revisited,* p. 9.

58. Americas Watch, *Year of Reckoning,* pp. 128–29.

59. Bonner, *Weakness and Deceit,* pp. 103–4.

60. Americas Watch and ACLU, *As Bad as Ever*, pp. 36–37.

61. Americas Watch and ACLU, *Third Supplement*, p. 37; and William Montalbano, "Salvador Death Squads Assailed," *Los Angeles Times*, May 14, 1983.

62. Americas Watch and ACLU, *Third Supplement*, p. 38.

63. Ibid., pp. 41–42.

64. Douglas Farah, "Campaigner's Death Stirs El Salvador," *Washington Post*, December 14, 1988.

65. Committee to Protect Journalists, "Backgrounder," New York, February 11, 1990, pp. 7–8. The FMLN was apparently responsible for the November 1989 disappearance of five journalists working for a government-run information agency. Americas Watch, *Update on El Salvador*, pp. 22–24; and Americas Watch, *Year of Reckoning*, pp. 88–89.

66. Americas Watch, *Continuing Terror*, p. 151; and Americas Watch and ACLU, *Report*, pp. 124–26.

67. Americas and ACLU, *Report*, p. 60; Americas Watch, *Continuing Terror*, p. 151.

68. Americas Watch and ACLU, *Supplement*, p. 80.

69. Ibid., p. 92.

70. Americas Watch, *Continuing Terror*, p. 153.

71. Americas Watch, *Year of Reckoning*, p. 28.

72. Americas Watch and ACLU, *Report*, pp. 58, 141.

73. Lawyers Committee, *Critique for 1989*, p. 73.

74. Americas Watch and ACLU, *Report*, pp. 129–30. For details on the Hernández and Figueroa cases, the aftermath of the strike, and the Menéndez and Ulloa cases see ibid., pp. 130, 141.

75. Americas Watch, *Continuing Terror*, pp. 154–55.

76. Americas Watch and ACLU, *Supplement*, p. 120.

77. Americas Watch and ACLU, *As Bad as Ever*, p. 31.

78. Americas Watch, *Continuing Terror*, pp. 155–56.

79. Americas Watch, *Year of Reckoning*, pp. 36–37. For details on the rest of the cases in this section see ibid., pp. 66, 25–26, 42–43.

80. Article 3, which is common to the four Geneva conventions of 1949, reads: "The wounded and sick shall be collected and cared for." Article 7 says: "1. All the wounded, sick and shipwrecked, whether or not they have taken part in the armed conflict, shall be respected and protected. 2. In all circumstances they shall be treated humanely and shall receive, to the fullest extent practicable and with the least possible delay, the medical care and attention required by their condition." Protocol Additional to the Geneva Conventions of 12 August 1949, and Relating to the Protection of Victims of Non-International Armed Conflicts (Protocol II).

The three articles in Protocol II expressly protect medical personnel: Article 9 ("Medical and religious personnel shall be respected and protected and shall be granted all available help for the performance of their duties. They shall not be compelled to carry out tasks which are not compatible with their humanitarian mission"), Article 10 ("Under no circumstances shall any person be punished for having carried out medical activities compatible with medical ethics, regardless of the person benefiting therefrom"), and Article 11 ("Medical units and transports shall be respected and protected at all times and shall not be the object of attack").

81. Americas Watch, *Carnage Again*, pp. 28–29.

82. Ibid., pp. 72–73; Americas Watch, *Year of Reckoning*, p. 56.
83. Americas Watch, *Civilian Toll*, p. 290.
84. Americas Watch and ACLU, *Report*, pp. 144–45.
85. Americas Watch and ACLU, *Supplement*, p. 59; Americas Watch, *Civilian Toll*, p. 288.
86. Americas Watch and ACLU, *Second Supplement*, p. 47.
87. Americas Watch and ACLU, *Third Supplement*, pp. 32–34.
88. Americas Watch, *Civilian Toll*, p. 284.
89. Americas Watch, *Nightmare Revisited*, p. 39.
90. Americas Watch, *Civilian Toll*, p. 76.

CHAPTER 3: COMBAT-RELATED ABUSES BY GOVERNMENT FORCES

1. Americas Watch and ACLU, *Report*, pp. 168–69.
2. Ibid., pp. 169–70.
3. Americas Watch and ACLU, *Supplement*, p. 25.
4. Ibid., pp. 26–27.
5. "Major Massacre Is Reported in Salvadoran Village," *New York Times*, January 27, 1982; "Salvadoran Peasants Describe Mass Killing," *Washington Post*, January 27, 1982.
6. Lawyers Committee and Human Rights Watch, *El Salvador*, p. 50.
7. Americas Watch and ACLU, *Third Supplement*, pp. 17–23.
8. Americas Watch and ACLU, *As Bad as Ever*, pp. 20–22.
9. *Philadelphia Inquirer*, December 7, 1983.
10. Julia Preston, "Salvadoran Troops Are Accused in Slaying," *Boston Globe*, September 9, 1984. See also Sam Dillon, "Troops Stalk and Kill Rebels' Civilian Allies," *Miami Herald*, September 9, 1984; James LeMoyne, "Salvadoran Villagers Report Army Massacre," *New York Times*, September 9, 1984; and Americas Watch, *Draining the Sea*, pp. 3–11.
11. "Salvadoran Villagers Report Attack by Army," *New York Times*, September 15, 1984. See also Americas Watch, *Draining the Sea*, pp. 11–18.
12. Americas Watch, *Draining the Sea*, p. 13.
13. "Nightline," ABC television, February 13, 1985.
14. Ibid.; Americas Watch, *Draining the Sea*, p. 18.
15. Tutela Legal, Testimonio no. 13, Informe no. 17, September 1983. See also Americas Watch and ACLU, *As Bad as Ever*, pp. 18–20.
16. Americas Watch, *Civilian Toll*, pp. 157–66.
17. The text of the cable is reproduced in Americas Watch, *Protection of the Weak and Unarmed*, pp. 14–29. The quotations appear on p. 23.
18. Ibid., pp. 30–45.
19. Interview, July 11, 1984, cited in Americas Watch and Lawyers Committee, *Free Fire*, pp. 34–36.
20. See Americas Watch and Lawyers Committee, *Free Fire*; and Americas Watch, *Draining the Sea*.
21. The U.S. Department of State distributed copies, asserting that the information

about the rules of engagement was extracted from Presidential Directive C-111–03–982. See also Americas Watch, *Draining the Sea*, pp. 29–30.

22. See Americas Watch and Lawyers Committee, *Free Fire*, pp. 61–63. The Americas Watch representatives who discussed arrests and abductions by the air force with Col. López Nuila during a July 1984 mission were Juan Méndez and Aryeh Neier.

23. *Prensa Gráfica*, January 9 and 11, 1985; *El Mundo*, January 11, 1985.

24. See Dan Williams, "El Salvador Intensifies Its Air War against Guerrillas," *Los Angeles Times*, July 17, 1985. See also Americas Watch, *Continuing Terror*, pp. 29–32.

25. Lane, "Pilot Shark of El Salvador," p. 28.

26. M.P.'s account is from Americas Watch, *Continuing Terror*, pp. 13–18.

27. Ricardo Chavira, "Inside Guerrilla Territory," *Time*, January 20, 1986. See also Americas Watch, *Settling into Routine*, pp. 7–19.

28. James LeMoyne, "Salvador Prelate Accuses Air Force," *New York Times*, January 13, 1986; and Americas Watch, *Settling into Routine*, pp. 19–20.

29. James LeMoyne, "Bombings in El Salvador Appear to 'Bend the Rules,'" *New York Times*, December 20, 1985.

30. Americas Watch, *Settling into Routine*, pp. 32–34.

31. Ibid., p. 26. See also *Proceso*, February 17, 1986

32. Marjorie Miller, "Salvadoran Civilians in Crossfire," *Los Angeles Times*, April 11, 1986.

33. James LeMoyne, "Salvadoran Air Raid Reported in Town," *New York Times*, February 1, 1987. See also Americas Watch, *Civilian Toll*, pp. 48–49.

34. An Americas Watch researcher, Jemera Rone, visited the site that afternoon and the following day to gather evidence. The affected community has since been renamed Communidad Ignacio Ellacuría, after the Jesuit rector of the Central American University who was killed by the army on November 16, 1989.

35. See "Army Admits Blame in Refugee Deaths," *Miami Herald*, February 18, 1990; *El Mundo*, February 21, 1990; and Americas Watch, *Year of Reckoning*, pp. 39–41.

36. Americas Watch, *Civilian Toll*, pp. 28–34.

37. For more on the San Francisco massacre see Americas Watch, *Nightmare Revisited*, p. 18; and Americas Watch, "El Salvador: Army Massacre."

38. See Americas Watch, "El Salvador: Impunity," pp. 8–9.

39. Americas Watch, *Human Rights*, p. 12.

40. Americas Watch, *Year of Reckoning*, pp. 27–28.

41. Americas Watch, *Update on El Salvador*, pp. 58–59.

CHAPTER 4: ABUSES BY THE GUERRILLAS

1. See Americas Watch, *Land Mines;* and Americas Watch, *Nightmare Revisited*, pp. 48–49.

2. Americas Watch and Lawyers Committee, *Free Fire*, pp. 54–59.

3. Protocol II of 1977 to the Geneva Conventions, Article 3(c).

4. Americas Watch, *Draining the Sea*, pp. 59–61.

5. Ibid., pp. 54–55.

6. James LeMoyne, "Salvadoran Rebels Reported to Execute Nine," *New York Times*, November 4, 1984; and Americas Watch, *Settling into Routine*, p. 71.

7. See Americas Watch, *Settling into Routine*, pp. 76–78; and Protocol II of 1977 to the Geneva Conventions, Article 4(2)(c).

8. Americas Watch, *Continuing Terror*, pp. 111–22.

9. Americas Watch, *Settling into Routine*, pp. 72–75.

10. Americas Watch, *Land Mines*, p. 30.

11. Americas Watch, *Civilian Toll*, pp. 143, 121–35.

12. Ibid., pp. 130–33.

13. Tutela Legal attributed one of the 1987 deaths to an FMLN mine and three to army mines; twenty-five were unattributed. In 1988 the guerrillas were blamed for eleven civilian deaths from land mines, the army for ten, and unknown authors for forty-four.

14. Americas Watch, *Human Rights*, p. 8.

15. Americas Watch, *Nightmare Revisited*, p. 45.

16. For details on all of them see Americas Watch, *Year of Reckoning*, pp. 72–73, 74, 76–77.

17. Americas Watch, *Nightmare Revisited*, p. 44.

18. For early criticisms see, for example, Americas Watch, *Civilian Toll*, pp. 121–35; and Americas Watch, *Nightmare Revisited*, pp. 43–48. For the review of twenty-nine killings see Americas Watch, *Violations*, pp. 23–27. The quotation is on p. 3.

19. Americas Watch, *Year of Reckoning*, pp. 90, 3.

20. See two Americas Watch reports on the offensive: *Carnage Again* and *Update on El Salvador*.

21. Americas Watch, *Year of Reckoning*, pp. 88–89.

CHAPTER 5: THE ADMINISTRATION OF JUSTICE

1. Americas Watch, *Nightmare Revisited*, pp. 7–8.

2. Americas Watch, *Update on El Salvador*, p. 27. In March 1990 after the state of emergency was lifted, the military courts still had jurisdiction over political cases that arose during the state of emergency (even if the defendant was arrested after the emergency), and civilian courts tried older political cases. Americas Watch, *Year of Reckoning*, p. 135.

3. See, for example, International Human Rights Law Group, *Waiting for Justice*.

4. Ibid., p. 57.

5. Ibid., p. 64; Americas Watch, *Year of Reckoning*, p. 139n.

6. Americas Watch, *Settling into Routine*, pp. 97–104.

7. Americas Watch, *Year of Reckoning*, pp. 131–32.

8. Americas Watch and ACLU, *Second Supplement*, p. 62; Americas Watch, *Settling into Routine*, pp. 57–58.

9. Americas Watch and ACLU, *As Bad as Ever*, pp. 27–28.

10. Americas Watch and ACLU, *Second Supplement*, p. 52.

11. Americas Watch and ACLU, *Third Supplement*, p. 54.

12. Americas Watch and ACLU, *As Bad as Ever*, p. 27; Americas Watch, *Settling into Routine*, p. 53; Americas Watch, *Civilian Toll*, p. 66.

13. Americas Watch, *Civilian Toll*, pp. 19–20, 67; International Human Rights Law Group, *Waiting for Justice*, pp. 4, 5.

14. Lawyers Committee, *Underwriting Injustice*, p. 12; Americas Watch, *Year of Reckoning*, p. 136.

15. Americas Watch and ACLU, *Report*, p. 124.

16. Ibid., pp. 102–3.

17. Ibid., p. 103.

18. Americas Watch and ACLU, *Supplement*, p. 47.

19. Americas Watch and ACLU, *Report*, pp. 103–4.

20. U.S. Department of State, *Country Reports for 1985*, p. 517.

21. Americas Watch, *Civilian Toll*, pp. 242–244.

22. Americas Watch, *Nightmare Revisited*, pp. 41–42.

23. Lawyers Committee, *Underwriting Injustice*, p. 6.

24. Ibid.

25. Americas Watch, *Update on El Salvador*, pp. 39–40.

26. *El Diario de Hoy*, April 17, 1990; *El Mundo*, April 16, 1990.

27. Tutela Legal, *Weekly Report*, June 8–14, 1990.

28. Ibid., July 20–26, 1990.

29. Americas Watch and ACLU, *Supplement*, p. 45; Americas Watch and ACLU, *As Bad as Ever*, p. 63; U.S. Department of State, *Country Reports for 1989*, p. 570.

30. Lawyers Committee, *Underwriting Injustice*, p. 38.

31. The United States has obligated $13.7 million in aid to this project but had spent only $7 million by April 1991. Americas Watch interview with David Robinson, U.S. Department of State, April 3, 1991.

32. Lawyers Committee, *Underwriting Injustice*, pp. 43, 44; Americas Watch interview with David Robinson.

33. Lawyers Committee, *Underwriting Injustice*, p. 49.

34. Americas Watch, "El Salvador: Impunity," p. 7.

35. Lawyers Committee, *Underwriting Injustice*, p. 68.

36. See the May 1985 testimony of the assistant secretary of state for human rights and humanitarian affairs, Elliott Abrams, cited in Burkhalter and Paine, "Our Overseas Cops," p. 197.

37. U.S. Department of State, AID, Office of Public Safety, "Termination Phase-out Study, Public Safety Project, El Salvador," report prepared by Richard R. Martinez (May 1974), pp. 1–27; and U.S. Department of State, AID, Office of Public Safety, "Report on Visit to Central America and Panama to Study AID Public Safety Programs," report prepared by C. Allan Stewart (Undated; declassified April 4, 1980), p. 5.

38. U.S. Department of State, AID, Office of Public Safety, "Report on Visit to Central America," p. 24; and prepared statement of Hon. George Miller, in U.S. Congress, House, Committee on Foreign Affairs, *Central American Counterterrorism Act*, p. 67.

39. McClintock, *American Connection*, 1:18; U.S. Congress, Arms Control and Foreign Policy Caucus, "Police Aid to Central America," p. 20 n. 22.

40. U.S. Congress, Arms Control and Foreign Policy Caucus, "Police Aid to Central America," p. 14.

41. In 1984 the three Salvadoran security forces had been placed under the jurisdiction of the vice minister of public security. See Yu, "U.S. Assistance for Foreign Police Forces," p. 23.

42. U.S. Congress, House, Committee on Foreign Affairs, *Central American Counterterrorism Act*, p. 74.

43. Yu, "U.S. Assistance for Foreign Police Forces," app. E and pp. 16–17. Section 660(d) of the Foreign Assistance Act waived the prohibition on police training for El Salvador and Honduras for two years, until the end of fiscal year 1987. The first certification for El Salvador was issued in October 1985. In it Secretary of State George Shultz claimed that "there is no credible evidence that human rights violations of any kind occur with even tacit government consent." The standard practice is for reprogrammings to be presented to four congressional committees, which then can review the request. The committees' recommendations are not legally binding on the administration, but it normally heeds them.

44. In September 1985 the Reagan administration had submitted a Central American Counterterrorism Act to the Congress to expand to all of Central America the exemptions to Section 660 granted to El Salvador and Honduras. The Congress as a whole never acted on the program, however, both because of its introduction late in the session and because of political objections to a large increase in police and military aid. The extension of Section 660(d) for two additional fiscal years preserved and expanded the previous certification requirement and provided that police aid would be confined to training in human rights, civil law, and investigative techniques. See *Congressional Quarterly Almanac* (1989): 591–93.

45. In October 1983, for example, a terrorist attack on the U.S. Embassy compound in Beirut, Lebanon, left over two hundred marines dead.

46. Information provided to Americas Watch by David Epstein, ATA Program, September 26, 1990.

47. U.S. Congress, Arms Control and Foreign Policy Caucus, "Police Aid to Central America," p. 13; Watch Committees and Lawyers Committee, *Reagan Administration's Record in 1986*, p. 55; Yu, "U.S. Assistance for Foreign Police Forces," p. 25.

48. Yu, "U.S. Assistance for Foreign Police Forces," pp. 12–13.

49. U.S. Congress, Arms Control and Foreign Policy Caucus, "Police Aid to Central America," p. 13.

50. Americas Watch interview with David Kriskovich, U.S. Department of Justice, ICITAP, September 26, 1990, and October 18, 1990; and Speaker's Task Force on El Salvador, "Interim Report," pp. 27–29.

51. Americas Watch interview with Joe Keefe, DEA, October 4, 1990.

52. Farah, "Death Squad Began as Scout Troop," *Washington Post*, August 29, 1988; and Farah, "Salvadoran Death Squads Threaten Resurgence," *Washington Post*, August 28, 1988.

CHAPTER 6: IMPUNITY

1. In a few cases, low-ranking members of the armed forces have been convicted and punished for human rights abuses. The prosecutions of the killers of four U.S. churchwomen and two U.S. labor advisers and their Salvadoran colleague are discussed later in this chapter. In addition, on June 17, 1987, a sergeant of the Third Brigade and his brother-in-law, a former soldier, were convicted for the November 1984 murder of the Rev. David Ernesto Fernández, a Lutheran minister; in May 1987 three municipal police from Quetzaltepeque, La Libertad, were convicted of two separate murders committed in January 1983; and in 1990 a soldier was convicted and sentenced to sixteen years in prison for the October 13, 1982, murder of a U.S. citizen, Michael David Kline.

Americas Watch, *Civilian Toll*, p. 236; *El Mundo*, June 13, 1990; and *El Diario de Hoy*, June 14, 1990.

The officers facing formal charges are Maj. Mauricio Beltrán, for the massacre of ten peasants at San Francisco, San Vicente, in September 1988, and Col. Guillermo Alfredo Benavides Morales, Lt. Yusshy René Mendoza Vallecillos, Lt. José Ricardo Espinoza Guerra, and 1st Lt. Gonzalo Guevara Cerritos, for the massacre of six Jesuit priests, their housekeeper, and her daughter in November 1989. In a related charge, Lt. Col. Camilo Hernández, acting deputy director of the Military School at the time of the massacre of the Jesuits, has been accused of ordering the destruction of the school's logbooks for the night of the crime. Lt. Nelson Saúl Solano Reyes has been charged in the shooting death of one journalist and the wounding of another in March 1989.

Guerrillas have rarely been prosecuted for political killings either, though for different reasons. The one exception has been the FMLN massacre of four U.S. Marines and nine civilians at a café in San Salvador in 1985.

2. Christopher Marquis, "Angry U.S. Cuts Salvador Legal Aid after Court's Murder Probes Wither," *Miami Herald*, August 16, 1990. The U.S. State Department has refused to confirm or deny the suspension of aid.

3. Americas Watch, *Update on El Salvador*, pp. 17–19; and Americas Watch, "El Salvador: Impunity," pp. 7–8.

4. Douglas Mine, "Jesuit Investigation: Exception That Confirms Rule of Military Impunity," Associated Press, February 16, 1990.

5. Americas Watch, "El Salvador: Impunity" p. 9.

6. Americas Watch, *Nightmare Revisited*, pp. 1–8.

7. Information on the number of prisoners released comes from International Committee of the Red Cross, *1987 Annual Report*, p. 41.

8. Americas Watch, *Year of Reckoning*, p. 139.

9. "Government Proposes Amnesty for Military," *El Salvador On Line* (Mimeo, July 30, 1990), p. 2.

10. Americas Watch and ACLU, *Report*, pp. 102–3, 55–56; Lawyers Committee, *Decade of Failed Promises*, p. 12n. The Lawyers Committee report is the most detailed published account of the official investigation into the assassination. It was written by Robert Weiner, a New York attorney, based in part on work he did for Americas Watch.

11. See Morley, "Demonizing D'Aubuisson."

12. Although President Cristiani declared in June 1990 that the investigation had not been closed, there is no evidence that it is being actively pursued. *El Mundo*, June 7, 1990. In July 1990, Attorney General Roberto Mendoza expressed doubt that the case would ever be solved: "Legally, the possibilities of resolving the case have been exhausted, and a lot of time has passed." Cited in El Rescate Human Rights Department, *Report from El Salvador*, July 23–30, 1990, p. 4.

13. Lawyers Committee, *Decade of Failed Promises*, pp. 11, 6.

14. U.S. Congress, Senate, Committee on Foreign Relations, *Situation in El Salvador*, p. 117.

15. Laurie Becklund, "US Cables Reportedly Tie Salvador Right to Slaying," *Los Angeles Times*, April 13, 1983.

16. Hearings before the Subcommittees on Human Rights and International Organizations and on Western Hemisphere Affairs of the Committee on Foreign Affairs, House of Representatives, February 6, 1984, p. 50.

17. "Salvador Ex-Intelligence Aide Links Brass, Killers," *Chicago Tribune*, March

22, 1985; transcript of interview with Santiváñez by the filmmaker Alan Francovich, September 1985, p. 6 (hereafter Santiváñez Transcript).

18. Ana Arana, "Salvador Officers Met Just before Jesuit Massacre," *Baltimore Sun*, February 4, 1990.

19. Robert Parry, "Salvadoran Says Top Nicaraguan Rebel Had Role in 1980 Killing of Archbishop," *Boston Globe*, March 22, 1985; Don Oberdorfer, "Wealthy Exiles Implicated in Salvadoran Bishop's Death," *Washington Post*, March 22, 1985.

20. Joel Brinkley, "Contra Official Linked to Death Squads," *El Paso Herald Post*, March 22, 1985. Although the D'Aubuisson diary was in the hands of Salvadoran and U.S. authorities from the time it was seized, Salvadoran investigators and U.S. officials apparently ignored it until Antonio Amado Garay, whose name appears in the diary, returned to El Salvador in 1987 to testify that Saravia and D'Aubuisson were involved in Romero's murder. Lawyers Committee, *Decade of Failed Promises*, pp. 92, 10.

21. Lawyers Committee, *Decade of Failed Promises*, p. 12.

22. Ibid., pp. 14–17. D'Aubuisson denied knowing that Salazar's testimony was fabricated; he said the Pedro Lobo tape had been given to ARENA by unknown individuals. Lawyers Committee, *Underwriting Injustice*, p. 22.

23. Garay was located by U.S. and Salvadoran officials working with the U.S.-funded Special Investigative Unit. His name appears on the last page of the D'Aubuisson diary.
One journalist, Jefferson Morley, has suggested that Garay's testimony could be exculpatory, rather than supportive of the evidence against D'Aubuisson. D'Aubuisson's surprise at the news that Romero was dead could indicate that his plot to assassinate Romero had been preempted by another killer. Morley said that the "widespread assumption that D'Aubuisson is responsible for Romero's death may be a new case of that old tale, 'They framed a guilty man.'" "Demonizing D'Aubuisson."

24. Lawyers Committee, *Underwriting Injustice*, pp. 23–24.

25. Sister María del Socorro Iraheta testified in 1985 that she saw a man leaning over the window of a car as if he was hiding something. She believed the man to be D'Aubuisson. Lawyers Committee, *Decade of Failed Promises*, p. 17.

26. Americas Watch, *Human Rights*, p. 10.

27. Morley, "Demonizing D'Aubuisson," pp. 625–26.

28. D'Aubuisson, who has repeatedly denied involvement in the killing, reiterated his innocence in televised appearances on February 10 and 12. Lawyers Committee, *Decade of Failed Promises*, p. 23.

29. Farah, "Death Squad Began as Scout Troop," *Washington Post*, August 29, 1988.

30. Ibid.; Americas Watch, *Civilian Toll*, p. 241. The names Pérez Linares and Regalado appear frequently in the D'Aubuisson diary.

31. Craig Pyes, "Salvadoran Army Officer Implicated in Slaying of Archbishop," *Albuquerque Journal*, May 19, 1983.

32. Lawyers Committee, *Decade of Failed Promises*, p. 3.

33. Ibid., p. 19 n. 31; Morley, "Demonizing D'Aubuisson," p. 625.

34. Americas Watch and Lawyers Committee, *Free Fire*, p. 69.

35. Lawyers Committee and Human Rights Watch, *El Salvador*, pp. 63–64; and Tyler, *Churchwomen Murders*, pp. 16–17.

36. Tyler, *Churchwomen Murders*, pp. 16–19.

37. Ibid., pp. 22–24, 8, 32.

38. Americas Watch and Lawyers Committee, *Free Fire*, p. 69.

39. Americas Watch, *Human Rights*, p. 22. This ruling notwithstanding, it is clear that the guardsmen acted with a political motivation. The women were pursued after the guardsman reported that they looked suspicious because their handbags were large enough to conceal weapons; and after they were killed, Colindres Aléman repeatedly referred to them as subversives. Tyler, *Churchwomen Murders*, p. 37.

40. Tyler, *Churchwomen Murders*, pp. 10, 54; Santiváñez Transcript, p. 9.

41. Tyler, *Churchwomen Murders*, pp. 10, 51.

42. Larry Rohter, "Salvador Defense Lawyer Charges Cover-up in Slaying of U.S. Nuns," *New York Times*, May 6, 1985.

43. Ibarra worked among Salvadoran refugees in Texas until his return to El Salvador in 1987. On November 16, 1989, he was again detained by the National Guard after he accompanied twelve foreigners who had been arrested to guard headquarters. Ibarra was held for nine days, interrogated, kicked, and threatened. Upon his release to a visiting U.S. congressional delegation, a National Guard colonel said there were "five antecedents" in Ibarra's caseand mentioned specifically his defense of Contreras Palacios. Further persecution in December 1989 led Ibarra again to flee the country. Americas Watch, *Update on El Salvador*, p. 40.

44. Bonner, *Weakness and Deceit*, p. 52; Craig Pyes, "Two Dinner Parties Meet, and Two Americans Die," *Albuquerque Journal*, December 19, 1983.

45. Lawyers Committee, *Underwriting Injustice*, p. 30; Pyes, "Two Dinner Parties Meet"; and Lawyers Committee and Human Rights Watch, *El Salvador*, p. 19.

46. Lawyers Committee and Human Rights Watch, *El Salvador*, p. 20n; and Bonner, *Weakness and Deceit*, p. 45.

47. James LeMoyne, "No Salvador Action Yet on Officer Tied to Killings," *New York Times*, June 28, 1985; and Pyes, "Two Dinner Parties Meet."

48. LeMoyne, "No Salvador Action Yet"; Lawyers Committee and Human Rights Watch, *El Salvador*, p. 17.

49. Lawyers Committee and Human Rights Watch, *El Salvador*, pp. 19–20.

50. Although the U.S. Embassy claimed that the captain of the Sonsonate military base had been arrested after the massacre, a *New York Times* correspondent, Lydia Chávez, reported in July 1983 that Capt. Carlos Alfonso Figueroa Morales was back at the barracks and in charge of intelligence in the area: "It now appears the writing of the press release was as far as the arrest went." "Salvadoran Tied to Killings Now in Intelligence Job," *New York Times*, July 9, 1983.

51. Lawyers Committee and Human Rights Watch, *El Salvador*, p. 51.

52. "Corte resuelve casación en massacre de 'Las Hojas' confirmando amnistía," *El Mundo*, July 21, 1988; and "Confirma sobreseimiento corte en caso Las Hojas," *El Diario de Hoy*, July 22, 1988.

53. See Americas Watch, *Civilian Toll*, pp. 237–245; Americas Watch, *Nightmare Revisited*, pp. 40–42; and Americas Watch, "El Salvador: Impunity."

54. The activities of Colonel Staben, a suspect in the case, are outlined in n. 55. Lt. López Sibrián, also a suspect, was implicated in the Sheraton killings; and both of them, as well as Lt. Col. Joaquín Astasio Zacapa and Antonio Cornejo Arango, were caught plotting a coup with D'Aubuisson in May 1980. A former death squad member also named Cornejo in connection with death squads operated out of the Constituent Assembly in 1982 and 1983. Farah, "Death Squad Began as Scout Troop."

55. Colonel Staben is one of the officers whose name comes up most frequently in connection with gross violations of human rights. Until 1984, Staben commanded the

army barracks next to El Playón, an infamous dumping ground for the bodies of death squad victims. More recently, in December 1989, he was in charge of the army unit responsible for an area where soldiers kidnapped six cooperative members, who were never seen again (see chap. 2). In 1990, Staben was transferred to Honduras, where he serves as the military attaché, apparently because of his alleged involvement in corrupt activities as well as human rights abuses.

56. Morley, "Salvador Justice," pp. 13–14. Morley's article also criticizes the U.S. Embassy for maintaining its silence on Staben's involvement in the kidnapping ring, although it had access to evidence against him. Indeed, the *New York Times* described Colonel Staben as a "favorite of the Central Intelligence Agency and American military advisers who have seen him as a successful combat commander." James LeMoyne, "Officers Held in Salvador Abductions," *New York Times*, April 25, 1986. Years later, in response to Morley's Freedom of Information Act request for information about Staben and the military kidnapping ring, the CIA acknowledged generating eight reports in April and May 1986. Citing a law prohibiting the disclosure of the names of CIA employees, the agency declined to release the reports. Jefferson Morley, "What We're Paying For in El Salvador," *Los Angeles Times*, June 17, 1990.

57. Lawyers Committee, *Underwriting Injustice*, p. 132; and Douglas Farah, "Salvadoran Court Ruling Is Reversed," *Washington Post*, April 5, 1989.

58. *El Diario de Hoy*, April 24, 1990; *El Mundo*, April 26, 1990; *Diario Latino*, April 26, 1990.

59. *Diario Latino*, Feb. 27, 1990.

60. Americas Watch, *Year of Reckoning*, pp. 32–34.

61. *El Diario de Hoy*, June 7, 1990; *El Mundo*, June 7, 1990; El Rescate Human Rights Department, *El Salvador Chronology*, June 1990, p. 13.

62. Douglas Mine, "Jury Absolves Soldier in Journalist Slaying," Associated Press, June 7, 1990.

63. Americas Watch, *Year of Reckoning*, pp. 29–32.

64. The victims were Fathers Juan Ramón Moreno, Amando López Quintana, Ignacio Ellacuría, Segundo Montes, Ignacio Martín-Baró, Joaquín López y López; Julia Elba Ramos; and Celina Mariceth Ramos. Americas Watch, *Carnage Again*, pp. 13–28; Americas Watch, *Update on El Salvador*, pp. 6–15; Americas Watch, *Year of Reckoning*, pp. 9–24; and Lawyers Committee, "Status of Jesuit Murder Investigation."

Eight of the nine members of the armed forces have been detained: Colonel Benavides Morales, Lt. Yusshy René Mendoza Vallecillos, Lt. José Ricardo Espinoza Guerra, 1st Lt. Gonzalo Guevara Cerritos, Sgt. Antonio Ramiro Avalos Vargas, Sgt. Thomas Zarpate Castillo, Cpl. Angel Pérez Vásquez, and Pvt. Oscar Maríano Amaya Grímaldi. Pvt. Jorge Alberto Sierra Ascencio deserted before the arrests were made. In addition, Lt. Col. Camilo Hernández has been charged with ordering that the logbooks kept at the Military School be burned. He was released on bail on July 31, 1990. In recent months three soldiers—Sgt. Oscar Armando Solórzano Esquivel, Héctor Antonio Guerrero Maravilla, and Rufino Barrientos Ramos—have been charged with perjury. Lawyers Committee, "Update on Investigation," pp. 3–4.

65. "Soldiers Face New Charges in Deaths of Jesuit Priests," *Los Angeles Times*, November 21, 1990. An investigation by the SIU, including ballistics tests to match weapons, narrowed the field of suspects to a forty-five-member commando unit of the Atlacatl Battalion, Colonel Benavides Morales, and Lieutenant Mendoza. A special

Honor Commission consisting of five military officers and two civilian lawyers employed by the armed forces was subsequently designated to identify the ones to charge with the murders. After a six-day period in which, according to the commission members, they exhorted suspects to tell the truth about the crime, nine were singled out and charged. The only public record of the commission's activities is a vague seven-page document that is now in the court record but whose existence was denied for months by commission members and President Cristiani.

66. Speaker's Task Force on El Salvador, "Interim Report" (Moakley Report).

67. "Statement by Congressman Joe Moakley on the Jesuits' Case and the Salvadoran Negotiations," August 15, 1990.

68. "Statement of Rep. Joe Moakley, Chairman—Speaker's Special Task Force on El Salvador," October 18, 1990.

69. Ibid.; and Lindsey Gruson, "Salvadoran Judge Orders Trial in Slaying of Priests," *New York Times,* December 9, 1990.

CHAPTER 7: REFUGEES AND THE DISPLACED

1. Linda S. Peterson, "Central American Refugee Flows, 1978 to 1984" (U.S. Bureau of the Census, March 1985), pp. 13–14, presented as testimony by the Bureau of the Census before the Subcommittee on Census and Population of the House Committee on Civil Service and Post Office on June 27, 1985. See, for example, Crittenden, *Sanctuary,* for a discussion of the flight of Salvadoran refugees to the United States.

2. Crittenden, *Sanctuary,* p. 361.

3. See Americas Watch and Lawyers Committee, *El Salvador's Other Victims,* pp. 256–57.

4. Ibid., p. 116.

5. Ibid., p. 117.

6. These figures are based on U.S. Department of State, AID, *Congressional Presentation, Fiscal Year 1985* (Washington, D.C.: Department of State, 1985), p. 62; a report of the Salvadoran government agency that ministers to the registered displaced, the National Commission of Displaced Persons (CONADES), *1982 Study* (San Salvador: CONADES, 1982), pp. 6–7; and Americas Watch and Lawyers Committee, *El Salvador's Other Victims,* p. 119.

7. Universidad Centroamericana Jose Simeón Cañas, "On the Situation of Refugees in El Salvador," in *Estudios Centroamericanos (ECA), Revista de Extensión Cultural,* March 1981, p. 253; and Americas Watch and Lawyers Committee, *El Salvador's Other Victims,* p. 74.

8. August 1981 interview with a photojournalist who requested anonymity, in Americas Watch and ACLU, *Report,* p. 164.

9. Americas Watch and ACLU, *Report,* p. 163.

10. Americas Watch and Lawyers Committee, *El Salvador's Other Victims,* pp. 135–36; visit by Aryeh Neier of Americas Watch with Dr. Arthur Warner, January 13, 1984.

11. Americas Watch and Lawyers Committee, *El Salvador's Other Victims,* pp. 76–78.

12. See ibid., pp. 221–27, for a complete description of this case.

13. Cynthia J. Arnson and Aryeh Neier of Americas Watch interviewed them in Mariona and Ilopango prisons on January 11 and 12, 1984.

14. All are cited in Americas Watch and Lawyers Committee, *El Salvador's Other Victims*, pp. 227–31,64–69. For details on the Ibarra case see Americas Watch and ACLU, *Third Supplement*, p. 47; and Americas Watch and ACLU, *As Bad as Ever*, p. 38.

15. Americas Watch and Lawyers Committee, *Free Fire*, pp. 39–40.

16. Americas Watch, *Nightmare Revisited*, pp. 66–67.

17. According to the Salvadoran government, 29,168 refugees returned home between 1984 and March 1990, of which approximately eight thousand repatriated in January and February 1990. "Summary of the Official Document of the Republic of El Salvador," First International Meeting of the Follow-up Committee of the International Conference on Central American Refugees, New York, June 27–28, 1990, p. 1.

18. Americas Watch, *Nightmare Revisited*, pp. 69–80.

19. Americas Watch, *Civilian Toll*, pp. 157–66; and Americas Watch, *Nightmare Revisited*, p. 80.

20. Americas Watch, *Nightmare Revisited*, pp. 74–75, 72–73.

CHAPTER 8: THE ROLE OF THE UNITED STATES

1. U.S. Congress, House, Committee on International Relations, Subcommittee on International Organizations, *The Recent Presidential Elections in El Salvador: Implications for U.S. Policy. Hearings, March 9 and 17, 1977*, 95th Cong., 1st sess. (Washington, D.C.: Government Printing Office, 1977), p. 15.

2. Arnson, *Crossroads*, p. 41.

3. Between 1950 and 1979 the United States provided $16.7 million in weapons and training to the Salvadoran army. U.S. aid was cut off in 1976, after a senior Salvadoran officer was convicted of trying to sell several thousand machine guns to the Mafia.

4. Arnson, *Crossroads*, pp. 53, 54.

5. Deane Hinton, cited in Arnson, *Crossroads*, p. 58.

6. The figure is for January 1981. Brown, ed., *With Friends Like These*, p. 118.

7. Arnson, *Crossroads*, p. 61.

8. Americas Watch Committee and ACLU, *Second Supplement*, p. 66.

9. Deane Hinton, "A Statistical Framework for Understanding Violence in El Salvador, January 15, 1982" (Washington, D.C.: Department of State, 1982), p. 8; and Americas Watch, *U.S. Reporting on Human Rights*, pp. 19–24.

10. Americas Watch and ACLU, *Third Supplement*, pp. 78–79.

11. Americas Watch and ACLU, *Second Supplement*, pp. 67–70, 115–16.

12. Americas Watch, *Managing the Facts*, pp. 39–41; Americas Watch, *Protection of the Weak and Unarmed*, pp. 14–18; Americas Watch and ACLU, *Second Supplement*, p. 48.

13. Americas Watch, *U.S. Reporting on Human Rights*, pp. 20–21, 3–65; and U.S. Congress, House, Permanent Select Committee on Intelligence, Subcommittee on Oversight and Evaluation, *U.S. Intelligence Performance*, pp. 18–19.

14. Arnson, *Crossroads*, p. 97.

15. Americas Watch and ACLU, *Third Supplement*, p. 7.

16. Americas Watch and ACLU, *As Bad as Ever*, p. 64.

17. U.S. Congress, House, Committee on Appropriations, Subcommittee on Foreign Operations, *Foreign Assistance and Related Programs for 1981*, pp. 345–46.

18. Americas Watch, *Managing the Facts*, p. 15.

19. U.S. Congress, Senate, Select Committee on Intelligence, *Recent Political Violence in El Salvador,* p. 11. The report noted that "numerous Salvadoran officials in the military and security forces as well as other official organizations have been involved in encouraging or conducting death squad activities or other violent human rights abuses. . . . The death squad and other abuses involving Salvadoran officials or encouraged or condoned by them have originated from the security services—especially in recent years the Treasury Police but also the National Police and National Guard. Personnel from military units have also been involved." Ibid., p. 15.

20. Americas Watch and ACLU, *Second Supplement,* p. 81. Hinton has named William Clark, then national security adviser, as the "anonymous" official.

21. Arnson, *Crossroads,* p. 99.

22. Americas Watch and ACLU, *As Bad as Ever,* 11.

23. Arnson, *Crossroads,* p. 136; and Douglas Farah, "Salvadoran Death Squads Threaten Resurgence," *Washington Post,* August 28, 1988. Within two years of the Bush visit, two officers who had been transferred—Lt. Col. Mario Denis Morán, a provincial army commander, and Maj. José Ricardo Pozo, intelligence chief of the Treasury Police—were promoted to full colonel and lieutenant colonel respectively. In addition, the lone civilian reportedly on Bush's list, Héctor Regalado, security chief of the Legislative Assembly, had returned to El Salvador in 1988 and reportedly was a key figure in an effort to rebuild the death squads. See Foreign Broadcast Information Service, "COPREFA Releases Changes within Armed Forces," January 2, 1986, p. P1; and Farah, "Salvadoran Death Squads Threaten Resurgence."

24. Scarcely four months earlier, Elliott Abrams, assistant secretary of state for human rights, had maintained that "the assumption that the death squads are active security forces remains to be proved. It might be right, though I suspect it probably isn't right." Americas Watch and ACLU, *As Bad as Ever,* p. 52.

25. Americas Watch, *Protection of the Weak and Unarmed,* pp. 14–17.

26. Americas Watch and ACLU, *As Bad as Ever,* pp. 52–53.

27. Americas Watch and Lawyers Committee, *Free Fire,* pp. iii–36. See also chap. 3, above.

28. George Shultz, "Project Democracy" (U.S. Department of State, Current Policy no. 456; originally his statement before the Subcommittee on International Operations of the House Foreign Affairs Committee on February 23, 1983), p. 2; U.S. Congress, House, Committee on Foreign Affairs, Subcommittee on Human Rights and International Organizations, *The Phenomenon of Torture. Hearings and Markup, May 15, 16; September 6, 1984,* 98th Cong., 2d sess. (Washington, D.C.: Government Printing Office, 1984), p. 158.

29. The administration viewed the problem of judicial reform as technical and administrative, rather than involving political will. Between fiscal year 1984 and fiscal year 1989 the administration spent $5 million dollars to reform El Salvador's judiciary, out of $13.7 million authorized by the Congress. U.S. General Accounting Office, *Foreign Aid: Efforts to Improve the Judicial System in El Salvador* (NSIAD-90-81, May 1990), p. 4.

30. "U.S. Envoy Reportedly Target of Salvadoran Rightists' Plot," *Washington Post,* June 23, 1984; James LeMoyne, "Salvadoran Right Reportedly Plotted to Assassinate U.S. Ambassador," *New York Times,* June 23, 1984; Joanne Omang, "U.S. Feared Slaying of Envoy Here," *Washington Post,* June 27, 1984.

31. Americas Watch, *Draining the Sea,* pp. 28–37.

32. Americas Watch, *Settling into Routine*, pp. 3, 141.

33. See, for example, James LeMoyne, "Salvadoran Rebels Step Up Action in the Capital," *New York Times*, June 4, 1987; Chris Hedges, "Salvadorans Reported Angry at Leftists' Push," *Dallas Morning News*, August 23, 1987.

34. The categories were guerrillas, possibly guerrillas, far right, possibly the far right, and unknown assailants. Americas Watch, *Continuing Terror*, pp. 131–32.

35. Washington Office on Latin America, "El Salvador: Stepping Ahead toward More War," *Update*, vol. 10 (July–August 1985), p. 6.

36. The Congress adopted a waiver to Section 660 of the Foreign Assistance Act, which bans assistance to foreign police forces. The waiver covered El Salvador and Honduras for fiscal years 1986 and 1987, but unbeknownst to the Congress, such aid had been provided all along. Several battalions of Treasury Police had been trained on the grounds that they had military, not police, functions.

37. The Atlacatl was the first rapid-reaction battalion created from scratch by the United States in 1981. It was involved in massacres of civilians in El Mozote (1981); Tenancingo (1983); Copapayo, San Nicolas, and La Escopeta (1983); Los Llanitos (1984); and Gualsinga (1984). In February 1989, Atlacatl troops violated medical neutrality when they murdered a doctor, nurse, three paramedics, and five wounded guerrillas in Chalatenango. In July 1989, Atlacatl and First Brigade soldiers tortured seven prisoners, resulting in the death of two men. In November 1989 soldiers from the Atlacatl Battalion assassinated six Jesuit priests, their housekeeper, and her daughter. See chap. 2.

38. Americas Watch, *Civilian Toll*, p. 209; Lawyers Committee and Human Rights Watch, *Reagan Administration's Record in 1986*, pp. 53–55; Vince Bielski and Dennis Bernstein, "U.S. Trained Salvador 'Death Squads,' Critics Say," *Cleveland Plain Dealer*, August 10, 1986.

39. By this time the U.S. Embassy in El Salvador was headed by Ambassador Edwin G. Corr and Deputy Chief of Mission David Dlouhy.

40. Lawyers Committee and Human Rights Watch, *Reagan Administration's Record in 1986*, pp. 47–48 (quotations); Americas Watch, *Settling into Routine*, p. 140.

41. Hatfield, Leach, and Miller, "Bankrolling Failure," p. 14.

42. Americas Watch, *Labor Rights in El Salvador*; Holly Burkhalter and James A. Goldston, "Shame on Duarte, Not Americas Watch," *Washington Post*, March 19, 1988.

43. The Americas Watch petitions listed assassinations, disappearances, and jailings of trade union and peasant association members in 1986 and 1987, giving a chronology of twenty-seven cases, from September 1985–February 1986, in which labor union leaders and members were arrested. Section 502(b)(8) of the Trade Act of 1974, as amended, denies preferential treatment under the Generalized System of Preferences to countries that violate internationally recognized workers' rights.

In a cable circulated on Capitol Hill, Ambassador Corr accused Americas Watch of orchestrating "what is clearly a politically motivated attack on the human rights principles of the Salvadoran government." Corr insisted that "the time has come to cease and desist in efforts to move the El Salvador debate from human rights to labor rights." AmEmbassy San Salvador to SecState WashDC, "Congressional Correspondence: Rep. Don J. Pease," (Unclassified cable, July 1988), p. 13.

44. Lawyers Committee and Human Rights Watch, *Reagan Administration's Record in 1987* (1987), pp. 50–51; Americas Watch, *Civilian Toll*, pp. 297–98; Americas

Watch, *Labor Rights in El Salvador*, pp. 97–101. See also Americas Watch, *Settling into Routine*, pp. 104–13. The special representative for El Salvador of the U.N. Commission on Human Rights made the same point when he labeled the October 1989 bombing of the headquarters of the left-leaning trade union FENASTRAS "mass summary executions." Quoted in International Commission of Jurists, "El Salvador," *Review*, no. 44 (June 1990), p. 5.

45. Americas Watch, *Civilian Toll*, pp. 282–87.

46. Ibid., pp. 300–302.

47. Ibid., pp. 304–5.

48. Lawyers Committee and Human Rights Watch, *Reagan Administration's Record in 1986*, pp. 48–49.

49. Lawyers Committee and Human Rights Watch, *Reagan Administration's Record in 1987*, pp. 54–55. See also Lawyers Committee and Human Rights Watch, *Critique for 1987* (1988), p. 45.

50. Americas Watch, *Nightmare Revisited*, p. 82.

51. Manuel, "Killing Fields."

52. Americas Watch, *Nightmare Revisited*, pp. 81, 33.

53. Americas Watch, "El Salvador: Army Massacre."

54. Lawyers Committee and Human Rights Watch, *Reagan Administration Record in 1988* (1989), p. 53.

55. Ann Devroy, "Quayle Gives Salvadorans Human Rights Warning," *Washington Post*, February 4, 1989.

56. Douglas Farah, "Quayle's Salvadoran Visit Prompts Mixed Reaction," *Washington Post*, February 5, 1989; and Robert Pear, "Quayle, on Visit, Pressed Salvador on Massacre," *New York Times*, February 15, 1989.

57. Douglas Farah, "El Salvador Acts against Army Officers," *Washington Post*, March 9, 1989; Americas Watch, "El Salvador," pp. 12–13.

58. Douglas Farah, "U.S. Expands Contacts with Salvadoran Rightists," *Washington Post*, June 20, 1989.

59. Testimony of Bernard W. Aronson, assistant secretary of state for inter-American affairs, before the Senate Foreign Relations Committee, November 17, 1989.

60. Americas Watch, *Carnage Again*, pp. 75–76; and Americas Watch, *Update on El Salvador*, chaps. 2–4.

61. Americas Watch, *Carnage Again*, pp. 77–78.

62. U.S. Department of State, Office of the Assistant Secretary / Spokesman, "Secretary's Letter to President Cristiani," December 11, 1989; and Americas Watch, *Carnage Again*, pp. 82–83, 77–78.

63. Speaker's Task Force on El Salvador, "Interim Report" (Moakley Report), pp. 22–26; Lawyers Committee and Human Rights Watch, *Jesuit Murders*, pp. 16–37.

64. Speaker's Task Force on El Salvador, "Interim Report" (Moakley Report), pp. 26–34. The task force also stated its belief that the case might never have been broken if the U.S. major had not come forward.

65. Eric Warren Buckland, affidavit to the FBI, Washington, D.C., January 11, 1990. Buckland also stated that Avilés told him on the day of the murders that the military was going to carry out an operation against the Catholic University. See Memorandum from Jim McGovern and Bill Woodward to Hon. Joe Moakley, "Staff Trip to El Salvador," January 7, 1991; and Lawyers Committee, *Jesuit Case a Year Later*, pp. 3–4.

66. Bennet, "Burying the Jesuits," p. 118.

67. "Statement by Congressman Joe Moakley on the Jesuits' Case and the Salvadoran Negotiations," August 15, 1990, p. 1. Moakley later revealed that the embassy shared a videotape of Buckland's statement with President Cristiani in February 1990.

68. Bennet, "Burying the Jesuits," pp. 118, 115.

69. Speech of Ambassador Edwin G. Corr before the American Chamber of Commerce in San Salvador, July 14, 1988, p. 3.

CHAPTER 9: CONCLUSION

1. Americas Watch, *Settling into Routine*, pp. 88–89; and Lane, "Pilot Shark of El Salvador," *New Republic*, September 24, 1990, p. 28.

SELECT BIBLIOGRAPHY

BOOKS

Americas Watch and American Civil Liberties Union. *Report on Human Rights in El Salvador, January 26, 1982.* New York: Vintage, 1982.

Anderson, Thomas P. *Matanza: El Salvador's Communist Revolt of 1932.* Lincoln: University of Nebraska Press, 1971.

————. *Politics in Central America: Guatemala, El Salvador, Honduras, and Nicaragua.* New York: Praeger Publishers, 1982.

————. *The War of the Dispossessed: Honduras and El Salvador, 1969.* Lincoln: University of Nebraska Press, 1981.

Arías Gómez, José. *Farabundo Martí.* San José, C.R.: Editorial Universitaria Centroamericana, 1971.

Armstrong, Robert, and Janet Shenk. *El Salvador: The Face of Revolution.* Boston: South End Press, 1982.

Arnson, Cynthia J. *Crossroads: Congress, the Reagan Administration, and Central America.* New York: Pantheon Books, 1989.

————. *El Salvador: A Revolution Confronts the United States.* Washington, D.C.: Institute for Policy Studies, 1982.

Bacevich, A. J., Mames D. Hallums, Richard H. White, and Thomas F. Young. *American Military Policy in Small Wars: The Case of El Salvador.* Cambridge, Mass.: Institute for Foreign Policy Analysis, 1988.

Baloyra, Enrique A. *El Salvador in Transition.* Chapel Hill: University of North Carolina Press, 1982.

Barry, Tom. *El Salvador: A Country Guide.* Albuquerque, N.Mex.: Inter-Hemispheric Education Resource Center, 1990.

Berryman, Phillip. *Liberation Theology.* New York: Pantheon Books, 1987.

————. *The Religious Roots of Rebellion: Christians in Central American Revolutions.* Maryknoll, N.Y.: Orbis Books, 1984.

Blachman, Morris J., William M. LeoGrande, and Kenneth Sharpe, eds. *Confronting Revolution: Security through Diplomacy in Central America.* New York: Pantheon Books, 1986.

Black, George. *The Good Neighbor: How the United States Wrote the History of Central America and the Caribbean.* New York: Pantheon Books, 1988.

Bonner, Raymond. *Weakness and Deceit: U.S. Policy and El Salvador.* New York: Times Books, 1984.

Brockman, James R. *Romero: A Life.* Maryknoll, N.Y.: Orbis Books, 1989.

————. *The Violence of Love: The Pastoral Wisdom of Archbishop Oscar Romero.* New York: Harper and Row, 1988.

Brown, Cynthia, ed. *With Friends Like These: The Americas Watch Report on Human Rights and U.S. Policy in Latin America.* New York: Pantheon Books, 1985.

Browning, David. *El Salvador: Landscape and Society.* London: Clarendon Press, 1971.

Bulmer-Thomas, Victor. *The Political Economy of Central America since 1920.* Cambridge: Cambridge University Press, 1987.

Carranza, Salvador, ed. *Martires de la UCA: 16 de noviembre de 1989.* San Salvador: UCA editores, 1990.

Carrigan, Ana. *Salvador Witness: The Life and Calling of Jean Donovan.* New York: Simon and Schuster, 1984.

Castro, Rodolfo Barón. *La población de El Salvador.* San Salvador: UCA, 1978.

Cayetano Carpio, Salvador. *Secuestro y capucha.* San José, C.R.: Editorial Universitaria Centroamericana, 1979.

Chace, James. *Endless War: How We Got Involved in Central America—and What Can Be Done.* New York: Vintage, 1984.

Clements, Charles. *Witness to War: An American Doctor in El Salvador.* New York: Bantam Books, 1984.

Crittenden, Ann. *Sanctuary.* New York: Weidenfeld and Nicholson, 1988.

Dalton, Roque. *Las historias prohibidas del Pulgarcito.* Mexico City: Siglo Veintiuno, 1974.

———. *Miguel Mármol.* Trans. Kathleen Ross and Richard Schaaf. Willimantic, Conn.: Curbstone Press, 1987.

Didion, Joan. *Salvador.* Toronto: Lester and Orphen Dennys, 1983.

Diskin, Martin, ed. *Trouble in Our Backyard: Central America and the United States in the Eighties.* New York: Pantheon Books, 1984.

Duarte, José Napoleón, with Diana Page. *Duarte: My Story.* New York: Putnam, 1986.

Dunkerley, James. *The Long War: Dictatorship and Revolution in El Salvador.* London: Junction Books, 1982.

———. *Power in the Isthmus: A Political History of Modern Central America.* London: Verso, 1988.

Erdozain, Placido. *Archbishop Romero: Martyr of El Salvador.* Maryknoll, N.Y.: Orbis Books, 1980.

Feinberg, Richard E., ed. *Central America: International Dimensions of the Crisis.* New York: Holmes and Mercer, 1982.

Forche, Carolyn. *The Country between Us.* New York: Harper and Row, 1982.

Gettleman, Marvin E., Patrick Lacefield, Louis Menasche, David Mermelstein, and Ronald Radosh, eds. *El Salvador: Central America in the New Cold War.* New York: Grove Press, 1981.

Guerra, Tomás. *El Salvador: Octubre sangriento.* San José, C.R.: Centro Víctor Sanabría, 1980.

Guidos Vejar, Rafael. *El ascenso del militarismo en El Salvador.* San Salvador: UCA, 1980.

Gutiérrez, Gustavo. *A Theology of Liberation.* New York: Orbis Books, 1977.

Hahn, Walter F., ed. *Central America and the Reagan Doctrine.* Washington, D.C.: University Press of America, 1987.

Hamilton, Nora, et al. *Crisis in Central America: Regional Dynamics and U.S. Policy in the 1980s.* Boulder, Colo.: Westview Press, 1988.

Hirezi, Héctor Dada. *La economía de El Salvador y la integración Centroamericana, 1945–1980.* San Salvador: UCA, 1978.

LaFeber, Walter. *Inevitable Revolutions: The United States in Central America.* New York: W. W. Norton, 1983.

Leiken, Robert S., ed. *Central America: Anatomy of a Conflict.* Oxford: Pergamon Press, 1984.

Leonard, Jeffrey H. *Natural Resources and Economic Development in Central America: A Regional Environmental Profile.* New Brunswick, N.J.: Transaction Books, 1987.

Lernoux, Penny. *Cry of the People: United States Involvement in the Rise of Fascism, Torture, and Murder and the Persecution of the Catholic Church in Latin America.* New York: Doubleday, 1980.

McClintock, Michael. *The American Connection: State Terror and Popular Resistance in El Salvador.* 2 vols. London: Zed Books, 1985.

McNeil, Frank. *War and Peace in Central America.* New York: Charles Scribner's Sons, 1988.

Manwaring, Max G., and Court Prisk, eds. *El Salvador at War: An Oral History of Conflict from the 1979 Insurrection to the Present.* Washington, D.C.: National Defense University Press, 1988.

Martínez, Ana Guadalupe. *Las cárceles clandestinas de El Salvador.* San Salvador, 1978.

Menjivar, Rafael. *Acumulación originaria y desarrollo del capitalismo en El Salvador.* San José, C.R.: Editorial Universitaria Centroamericana, 1980.

―――. *Crisis del desarrollismo: Caso de El Salvador.* San José, C.R.: Editorial Universitaria Centroamericana, 1977.

―――. *Formación y lucha del proletariado industrial salvadoreño.* San Salvador: UCA, 1979.

―――. *El Salvador: El eslabón mas pequeño.* San José, C.R.: Editorial Universitaria Centroamericana, 1980.

Montgomery, Tommie Sue. *Revolution in El Salvador: Origins and Evolution.* Boulder, Colo.: Westview Press, 1982.

Munro, Dana G. *The Five Republics of Central America: Their Political and Economic Development and Their Relations with the United States.* New York: Oxford University Press, 1918.

O'Malley, William. *The Voice of Blood.* Maryknoll, N.Y.: Orbis Books, 1980.

Pearce, Jenny. *Promised Land: Peasant Rebellion in Chalatenango, El Salvador.* New York: Monthly Review Press, 1986.

―――. *Under the Eagle: U.S. Intervention in Central America and the Caribbean.* London: Latin American Bureau, 1981.

Raynolds, David R. *Rapid Development in Small Economies: The Example of El Salvador.* New York: Praeger Publishers, 1967.

Rodríquez, Mario Menéndez. *El Salvador: Una auténtica guerra civil.* San José, C.R.: Editorial Universitaria Centroamericana, 1981.

Romero, Oscar A. *"Cese la Represión!"* Madrid: Editorial Popular, Instituto de Estudios Políticos de America Latina y Africa, 1980. A collection of the archbishop's writings and homilies.

Rowles, James. *El conflicto Honduras–El Salvador.* San José, C.R.: Editorial Universitaria Centroamericana, 1980.

Schoultz, Lars. *Human Rights and United States Policy toward Latin America.* Princeton: Princeton University Press, 1981.

————. *National Security and United States Policy toward Latin America*. Princeton: Princeton University Press, 1987.

Sobrino, J., I. Martín-Baró, and J. Cardenal, eds. *La voz de los sin voz: La palabra viva de monseñor Romero*. San Salvador: UCA, 1980.

Swedish, Margaret. *Like Grains of Wheat*. Washington, D.C.: Religious Task Force on Central America, 1989.

Thomson, Marilyn. *Women of El Salvador: The Price of Freedom*. Philadelphia: Institute for the Study of Human Issues, 1986.

Universidad Centroamericana, ed. *Rutilio Grande: Mártir de la evangelización rural en El Salvador*. San Salvador: UCA, 1978.

Webre, Stephen. *José Napoleón Duarte and the Christian Democratic Party in Salvadoran Politics (1960–1972)*. Baton Rouge: Louisiana State University Press, 1979.

Wheaton, Philip. *Agrarian Reform in El Salvador: A Program of Rural Pacification*. Washington, D.C.: Ecumenical Program for Interamerican Communication and Action, 1980.

White, Alistair. *El Salvador*. New York: Praeger Publishers, 1973.

Wiarda, Howard, ed. *Rift and Revolution: The Central American Imbroglio*. Washington, D.C.: American Enterprise Institute, 1984.

Wortman, Miles, L. *Government and Society in Central America, 1680–1840*. New York: Columbia University Press, 1982.

ARTICLES AND REPORTS

Americas Watch. *Carnage Again: Preliminary Report on Violations of the Laws of War by Both Sides in the November 1989 Offensive in El Salvador, November 24, 1989*. New York: Americas Watch, 1989.

————. *The Civilian Toll, 1986–1987: Ninth Supplement to the Report on Human Rights in El Salvador, August 30, 1987*. New York: Americas Watch, 1987.

————. *Compliance with the Human Rights Provisions of the Central American Peace Plan, August 1987–August 1988*. New York: Americas Watch, 1988.

————. *Compliance with the Human Rights Provisions of the Central American Peace Plan, January 1988*. New York: Americas Watch, 1988.

————. *The Continuing Terror: Seventh Supplement to the Report on Human Rights in El Salvador, September 1985*. New York: Americas Watch, 1985.

————. *Draining the Sea: Sixth Supplement to the Report on Human Rights in El Salvador, March 1985*. New York: Americas Watch, 1985.

————. "El Salvador: The Army Massacre at San Francisco." *News from Americas Watch*. September 1989.

————. "El Salvador: Impunity Prevails in Human Rights Cases." *News from Americas Watch*. September 1990.

————. *Human Rights in El Salvador on the Eve of Elections, March 1988*. New York: Americas Watch, 1988.

————. *Labor Rights in El Salvador, March 1988*. New York: Americas Watch, 1988.

————. *Land Mines in El Salvador and Nicaragua: The Civilian Victims, December 1986*. New York: Americas Watch, 1986.

————. *Managing the Facts: How the Administration Deals with Reports of Human Rights Abuses in El Salvador, December 1985.* New York: Americas Watch, 1985.

————. *Messengers of Death: Human Rights in Guatemala, November 1988–February 1990.* New York: Americas Watch, 1990.

————. *Nightmare Revisited, 1987–88: Tenth Supplement to the Report on Human Rights in El Salvador, September 1988.* New York: Americas Watch, 1988.

————. "Petition before the U.S. Trade Representative on Labor Rights in El Salvador." Washington, D.C., May 1990.

————. *Protection of the Weak and Unarmed: The Dispute over Counting Human Rights Violations in El Salvador, February 1984.* New York: Americas Watch, 1984.

————. *Settling into Routine: Human Rights Abuses in Duarte's Second Year: Eighth Supplement to the Report on Human Rights in El Salvador, May 1986.* New York: Americas Watch, 1986.

————. *Update on El Salvador: The Human Rights Crisis Continues in the Wake of the FMLN Offensive, December 16, 1989.* New York: Americas Watch, 1989.

————. *U.S. Reporting on Human Rights in El Salvador: Methodology at Odds with Knowledge, June 1982.* New York: Americas Watch, 1982.

————. *Violations of Fair Trial Guarantees by the FMLN's Ad Hoc Courts, May 1990.* New York: Americas Watch, 1990.

————. *A Year of Reckoning: El Salvador a Decade after the Assassination of Archbishop Romero, March 1990.* New York: Americas Watch, 1990.

Americas Watch and American Civil Liberties Union. *As Bad as Ever: A Report on Human Rights in El Salvador, January 31, 1984, Fourth Supplement.* New York: Americas Watch, 1984.

————. *Supplement to the Report on Human Rights in El Salvador, July 20, 1982.* Washington, D.C.: Center for National Security Studies, 1982.

————. *Second Supplement to the Report on Human Rights in El Salvador, July 19, 1982.* Washington, D.C.: Center for National Security Studies, 1982.

————. *Third Supplement to the Report on Human Rights in El Salvador, July 19, 1983.* Washington, D.C.: Center for National Security Studies, 1983.

Americas Watch and Lawyers Committee for Human Rights. *Free Fire: A Report on Human Rights in El Salvador, August 1984, Fifth Supplement.* New York: Americas Watch and Lawyers Committee, 1984.

————. *El Salvador's Other Victims: The War on the Displaced, April 1984.* New York: Americas Watch and Lawyers Committee, 1984.

Amnesty International. *Amnesty International Annual Report, 1980.* Amnesty International, 1980. See various years, especially 1979–90.

————. *El Salvador: "Death Squads"—A Government Strategy.* London: Amnesty International, 1988.

Anderson, Kenneth H. "Action Specific Human Rights Legislation for El Salvador." *Harvard Journal on Legislation,* vol. 22 (Winter 1985): 255–68.

Anderson, Thomas P. "El Salvador's Dim Prospects." *Current History,* vol. 85 (January 1986): 9–11.

Baloyra, Enrique A. "Dilemmas of Political Transition in El Salvador." *Journal of International Affairs,* vol. 38 (Winter 1985): 221–42.

————. "The Seven Plagues of El Salvador." *Current History,* vol. 86 (December 1987): 413–16.

Bennet, Philip. "Burying the Jesuits." *Vanity Fair*, November 1990, pp. 110–23.

Blachman, Morris J., and Kenneth E. Sharpe. "Things Fall Apart: Trouble Ahead in El Salvador." *World Policy Journal*, vol. 6 (Winter 1988–89): 107–39.

Burke, Melvin. "El sistema de plantación y la proletarización del trabajo agrícola en El Salvador." *Estudios Centroamericanos*, nos. 335–36 (September–October 1976).

Burkhalter, Holly, and Alita Paine. "Our Overseas Cops." *Nation*, September 14, 1985, p. 197.

Dickey, Christopher. "Behind the Death Squads." *New Republic*, December 26, 1983, pp. 16–21.

Dillon, Sam. "Dateline El Salvador: Crisis Renewed." *Foreign Policy*, no. 73 (Winter 1988–89): 153–70.

El Rescate Human Rights Department. *El Salvador Chronology*. Los Angeles, El Rescate Human Rights Department. See various months.

El Salvador. Ministry of Foreign Relations. "Human Rights and Fundamental Freedoms in El Salvador [1987]." *Dirección de Publicaciones e Impresos*. 1987.

"El Salvador after Duarte." *World Policy Journal*, vol. 5 (Fall 1988): 703–23.

Forche, Carolyn, and Philip Wheaton. *History and Motivation of U.S. Involvement in the Control of the Peasant Movement in El Salvador: The Rise of AIFLD in the Agrarian Reform Process, 1970–1980*. Washington, D.C.: Ecumenical Program for Interamerican Communication and Action, n.d..

Gibb, Tom, and Frank Smyth. *El Salvador: Is Peace Possible? A Report on the Prospects for Negotiations and U.S. Policy*. Washington Office on Latin America, April 1990.

Gleijeses, Piero. "The Case for Power Sharing in El Salvador." *Foreign Affairs*, vol. 61 (Summer 1983): 1048–63.

Gómez, Leonel, and Bruce Cameron. "El Salvador: The Current Danger." *Foreign Policy*, no. 43 (Summer 1981): 70–78.

Hatfield, Mark O., Jim Leach, and George Miller. "Bankrolling Failure: United States Policy in El Salvador and the Urgent Need for Reform." Report to the Arms Control and Foreign Policy Caucus. November 1987.

"Hemispheric Crisis: Issues and Options." *Foreign Policy*, no. 52 (Fall 1983): 42–117. Five articles by Nestor D. Sanchez, Guillermo Manuel Ungo, Abraham F. Lowenthal, Ronald T. Libbey, and Tom J. Farer.

International Commission of Jurists. *Review* (Geneva), no. 23 (December 1979).

International Commission for Central American Recovery and Development (Sanford Commission). *Poverty, Conflict, and Hope: A Turning Point in Central America*. Durham, N.C.: Duke University Press, 1989.

International Committee of the Red Cross, *1987 Annual Report*. Geneva: ICRC, 1988.

International Human Rights Law Group. *Waiting for Justice: Treatment of Political Prisoners under El Salvador's Decree 50, March 1987*. Washington, D.C.: International Human Rights Law Group, 1987.

Lane, Charles. "The Pilot Shark of El Salvador." *New Republic*, September 24, 1990.

Lawyers Committee for Human Rights. *Critique: Review of the Department of State's Country Reports on Human Rights Practices for 1989*. New York: Lawyers Committee, 1990.

————. *A Decade of Failed Promises: The Investigation of Archbishop Romero's Murder, March 1990.* New York: Lawyers Committee, 1990.

————. *The Jesuit Case a Year Later: An Interim Report.* New York: Lawyers Committee, 1990.

————. "Status of Jesuit Murder Investigation in El Salvador." Memorandum. July 27, 1990.

————. *Underwriting Injustice: AID and El Salvador's Judicial Reform Program.* New York: Lawyers Committee, 1989.

————. "Update on Investigation of Six Jesuit Priests in El Salvador." Memorandum. October 2, 1990.

Lawyers Committee for Human Rights and Human Rights Watch. *Critique: Review of the Department of State's Country Reports on Human Rights Practices for [Year].* New York: Lawyers Committee and Human Rights Watch. See especially 1987. See also critiques available for various years.

————. *El Salvador: Human Rights Dismissed, a Report on Sixteen Unresolved Cases, 1986.* New York: Lawyers Committee and Human Rights Watch, 1986.

————. *The Jesuit Murders: A Report on the Testimony of a Witness, December 15, 1989.* New York: Lawyers Committee and Human Rights Watch, 1989.

————. *Reagan Administration's Record on Human Rights in 1986.* New York: Lawyers Committee and Human Rights Watch, 1987. See also reports available for various years.

LeMoyne, James. "El Salvador's Forgotten War." *Foreign Affairs* (Summer 1989): 105–25.

LeoGrande, William M. "A Splendid Little War: Drawing the Line in El Salvador." *International Security,* vol. 6 (Summer 1981): 27–52.

McColm, R. Bruce. *El Salvador: Peaceful Revolution or Armed Struggle?* Perspectives on Freedom, no. 1. Washington, D.C.: Freedom House, 1982.

Manuel, Anne. "Killing Fields." *Nation,* July 2–9, 1988, p. 5.

Matheson, Catherine. "War of Words: Physical Attacks and Threats to Withdraw State Advertising from the Media Combine to Keep the Salvadoran Press in Line." *Index on Censorship,* vol. 15 (September 1986): 31–36.

Morley, Jefferson. "Demonizing D'Aubuisson." *Nation,* May 8, 1989.

————. "Jean vs. Jean." *New Republic,* January 28, 1985, pp. 35–39.

————. "Prisoner Duarte." *New York Review of Books,* December 4, 1986, pp. 15–19.

————. "Salvador Justice." *New Republic,* September 8, 1986, pp. 13–15.

Nairn, Allan. "Behind the Death Squads." *Progressive,* May 1984, pp. 20–29.

North American Congress on Latin America. "Duarte: Prisoner of War," *Report on the Americas* (New York), vol. 20 (January–March 1986): 13.

National Bipartisan Commission on Central America (U.S.). *The Report of the President's National Bipartisan Commission on Central America.* New York: Macmillan, 1984.

Pastor, Robert A. "Three Perspectives on El Salvador." *SAIS Review* (School of Advanced International Studies), Summer 1981, pp. 35–48.

Report on the Situation of Human Rights in El Salvador. Organization of American States, Inter-American Commission on Human Rights. OEA/Ser.L/V/II. 46, doc. 23, rev. 2, November 17, 1978.

Robinson, Linda. "Peace in Central America?" *Foreign Affairs*, vol. 66, no. 3 (1988): 591–613.

Sharpe, Kenneth E., and Martin Diskin. "El Salvador Revisited: Why Duarte Is in Trouble." *World Policy Journal*, vol. 3 (Summer 1986): 473–94.

———. "Facing Facts in El Salvador: Reconciliation or War." *World Policy Journal*, vol. 1 (Spring 1984): 517–47.

Stanley, William Deane. "Economic Migrants or Refugees from Violence? A Time-Series Analysis of Salvadoran Migration to the U.S." *Latin American Research Review*, vol. 22, no. 1 (1987): 132–54.

"Struggle in Central America." *Foreign Policy*, no. 43 (Summer 1981): 70–103. Five articles by Leonel Gómez and Bruce Cameron, W. Scott Thompson, J. Bryan Heir, Olga Pellicer, and Marlise Simons.

Tyler, Harold R., Jr. *The Churchwomen Murders: A Report to the Secretary of State.* New York, December 2, 1983. An account of the report was published in the *New York Times*, February 16, 1984.

U.S. Department of State. *Country Reports on Human Rights Practices for [Year].* Washington, D.C.: Government Printing Office. See especially 1979–89.

———. Agency for International Development. Office of Public Safety. *Report on Visit to Central America and Panama to Study AID Public Safety Programs, 1967.* Washington, D.C.: Department of State, 1967.

Yu, Alan K. "U.S. Assistance for Foreign Police forces." Report prepared for the Congressional Research Service, Library of Congress. July 18, 1989.

Zaid, Gabríel. "Enemy Colleagues: A Reading of the Salvadoran Tragedy." *Dissent*, Winter 1982, 13–40.

HEARINGS AND REPORTS OF THE U.S. CONGRESS

Speaker's Task Force on El Salvador. "Interim Report" (Moakley Report). Washington, D.C., April 30, 1990. Photocopy.

Arms Control and Foreign Policy Caucus. "Abuses of Human Rights Attributed to Atlacatl Battalion." Memorandum. April 13, 1990.

Arms Control and Foreign Policy Caucus. "Barriers to Reform: A Profile of El Salvador's Military Leaders." May 21, 1990.

Arms Control and Foreign Policy Caucus. "Police Aid to Central America: Yesterday's Lessons, Today's Choices." August 13, 1986.

House. Committee on Appropriations. Subcommittee on Foreign Operations. *Foreign Assistance and Related Programs for 1981.* Part 1, *Hearings.* 96th Cong., 2d sess. Washington, D.C.: Government Printing Office, 1980.

———. *Appropriations for 1982.* Part 2, *Hearings.* 97th Cong., 1st sess. Washington, D.C.: Government Printing Office, 1981.

House. Committee on Foreign Affairs, *The Central American Counterterrorism Act of 1985. Hearings, October 24 and November 19, 1985,* 99th Cong., 1st sess. Washington, D.C.: Government Printing Office, 1986.

———. *Foreign Assistance Legislation for Fiscal Year 1982.* Part 1, *Hearings, March 13, 18, 19, and 23, 1981.* 97th Cong., 1st sess. Washington, D.C.: Government Printing Office, 1981.

―――. *Foreign Assistance Legislation for Fiscal Years 1984–1985.* Part 1, *Hearings, February 8, 15, 16, 22, 23, 24; March 24, 1983.* 98th Cong., 1st sess. Washington, D.C.: Government Printing Office, 1984.

―――. *Foreign Assistance Legislation for Fiscal Years 1984–1985.* Part 2, *Hearings, February 23; March 3, 10, and 23, 1983.* 98th Cong., 1st sess. Washington, D.C.: Government Printing Office, 1984.

―――. *Presidential Certification on El Salvador.* Vol. 2, *Hearings and Mark-up, June 2, 22; July 29; August 3, 10, and 17, 1982.* 97th Cong., 2d sess. Washington, D.C.: Government Printing Office, 1982.

―――. *Prospects for Peace in El Salvador. Hearing, March 7, 1989.* 101st Cong., 1st sess. Washington, D.C.: Government Printing Office, 1989.

―――. Subcommittee on Inter-American Affairs. *Central America at the Crossroads. Hearings, September 11 and 12, 1979.* 96th Cong., 1st sess. Washington, D.C.: Government Printing Office, 1979.

―――. *Presidential Certification on El Salvador.* Vol. 1, *Hearings, February 2, 23, 25, and March 2, 1982.* 97th Cong., 2d sess. Washington, D.C.: Government Printing Office, 1982.

―――. *U.S. Policy Options in El Salvador. Hearings and Mark-up, September 24 and November 5 and 19, 1981.* 97th Cong., 1st sess. Washington, D.C.: Government Printing Office, 1981.

―――. *U.S. Policy toward El Salvador. Hearings, March 5 and 11, 1981.* 97th Cong., 1st sess. Washington, D.C.: Government Printing Office, 1981.

House. Committee on Foreign Affairs. Subcommittees on Human Rights and International Organizations and on Western Hemisphere Affairs. *Human Rights and Political Developments in El Salvador, 1987. Hearings, September 23 and 29, 1987.* 100th Cong., 1st sess. Washington, D.C.: Government Printing Office, 1988.

―――. *The Situation in El Salvador. Hearings, January 26, 1983, and February 6, 1984.* 98th Cong., 2d sess. Washington, D.C.: Government Printing Office, 1984.

―――. *U.S. Policy in El Salvador. Hearings, February 4, 28; March 7, 17, 1983.* 98th Cong., 1st sess. Washington, D.C.: Government Printing Office, 1983.

House. Committee on Foreign Affairs. Subcommittee on Western Hemisphere Affairs. *Developments in El Salvador. Hearing, January 31, 1985.* 99th Cong., 1st sess. Washington, D.C.: Government Printing Office, 1985.

House. Committee on International Relations. Subcommittee on International Organizations. *Human Rights in Nicaragua, Guatemala, and El Salvador: Implications for U.S. Policy. Hearings, June 8 and 9, 1976.* 94th Cong., 2d sess. Washington, D.C.: Government Printing Office, 1976.

―――. *Religious Persecution in El Salvador. Hearings, July 21 and 29, 1977.* 95th Cong., 1st sess. Washington, D.C.: Government Printing Office, 1977.

House. Permanent Select Committee on Intelligence. *Report on the Activities of the Permanent Select Committee on Intelligence of the House of Representatives during the 98th Congress.* Washington, D.C.: Government Printing Office, 1985.

―――. Subcommittee on Oversight and Evaluation. *U.S. Intelligence Performance on Central America: Achievements and Selected Instances of Concern, Staff Report, September 22, 1982.* 97th Cong., 2d sess. Washington, D.C.: Government Printing Office, 1982.

Senate. Committee on Appropriations. Subcommittee on Foreign Operations. *El Salvador: Military and Economic Reprogramming. Hearing.* 98th Cong., 1st sess. Washington, D.C.: Government Printing Office, 1983.

―――. Committee on Foreign Relations. *Certification Concerning Military Aid to El Salvador. Hearings, February 8 and March 11, 1982.* 97th Cong., 2d sess. Washington, D.C.: Government Printing Office, 1982.

―――. *Presidential Certifications on Conditions in El Salvador. Hearing, August 3, 1982.* 97th Cong., 2d sess. Washington, D.C.: Government Printing Office, 1982.

―――. *Security and Development Assistance. Hearings, February 22, 29, March 7, 8, 20, 21, 22, and 27, 1984.* 98th Cong., 2d sess. Washington, D.C.: Government Printing Office, 1984.

―――. *The Situation in El Salvador. Hearings, March 18 and April 9, 1981.* 97th Cong., 1st sess. Washington, D.C.: Government Printing Office, 1981.

Senate. Committees on Foreign Relations and Appropriations. *El Salvador: The United States in the Midst of a Maelstrom. Report, March 1982.* 97th Cong., 2d sess. Washington, D.C.: Government Printing Office, 1982.

―――. Select Committee on Intelligence. *Recent Political Violence in El Salvador.* Report no. 98–659, October 5, 1984. 98th Cong., 2d sess. Washington, D.C.: Government Printing Office, 1984.

PRESS

Albuquerque Journal (U.S.)
Associated Press (U.S.)
Baltimore Sun (U.S.)
Boston Globe (U.S.)
El Diario de Hoy (El Salvador)
Diario Latino (El Salvador)
Estudios Centroamericanos (El Salvador)
Foreign Broadcast Information Services (U.S. Government)
Los Angeles Times (U.S.)
Miami Herald (U.S.)
El Mundo (El Salvador)
New York Review of Books (U.S.)
New York Times (U.S.)
Philadelphia Inquirer (U.S.)
Prensa Grafica (El Salvador)
Proceso (El Salvador)
Progressive (U.S.)
Reuters (U.K.)
Time (U.S.)
Village Voice (U.S.)
Washington Post (U.S.)

INDEX

Abrams, Elliott (former U.S. assistant secretary of state), 52, 125, 181*n*

Administration of Justice Program, 81, 82–83

Agency for International Development (AID), 12. *See also* Administration of Justice Program; International Criminal Investigative Training Assistance Program; Office of Public Safety

Agrarian Law of *1907*, 2, 4

Agrarian reform. *See* Land reform

Air force. *See* Armed forces

Albuquerque Journal, 93

Alemán Alas, Cristobal (UCS leader), 29

Alfaro Peña, Luz Janeth (former CDHES-NG employee), 45, 130

Alliance for Progress era, 3, 4

Alvarez, Walter Antonio (alleged assassin of Archbishop Romero), 90–91, 93

Amaya Rosa, Francisco, Lt.: and Archbishop Romero's murder, 90, 93

American Chamber of Congress in El Salvador, 123–24

American Institute for Free Labor Development (AIFLD), 6, 28, 97, 122

Americas Watch, 19, 25, 30, 33, 50, 52, 62; and U.S. Embassy, 54, 128–29, 130; on Salvadoran air force, 55, 87; and Colomoncagua refugee camp, 56; and San Francisco massacre, 60, 100; on guerrillas, 64–65, 69–70; on displaced people, 109–13 passim; and USTR, 129, 182*n*

Amnesty, 87–88; for political prisoners, 7; for opposition forces, 12, 13, 79; for military, 14, 78; on death squads, 22; Amnesty International, 28, 42; on killings of teachers, 41; and Sheraton Hotel murders, 96

Anticommunist Command for Salvation of the University (CASU), 42

Anti-Terrorism Assistance (ATA), 84

Araujo, Arturo (former president of El Salvador), 3

Arce Rapid Reaction Battalion, 41, 99, 102; and Los Palitos massacre, 59–60; impunity of, 88

Archdiocese of San Salvador. *See* Catholic Church

Arguera, Amílcar Martínez (former Foreign Ministry official), 38

Armed forces, 6, 20–21, 32–41 passim, 47–63, 124, 127, 131, 138; and detention facilities, 7; and resistance to reform, 7, 8, 71, 82, 117; institutional use of torture, 7, 18, 24, 29, 33, 133; alliance with PDC, 9; size of, 9, 20; U.S. military aid to, 10, 15, 118, 180*n*; amnesty for, 14; impunity of, 14, 80, 83, 86–106, 117, 122, 136, 139; linking armed and peaceful opposition, 19; U.S. training of, 20, 167*n*; and *tandona*, 21; shooting of journalists, 41; attack on National University, 42; attacks on noncombatants, 47–49, 57, 59–62, 115; and aerial attacks, 53–59, 113–14, 124, 126; use of land mines, 68, 172*n*; and forced depopulation, 107, 124; and military sweeps, 109; and refugees and displaced people, 110, 114; stealing elections, 117; and attacks in Guazapa, 129. *See also* Arce Rapid Reaction Battalion; Atlacatl Battalion; Death squads; Jiboa Battalion; Press Office of the Armed Forces; Security forces; Transmission Instruction Center of the Armed Forces; *and various brigades (first, etc.)*

ABOUT HUMAN RIGHTS WATCH

Human Rights Watch conducts systematic investigations of human rights abuses in some sixty countries around the world. It addresses the human rights practices of governments of all political stripes, geopolitical alignments, and ethnic and religious persuasions. In internal wars—such as those in Afghanistan, Angola, Cambodia, and El Salvador—it documents abuses by governments and rebel groups. Human Rights Watch defends freedom of thought and expression, due process of law, and equal protection of the law; it denounces murders, disappearances, torture, arbitrary imprisonment, exile, censorship, and other abuses of internationally recognized human rights.

With a staff that includes over thirty country specialists, Human Rights Watch annually carries out more than one hundred investigative missions to gather current human rights information. In country after country, this ongoing effort makes a difference—saving lives, stopping torture, freeing prisoners, and helping to create the space for citizens to exercise their civil and political rights. Human Rights Watch reports are unique, up-to-date, firsthand sources of human rights information worldwide.

Human Rights Watch began in 1978 with the founding of Helsinki Watch by a group of publishers, lawyers, and other activists and now maintains offices in New York, Washington, D.C., Los Angeles, London, San Salvador, and Hong Kong. Today it includes Africa Watch, Americas Watch, Asia Watch, Helsinki Watch, Middle East Watch, and the Fund for Free Expression. Human Rights Watch is an independent, nongovernmental organization supported by contributions from private individuals and foundations. It accepts no government funds, directly or indirectly.

31935   323.4 ELS

El Salvador's reign of terror